Sign Languages in Contact

THE SOCIOLINGUISTICS IN DEAF COMMUNITIES SERIES

Ceil Lucas, General Editor

Sign Languages in Contact

David Quinto-Pozos, Editor

GALLAUDET UNIVERSITY PRESS

Washington, D.C.

Sociolinguistics in Deaf Communities
A Series Edited by Ceil Lucas

Gallaudet University Press
Washington, D.C. 20002

http://gupress.gallaudet.edu

ISBN 1-56368-356-3
ISSN 1080-5494

Contents

Series Editor's Introduction

It is with great pleasure that I welcome Volume 13 to the Sociolinguistics in Deaf Communities series! Work on language contact in Deaf communities has focused almost exclusively on the outcomes of contact between spoken and written majority languages and sign languages. Such work has been very valuable, as it has helped us see parallels and differences between language contact outcomes in exclusively spoken language communities and communities that involve both a spoken language and a signed language. Studies of the outcomes of contact between languages in two modalities—signed and spoken—have pushed us to re-think very basic concepts such as bilingualism, code-switching and code-mixing. Such studies have helped us understand unique phenomena such as fingerspelling and initialization. What has always been lacking is data-based research on the outcomes of contact between natural sign languages, the kind of research that this volume brings together. Following a comprehensive and useful introduction to the issues to consider when discussing contact between sign languages by guest editor David Quinto-Pozos, the volume provides information on contact situations that involve sign languages of Deaf communities from New Zealand, Japan, Israel, Russia, Albania, China, Taiwan, and the United States. The U.S. example is an examination of the contact between ASL and North American Indian signed languages, which demonstrates how sign languages of Deaf communities can interact with sign languages used by groups of hearing people who do not share the same spoken language. In these papers, we see parallels with spoken language contact situations but also issues unique to sign languages in contact such as iconicity, gesture, and the interlingual similarity of sign languages. It is my hope that this pioneering volume will provide a model for many more studies of sign languages in contact.

Ceil Lucas
Washington, D.C.

Editor's Introduction: Outlining

Considerations for the Study

of Signed Language Contact

David Quinto-Pozos

To my knowledge, this volume represents the first book-length collection of various accounts of contact between sign languages, and this brings with it excitement as well as the realization of challenges that lie ahead.[1] As many researchers who are interested in language contact might suggest, it is exciting because these chapters contribute to our understanding of the structural and social aspects of contact and how such contact affects language in the visual-gestural modality. They provide us with information about Deaf communities throughout the world, as well as language data that speak to the ways in which contact is manifested in those communities. This global perspective allows us to examine contact situations in search of commonalties and recurring patterns. It also enables us to see how some outcomes of contact between sign languages might or might not fit the general patterns of contact that have been demonstrated for spoken languages. Perhaps as a way to balance the excitement about this topic, the sobering truth is that we know so little about contact between sign languages. As a result, we are faced with the task of documenting examples of such contact and the challenge of examining the effects of visual meaning creation on linguistic structures that occur in these contact situations. By focusing on this area of inquiry, we stand to gain much knowledge about how language works.

The study of language contact among signed languages forces us to carefully consider how the visual-gestural modality of human communication influences language birth, development, change, and decay or loss from disuse. Sign languages and sign language varieties are emerging in various parts of the world, and they are developing quickly. It is unclear how such rapid birth and development are paralleled in spoken language situations, although likely candidates for

cross-modal comparisons would be spoken language pidgins and creoles. Some varieties of signed language might also be quickly declining
in use as a result of influence from other sign languages. This phenomenon is to be expected because it also occurs when spoken languages
come into contact, although what we know about these cases is minimal. I suggest that certain characteristics of language in the visual-gestural modality influence the results of contact between sign languages.
These factors and some of the relevant works from the literature are
discussed in this introductory chapter.

LANGUAGE CONTACT IN SPOKEN LANGUAGE LITERATURE

Language contact has been an active area of linguistic inquiry in the
past few decades. Within the last decade alone, several volumes have
been devoted to various approaches to the study of contact between spoken languages and the multitude of phenomena that result. For example,
one of the authors of a classic work on language contact (Thomason and
Kaufman 1988) has published an introductory book on the topic that
serves as a useful resource for various students and those who are interested in linguistics (Thomason 2001). Another work presents a framework composed of several models that have been suggested in previous
writings to account for various types of contact data — mostly from a
code-switching perspective (Myers-Scotton 2002). Holm (2004) presents data from various language varieties as he explores the concept of
"semi-creolization," although the author uses the term "partially structured grammars" in that work. As further testament to the importance
of publishing entire volumes on the topic of language contact,
Cambridge University Press has begun an interdisciplinary series devoted to the topic, and three volumes have been published to date
(Mufwene 2001; Clyne 2003; Heine and Kuteva 2005).

Language contact phenomena are as complex as the linguistic reper-
toires and social situations of the individuals and communities who engage in contact between languages or language varieties. Moreover,
there are many lenses through which to examine language contact. One
could focus on the social aspect — taking into consideration issues such
as prestige, power, and social class, which influence what languages or
language varieties are acceptable in any given situation. Alternatively,

one could zoom in the linguistic microscope to examine the numerous and sometimes overlapping types of influences languages exert on one another. Some of these commonly discussed topics are borrowings and loans, interference, convergence, transference, bilingualism, code switching, foreigner talk, language shift, language attrition, and even language decline and death. Keep in mind that these and other frequently used terms are, at times, defined in different ways by different authors. In addition to these topics, some researchers focus on the emergence of new varieties of language (e.g., pidgins and creoles) that arise in contact situations. Some authors focus on lexical items, whereas others address grammatical matters. Those who work on bilingualism could consider the subject at the level of the individual or the community (i.e., societal bilingualism).

The result of significant interest in the topic of language contact — as reflected in the spoken language literature — has been the development of a sizeable and still growing corpus of examples of contact data. In most cases, this reflects contact between languages that are centuries old, although there might also be work on younger varieties such as pidgins and creoles. This is worth noting because many sign languages do not have the long histories of development that characterize spoken language varieties. Furthermore, examples of spoken language contact enable us to examine interactions between structurally similar languages, as well as those that are substantially different from one another. That level of linguistic diversity may not entirely be the case with sign language contact.

LANGUAGE CONTACT IN SIGNED LANGUAGE LITERATURE

Perhaps the most-studied aspect of signed language contact has been the way in which sign languages interact with spoken and/or written languages. The degree of lexical similarity between various sign languages has also been extensively studied, and this is arguably an area of inquiry that is relevant to the study of contact. In particular, lexical comparisons can be useful when considering contact phenomena, although they present the challenge of addressing the role of visual iconicity in the development of sign lexicons. A smaller percentage of works have addressed issues such as the effects of contact between two sign languages, the use of International Sign (IS) by deaf people from various countries, and language attrition and/or death that result, in part, from contact.

Contact between Signed and Spoken/Written Languages

Some of the earliest writings on contact between English and American Sign Language (ASL) conceptualized the phenomenon as influencing the creation of language varieties that were labeled Pidgin Sign English (PSE) (Woodward 1973b), but a possible diglossic situation in the American Deaf community was also suggested (Stokoe 1970; Woodward 1973a). The label PSE seems to have come about because of the ways in which the purported intermediate varieties of language use, along a continuum of ASL and English at either end, show "reduction and mixture of grammatical structures of both languages as well as some new structures that are common to neither of the languages" (Woodward 1973b, 40). For instance, Woodward identified the variable uses of various structures such as articles, plural markers, and the copula — none of which are common to both English and ASL. That variable use was what Woodward and others referred to as PSE — a label that has continued to be used, at least in some circles, until the present day.

However, over the years, various authors have pointed out that, in several ways, PSE does not seem to resemble spoken language pidgins. For instance, Cokely (1983), by looking at ways in which deaf people interact with hearing people, argued in favor of an analysis that labeled such language use as instances of foreigner talk, judgments of proficiency, and ASL learners' attempts to master the target language. Lucas and Valli (1992) isolated and listed features of both ASL and English in the signing of various informants included in their dyad- and triad-based data. Their analysis suggested that the term *contact signing* was a more appropriate label for varieties of sign language that combine features of ASL and English and exhibit significant individual variation in terms of the occurrence of features. They also pointed out that, despite the individual variation, some linguistic features from ASL and English seldom occur in contact signing, such as ASL nonmanual syntactic markers that occur with topicalization and various bound morphemes from English (e.g., plural -*s*, third-person singular -*s*, possessive '*s*, past tense -*ed*, or comparative -*er*). Fischer (1996) also pointed out that the alleged pidgin, PSE, is the opposite of what is typically found in spoken language pidgins since its vocabulary comes from the substrate (ASL), whereas its grammar comes from the superstrate (English).

The work of Lucas and Valli (1992) represents one of the first extensive discussions of various facets of language contact in and around a Deaf community and was preceded by shorter works on the subject (e.g., Lucas and Valli 1988, 1989, 1991). In their writings, these authors discuss several possible outcomes of contact between a signed and a spoken language, but they are careful to distinguish between those contact phenomena that have parallels in spoken language contact and those that are unique to contact between a signed and a spoken language. They maintain that the latter can be found in fingerspelling, fingerspelling/sign combinations, mouthing, CODA-speak, TTY conversations, code switching, and contact signing (which they also termed *code mixing*). Lucas and Valli also suggest that code switching can occur between sign and spoken/written language as well, but the main difference when addressing it in the signed modality is that the simultaneous use of devices from both modalities (e.g., signs from the visual-gestural modality, along with mouth movements — and perhaps even vocalizations — from the auditory-oral modality) allows for *simultaneous* combinations of various linguistic devices from both languages. This differs from the most common form of spoken language code switching, in which the switching primarily takes place *sequentially.*

Lucas and Valli (1992) also make several other important points. First, the simultaneous or sequential use of ASL and English forms in a signed segment makes it very difficult to determine whether the signer is actually code switching or simply borrowing elements from one language and using them in another. As a result, they suggest the use of a third term, *contact signing,* to describe the result of frequent contact between ASL and English.[2] In their other main themes, the authors discuss issues that arise when one investigates language use by individuals, communities, and societies. One of their suggestions is that the locus of study for contact situations should really be the behavior of the individual, although they also claim that the occurrence of many ASL and English features of contact signing cannot be predicted solely by this method. In other words, one cannot predict which features of contact signing an "average" member of the Deaf community will use in any given situation. Yet, despite the unpredictable nature of an individual's signing in a specific situation, the authors were able to identify various common features of contact signing at the lexical, morphological, and syntactic levels. As a final note, Lucas and Valli remind the reader that, inasmuch as contact situations are dynamic rather than static, a similar (i.e., dynamic) perspective for the analysis of contact situations is necessary. Such a standpoint would take into account the fact that language behavior can change rapidly based on both the interlocutor and the linguistic background of the language user.

The code switching that some deaf users of ASL and Cued Speech engage in has also been viewed as a form of contact between ASL and English.[3] In this system, consonant and vowel sounds are represented by the hands, and, in theory, any spoken language can be cued. Hauser (2000) describes the signing of a ten-year-old girl who is fluent in both ASL and Cued English and gives examples of how she code-switches between the two forms of manual communication.

Fingerspelling has also been viewed as one of the products of contact between a signed and a spoken or written language, although some researchers highlight the ways in which fingerspelling has been incorporated into the signed language, while others describe it as more of a foreign element that lies outside the core lexicon. Taking the former viewpoint, Battison (1978) addressed the manner in which some fingerspelled words become lexicalized over time, and Akamatsu (1985) stated that fingerspelled words form "articulatory envelopes" that resemble signs in some ways. Davis (1989, 97) also suggests that fingerspelling is, by its nature, an ASL phonological event — not an example of borrowing — because, as he maintains, "ASL morphemes are never borrowed from the orthographic English event; they are simply used to *represent* [emphasis in the original] the orthographic event." Other researchers have also discussed the manner in which fingerspelled items can form compounds with ASL signs (Brentari and Padden 2001; Padden 1998), the suggestion that fingerspelling can be viewed as code switching between ASL and written English (Kuntze 2000), and the claim that fingerspelling can also be considered a form of borrowing (Miller 2001).

Another characteristic of contact between a signed and a spoken language is the mouthing of spoken words while producing signs. Several authors have addressed this phenomenon with data from ASL and English (Davis 1989, 1990), Swiss German Sign Language and German (Boyes Braem 2001), and other European sign languages (see Ann 2001 for a brief discussion of relevant works). In addition, a number of authors have described code switching and code mixing between a signed and a spoken language. For instance, researchers have looked at the manner in which code switching, as a function of the language background and use of the interlocutor, is performed by deaf adults (Hoffmeister and Moores 1987; Lee 1983) and deaf children (Kachman 1991).

In the present volume, Rachel Mckee, David Mckee, Kirsten Smiler, and Karen Pointon address contact between deaf and hearing people by discussing how, within an ethnic minority, the hearing members can affect the expression of identity by the deaf users of a sign language. Approximately 40 percent of the deaf users of New Zealand Sign Language (NZSL) have cultural and historical ties to the indigenous Māori culture. However, their deafness has historically precluded them from participation in Māori cultural events and activities. In recent years, the New Zealand deaf population with ties to Māori culture has begun to learn more about the minority culture, including its language-based references. This learning has resulted in an increase in the number of signs that are used in NZSL for references to Māori cultural concepts. However, the situation, which McKee et al. carefully describe, is far from simple inasmuch as the negotiation of new lexical elements by deaf Māori, hearing Māori, and trilingual (Māori, English, and NZSL) interpreters creates a complex interplay that is the perfect setting for a discussion of signed language contact.

Addressing Lexical Similarities between Sign Languages

Several studies that have compared lexical items across sign languages generally agree that sign languages are lexically more similar to each other than are spoken languages. Although this may not be a result of contact between sign languages, some researchers have investigated the likelihood of historical contact (e.g., McKee and Kennedy 2000; Davis, this volume). Higher degrees of lexical similarity clearly hold even for languages that are unrelated and whose users live in very disparate parts of the world. As a result, these works raise questions about the role of visual iconicity in the development of sign languages and in the comparison of sign lexicons.

A high degree of lexical similarity has been observed in comparisons of various European sign languages with Chinese Sign Language and Israeli Sign Language (Woll 1984); comparisons of North American sign languages (ASL and Mexican Sign Language [LSM]) with two from Europe (French Sign Language and Spanish Sign Language) and one from East Asia (Japanese Sign Language [JSL]; Guerra Currie, Meier, and Walters 2002); and comparisons of Spanish Sign Language with the sign languages of Northern Ireland, Finland, and Bulgaria (Parkhurst and

Parkhurst 2003). These works provide a snapshot of the lexical characteristics of sign languages from around the globe.

There is some debate, however, about the degree of similarity. In a comparison of pairs of twelve sign languages, Woll (1984) found that no pair had a similarity score of less than 40 percent, and some pairs showed 80 percent similarity. In their analysis of four different sign languages (Mexican Sign Language, Spanish Sign Language, French Sign Language, and Japanese Sign Language), Guerra Currie et al. claimed that even unrelated sign languages (i.e., those between which no known contact has occurred and which are embedded in hearing cultures that are very different from each other, e.g., LSM and JSL) show modest degrees of lexical similarity. In fact, the authors found that 23 percent of the selected sign lexicons of LSM and JSL were similarly articulated. Guerra Currie et al. suggest, as have other writers, that there likely exists a base level of similarity between the lexicons of all signed languages regardless of the existence of any historical ties. According to them, this base level of similarity may be 20 percent or more.

Parkhurst and Parkhurst (2003) focus on the importance of separating noniconic signs from those that could be interpreted iconically in interlingual lexical comparisons. They looked at four European sign languages (from Spain, Northern Ireland, Finland, and Bulgaria), as well as different dialects of the sign language of Spain (from Madrid, La Coruña, Granada, Valencia, and Barcelona). Among their conclusions is a recommendation for higher thresholds for determining relatedness between sign languages. What likely contributes to varying estimates of lexical similarity is that different authors have not always used the same criteria for their analyses. Despite that, it has clearly been shown that even unrelated sign languages have some lexical similarities, which is likely a result of the iconic nature of some signs.

In a comparison of the sign languages of the United Kingdom, Australia, New Zealand, and the United States, McKee and Kennedy (2000) have demonstrated that ASL is very different, at least lexically, from the varieties that have connections to nineteenth-century British Sign Language (BSL). This is true in spite of the claim that ASL may have been influenced somewhat by BSL of the late-eighteenth and early-nineteenth centuries as a result of the sign language used on Martha's Vineyard, which likely influenced the development of ASL. According to Groce (1985, 73), the "sign language used on the Vineyard seems to have had a considerable time depth and thus may have been based on an English sign language."

Two works in the present volume add to our knowledge of sign language histories by comparing signs from different sign languages. Jeff Davis takes a long overdue look at the signs used by Native Americans of North America during the beginning and development of ASL. Davis first compares signs used by various tribes and, based on an 80 to 90 percent degree of lexical similarity across the systems, concludes that they are variants of a single variety of North American Sign Language — what he refers to as Plains Indians Sign Language (PSL). Additionally, Davis compares PSL to early twentieth-century ASL. That comparison yields about a 50 percent lexical similarity, which, according to the metrics for lexical comparison proposed by Parkhurst and Parkhurst (2003), suggests that PSL and ASL are different languages but may have items that were borrowed from one language to the other in the nineteenth and twentieth centuries. Davis also provides some interesting accounts taken from the writings of nineteenth-century educators such as Thomas Hopkins Gallaudet, and those writings offer valuable information about possible contact and influence between the two North American sign languages.

Another work on the topic of lexical comparisons between sign languages, this time with the focus on two Asian sign languages, is authored by Daisuke Sasaki, who addresses lexical contact between JSL (also referred to as NS, or Nihon Syuwa, in some works but referred to as JSL in this volume) and Taiwan Sign Language (TSL). Historical accounts of the development of TSL cite JSL as one of the sign languages that influenced the development of TSL. Thus, Sasaki compares lexical items with an emphasis on the handshape parameter of articulation, and he further focuses the analytical lens on similarly articulated signs — those that differ only in one phonological parameter (i.e., handshape for Sasaki's analysis) but share the same meaning. Sasaki finds that a number of similarly articulated TSL-JSL signs show that TSL appears to contain handshapes that may be more difficult to articulate than those found in the JSL signs. The author suggests that this is due to conservatism on the part of TSL, which has allowed that language to retain older forms that may have also been a part of JSL but no longer exist in that language because of language internal changes that tend toward efficiency and ease of articulation.

Contact between Two or More Signed Languages

Lucas and Valli (1992) have briefly discussed several possible outcomes of contact between two signed languages: lexical borrowing; foreigner talk; interference; and the creation of pidgins, creoles, and mixed systems. Whereas these areas of inquiry have not yielded many published writings, there also likely exist unpublished works that provide descriptions of signed language contact. A list of characteristics of signed language that seem to influence such contact is found in the next section, but first I present a review of contact between sign languages in terms of lexical borrowing, code switching, interference, IS as a pidgin, and language attrition and death.

Lucas and Valli (1992) caution that it would be difficult to determine the difference between an instance of lexical borrowing and code switching (or code mixing) in signed language. The issue is that, in spoken language work, borrowings have often been characterized by the integration of the borrowed word into the phonology of the other language, but this integration may not be evident in signed language. The authors maintain that this is because sign language phonologies share many basic components. Thus, in an environment in which two sign languages are frequently used, it might be difficult to definitively determine which phonology (e.g., that of Language A or Language B) the signer is using in some instances. Because of this, the authors claim that using terms like *borrowing* and *code switching* may be problematic when looking at signed language contact situations.

Keeping in mind these points about code switching versus borrowing, my dissertation work (Quinto-Pozos 2002) provides evidence that U.S.-Mexico border signers of LSM and ASL engage in code switching. That work and another (Quinto-Pozos, Forthcoming-a) describe the sequential use of synonymous signs from ASL and LSM for the purposes of re-iteration — much like certain switches described in spoken languages (e.g., see Auer 1998; Eldridge 1996; Pakir 1989). In some cases, the reiterative switches seem to emphasize a particular sign, and at other times, they appear to be used to ensure that an interlocutor comprehends the message. However, there also seem to be examples of reiterative switches that do not place a focus on the switched item.

In addition, I present examples of nonreiterative switches and the complexity of dealing with items that may be articulated similarly in both sign languages and, as a result, are relatively transparent to the interlocutor (Quinto-Pozos, Forthcoming-a). Examples are various types of points, so-called classifier constructions, commonly used gestures, and the more mimetic-looking examples often referred to as *construction action*. When such meaningful devices exist within the sign stream, it is not clear how to label a particular utterance (e.g., a so-called classifier construction from Language A or Language B, an emblem from the ambient hearing community versus a sign, or the use of constructed action versus a language-specific lexical item).

As a result, investigators of code switching in signed language face the task of examining the way in which signers switch not only between the two languages but also between meaningful linguistic versus nonlinguistic elements. The latter (e.g., points, other gestural material) may even co-occur with the linguistic devices of the sign languages, and this must be addressed as well. The data presentation and analysis in my work (Quinto-Pozos 2002, Forthcoming-a) focus primarily on lexical phenomena, but ultimately an in-depth syntactic analysis of code switching between two sign languages is needed to compare this phenomenon across languages in the two modalities. For such phrase-level analyses, a framework for treating pointing, the use of gestures, and the use of mimetic devices in signed language must be employed.

Interference is another possible outcome of contact between two sign languages that Lucas and Valli (1992) have discussed. Interference can be described as the surfacing of the articulatory norms of one sign language in the production of another. Some instances of this phenomenon may be evident in the phonological parameters of sign formation. Lucas and Valli (ibid., 35) refer to this type of interference as follows: "It might be precisely the lack of phonological integration that might signal interference — for example, the involuntary use of a handshape, location, palm orientation, movement, or facial expression from one sign language in the discourse of the other." Interference may also be evident at other levels of language structure, such as the morphology or syntax of one or both of the signed languages.

Interference is also treated in my own work (Quinto-Pozos 2002, Forthcoming-b). The analyses focus primarily on the phonological parameter of handshape, the LSM and ASL nonmanual signals that are used for *wh*-question formation, and the mouthing that sometimes accompanies signed language production. The data indicate that signers, like users of spoken language, exhibit features of interference when they articulate items from their nonnative language. For example, a signer who grew up in Mexico signing LSM might sign ASL FAMILY with an LSM F handshape rather than an ASL F handshape. The two handshapes are similar, but they differ in the contact between thumb and index finger and also in the amount of spread between the nonselected fingers (i.e., the middle and ring fingers and the pinky). In terms of mouthing, signers from Mexico sometimes produce ASL signs while simultaneously mouthing Spanish words, although the production of LSM with English mouthing is also a common linguistic practice of some signers who live along the border. In most cases, whether such interference is always predictable based on the profile of the signer is unclear.

In terms of the creation of mixed systems as a result of contact, it is vital to include discussion of IS, a "type of signing used when deaf signers communicate across mutually unintelligible language boundaries" (Supalla and Webb 1995, 334). Deaf individuals who interact with each other, primarily at international gatherings, use IS for communication. As a result, IS could be said to be "foreigner talk." There do not appear to be native users of IS, which is employed only for restricted purposes. In these ways IS resembles spoken language pidgins, but Supalla and Webb suggest that it is much more structurally complex than spoken pidgins; in some ways IS more closely resembles full-fledged sign languages than pidgin languages.

The complexity of IS has been described in terms of the rule-governed nature of its syntactic structure and various features of its vocabulary. For example, Supalla and Webb (1995) claim that verb agreement, word order, and negation in IS are systematic and rule governed. They report that verbs are frequently inflected and in complex ways. The word order of IS is usually SVO, but it can also be described in terms of other structures in which pro-drop and object function account for the surface structure of the phrases. With regard to negation, Supalla and Webb (ibid., 346–47) claim that a signer of IS appears to use "a limited number of negative devices similar in structure and form to those used in full signed languages." In a more recent work, Rosenstock (2004) looks closely at the structure of IS and finds that it is indeed more complex than one would expect from a pidgin language. Rosenstock also reports that IS contains highly iconic signs, as well as more arbitrary ones that may be loans from full sign languages. By describing a number of grammatical and otherwise communicative devices used in IS, Rosenstock shows that IS contains an "extremely complex grammatical system with a rather limited lexicon" (212). Comprehension tasks conducted during Rosenstock's study show that IS is more easily understood than natural sign languages (for people who do not know those languages), but a significant amount of information is nevertheless not transparent to the viewer. Additionally, Rosenstock reports that there even seem to be differences between how interpreters and presenters produce IS. McKee and Napier (2002) also address IS, as produced by interpreters at a conference, and corroborate earlier research that claims that IS is structurally complex. In the present volume, Karin Hoyer also discusses IS.

In another study that is included in this volume, Yoel reports an unfortunate outcome of language contact. She focuses on the attrition of Russian Sign Language (RSL) in several individuals who immigrated to Israel and subsequently learned Israeli Sign Language (ISL). The data are taken from Yoel's master's thesis, which was completed in 2001. In the current volume, Yoel examines the situation of Russian Deaf immigrants to Israel from both linguistic and nonlinguistic perspectives. An analysis of language data obtained through two lexical naming tests yields evidence of attrition of RSL, which is attributed to influence from ISL. To understand the causes of attrition, Yoel adopts the social psychology framework of ethnolinguistic vitality as she examines various facets of the lives of the deaf immigrants to Israel. These analyses consider the situations in both Israel and the former Soviet Union. Her conclusions suggest that the attrition of RSL is linked to the types of opportunities that are encountered by Russian deaf immigrants in Israel.

Finally, language death has also been suggested, albeit minimally, to result from contact between sign languages. Much of this contact is a result of the work of foreign missionaries, foreign instructors, and even deaf people from those countries who have learned ASL and other Western sign languages and returned to their own country. Woodward (2000) claims that indigenous sign languages of Southeast Asia seem to be dying out and are apparently being replaced by signed languages influenced by ASL or French Sign Language (LSF). Many sign languages that are used in Africa have undergone significant contact with ASL (Lane, Hoffmeister, and Bahan 1996), although there are also suggestions that even that contact is not threatening the existence of the natural sign language. Schmaling (2001) suggests that ASL in contact with Hausa Sign Language (HSL) in northern Nigeria has resulted in the appearance of some ASL forms in HSL (e.g., loan signs and the use of the manual alphabet for the creation of initialized signs). Despite that, Schmaling indicates that some HSL users have little contact with native signers of ASL and that the influence of ASL on HSL remains limited. Her prognosis is that "Hausa Sign Language will survive as an independent, full-fledged sign language" (192).

That optimistic outlook, however, may not be shared by Nonaka (2004) in her account of indigenous sign languages of Thailand. In particular, she writes of the need to remember sign languages in discussions of language endangerment and in language preservation efforts. Nonaka discusses indigenous varieties of sign language in Thailand such as Ban Khor Sign Language and those referred to as Old Bangkok and Old Chiangmai sign varieties. Whereas the national sign language, Thai Sign Language, seems to be thriving, according to Nonaka, the future of the indigenous varieties is uncertain. It is clear that language contact can result not only in the creation of new varieties but also in the drastic alteration or destruction of others.

CHARACTERISTICS OF SIGNED LANGUAGE THAT LIKELY INFLUENCE CONTACT IN THE VISUAL-GESTURAL MODALITY

Based on various themes that repeatedly surface in writings about signed language contact, I propose that at least three prominent characteristics of signed languages influence the outcomes of contact in that modality. The characteristics are listed in Table 1, and each is addressed in the following section. The three characteristics are not necessarily mutually exclusive, and they may interact to various degrees. Whether or not these characteristics result in contact phenomena — over the long term — that are different from what is observed with spoken languages is unclear. However, they are important points to consider when addressing signed language contact.

The Prevalence of Iconicity

One of the most commonly discussed topics in the field of sign linguistics is the iconic characteristics of sign languages and the various implications of that iconicity (e.g., the effect on language structure, language acquisition, language learning, language processing, language

TABLE 1. Characteristics of Signed Language That Likely Influence Contact in the Visual-Gestural Modality

The prevalence of iconicity
The utilization of gestural (i.e., nonlinguistic) resources
The interlingual structural similarity of sign languages

change). In various cases, the fact that signed language contains much visual iconicity does not seem to alter the way in which it is acquired (e.g., Meier 1982; Newport and Meier 1985) or how it is processed and remembered (Poizner, Bellugi, and Tweney 1981). Despite the fact that iconicity is a prominent feature of sign languages, such languages also develop noniconic ways of communicating information (e.g., Frishberg 1975; Klima and Bellugi 1979; Cormier 2002). However, for the areas of inquiry that deal with signed language contact (either with another sign language or with users of spoken language), iconicity is particularly important because it likely allows people who do not use the same language to comprehend each other more easily than if they relied exclusively on spoken and/or written language. This could have a huge effect on the outcome of such contact.

Iconicity is present in various signed language devices. It is evident in the signs of so-called classifier constructions, which resemble some part of the referent (e.g., Klima and Bellugi 1979; Taub 2001; Liddell 2002; Quinto-Pozos 2007), and it is also present in metaphorical constructions (Taub 2001; Wilcox 2002). Aspects of iconicity are also evident in the ways in which signers use their entire upper bodies to portray postures and movements of an animate referent (Metzger 1995; Liddell and Metzger 1998; Taub 2001; Quinto-Pozos 2007).

Because visual iconicity is so prevalent in sign languages, its role in cross-linguistic signed communication should be carefully examined. The degree of iconicity in signed language can be considered a true modality difference between sign and speech: Both have iconicity, but signed languages are much more characterized by visual iconicity than spoken languages are by auditory iconicity (Liddell 2002). In some cases, iconicity can make certain signs and gestures transparent (to varying degrees) to a nonsigner of a particular sign language. As a result, investigators of signed language contact have to take into account the efficiency gained by having visual iconicity assist in the creation of meaning.

Visual iconicity perhaps allows deaf people to communicate with each other across the globe more easily than hearing people who speak different languages. Pizzuto and Volterra (2000) certainly found that to be the case when they compared the performance of deaf signing versus hearing nonsigning participants from throughout Europe in a test of their ability to comprehend transparent and nontransparent Italian Sign Language (LIS) signs. In general, some LIS signs are transparent to deaf and hearing people alike, whereas others are more difficult to decipher.

However, deaf signers consistently guessed the meanings of signs even though they were not LIS signers. As a result, the authors suggest that the data point to "the existence of potential universals across sign languages" (283). The "universals" that they refer to are mostly due to the prevalence of iconicity in the visual-gestural modality. The Pizzuto and Volterra study seems to echo some of the comments made by early writers on the topic of the interlinguistic intelligibility of sign languages (Battison and Jordan 1976; Jordan and Battison 1976; Mayberry 1978); specifically, it suggests that there are ways in which the viewer of an unknown sign language can understand a portion of what is being communicated. However, this certainly does not mean that sign languages are universal and easily understood by all. Rather, the use of iconic and mimetic forms — interspersed with linguistic material that is more abstract in nature — may allow the nonuser of a sign language to understand at least part of the message.

The Utilization of Gestural Resources

Signers take advantage of commonly used nonlinguistic gestures from the ambient hearing — and perhaps even Deaf — communities. Some of those gestures may become part of the lexicon or grammar of the sign languages as evidenced, in part, by changes in their articulation vis-à-vis the manner in which hearing people use those gestures. However, deaf signers also articulate gestures that, at least on the surface, do not appear to differ from some of those that hearing people use in conjunction with speech. As with iconic devices, such gestural resources — some of which become lexicalized or grammaticized over time and others that remain as gestures — present challenges for the researcher of signed language contact. One challenge for some analyses (e.g., a syntactic account of code switching) is to determine whether a meaningful form is, in some cases, a sign or a gesture.

Various authors have suggested ways in which the gestures — both manual and nonmanual — of hearing people can now be considered as part of a sign language. For example, Janzen and Shaffer (2002) maintain that some hand gestures have been grammaticalized as modals in ASL and that some facial gestures (specifically brow raise) have been incorporated as nonmanual signals that provide syntactic information (e.g., topic markers). McClave (2001) has also proposed that nonmanual signals (e.g., head shifts for direct quotes) in ASL have been influenced by the gestures of hearing people. Casey (2003a, 2003b) has shown that directional gestures and torso movements of nonsigners are similar to verb directionality and torso movement for role shift in signed language. She suggests that directionality in ASL (and other sign languages) originates from nonlinguistic gestures, but first- versus non-first-person distinctions have been grammaticized; thus not all of the directional gestures can be considered purely gestural.

Another way in which signers use the common gestures of the hearing communities in which they are situated is through their use of *emblems* or *emblematic gestures*. These meaningful gestures have been discussed by various authors (e.g., Efron 1941; Ekman and Friesen 1969; Kendon 1981, 1988; de Jorio 2000; McNeill 2002), who have described them as culture-specific displays that normally follow standards of form. In some instances, they actually substitute for spoken words, but they can accompany speech as well. Pietrosemoli (2001) writes about the emblems (or "cultural signs," in her terminology) that hearing Venezuelans commonly use and that signers of Venezuelan Sign Language (LSV) also produce. She reports that the emblematic signs appear to reflect a code switching of emblems with linguistic items or a borrowing of the emblems into LSV. Pietrosemoli suggests that code switching and lexical borrowing are related to deaf Venezuelans' interaction with hearing Venezuelans and the concept of politeness. She employs the Brown and Levinson (1987) model of politeness as a framework to show that the use of some emblematic signs by LSV signers is intentional (but not face threatening), whereas some serve as face-threatening acts. Additionally, she describes how cultural misunderstandings, due to the mutual inaccessibility of the languages in question, are the result of the use of emblematic signs.

In Quinto-Pozos (2002, 2004), I note that emblematic gestures alternate with lexical signs of LSM and ASL in the discourse of some deaf signers who live along the U.S.-Mexico border. For instance, the emblem that I have glossed as "well" (see Figure 1; consisting of palms turned upward and an optional shrug of the shoulders and/or tilt of the head to one side) occurs with high frequency in the contact data, and the emblem was produced by signers of both LSM and ASL.

Specifically, that emblem appeared 236 times within a data set of 6,477 lexical items, which translates into a frequency of approximately 36 per 1,000 signs. By way of comparison, the most frequent nonpronominal lexical item in the ASL corpus described in Morford and MacFarlane (2003) was NAME, with a frequency of 13.4 per 1,000 signs.

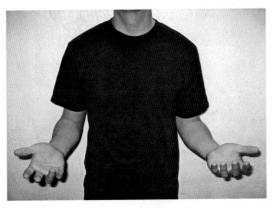

FIGURE 1. *The emblem/gesture* WELL *as produced in the LSM-ASL contact data.*

In the Morford and MacFarlane data set, WELL occurred with a frequency of 7.5 per 1,000 signs, although those authors seem to have considered that item an ASL sign as opposed to a commonly used gesture. One of my points (Quinto-Pozos 2004) is that emblems such as "well" should be categorized separately from the lexical signs of a sign language because it is not clear whether they are signs of the language (i.e., borrowings) or emblems that have been code switched. This could be particularly important if linguistic studies were to use emblems for data-elicitation tasks. The interaction of emblems with linguistic structures has been studied minimally at best; and at this point it is unclear whether they are processed differently than lexical signs.

Ways in which signers direct or "point" signs — either to present or hypothetical entities — should also be considered in signed language contact analyses. According to some accounts (e.g., Liddell 2002, 2003), some signs are directed at physically or conceptually present entities and can be described along linguistic and gestural parameters. The gestural parameters are presumably understood, at least to some degree, cross-linguistically, and this could impact cross-linguistic communication. Liddell (2002, 75) suggests that "Signers know where things are and direct signs toward them through the ability to point. The handshapes, orientation of the hand(s), the type of movement (straight, arc), are linguistically defined. The directionality of the signs is not linguistically defined. It is variable, depending completely on the actual or conceptualized location of the entity the sign is directed toward."

If Liddell's account is accurate, the variability of the directional component of the sign provides a challenge for contact researchers because they normally rely upon fixed linguistic components of lexical material (e.g., signs, words) from the two (or more) source languages to investigate the forms that the lexical items in the contact variety take. If there are no fixed components for directionality in some signs, as Liddell suggests, then the investigator must devise other means to determine what is influencing what in those cases.

The Interlingual Structural Similarity of Sign Languages

Based on the sign languages that have been studied thus far, it seems that the majority (if not all) share various structural features. Lucas and Valli (1992) suggest that sign language phonologies are more similar to each other than spoken language phonologies, and Newport and Supalla (2000) point out that sign languages show more typological similarity to each other than spoken languages, at least in terms of their morphological structure. If one uses an agreement analysis for sign language verbs, signs languages seem to favor object agreement over subject agreement.[4] Additionally, sign languages tend not to use lexical items for spatial descriptions (e.g., where a spoken language would use a preposition) but rather use the signing space for indicating such relationships. All sign languages seem to have a subset of verbs that do not indicate subject and object by using the sign space, and those verbs — commonly referred to as "plain verbs" — rely on word order for indicating the subject and object of a verbal construction within a clause (Padden 1983). However, certain sign languages have auxiliary verbs that indicate subject and/or object in the sign space — thus providing a way for most (if not all) of the verbs in those languages to use pointing for grammatical relationships (Rathmann 2000). Finally, all of the sign languages studied thus far contain so-called classifier constructions, which allow the signer to communicate various types of information such as figure, ground, motion, location, orientation, direction, manner, aspect, extant, shape, and distribution (Schembri 2003).

There are, of course, some differences across sign languages. For example, differences in phonetic inventories and phonological processes exist, but, compared to phonetic and phonological variations across spoken languages, they seem to be relatively few. As mentioned earlier, some sign languages have auxiliary verbs that aid in the use of the sign space to depict grammatical relationships, while some do not. Basic word order across sign languages is not as uniform as the use of space for showing grammatical relationships in conjunction with the verb (Newport and Supalla 2000). Moreover, signers certainly use nonmanual signals (e.g., head tilt, eyebrow raise and furrow) in different ways for grammatical and prosodic functions. As an example, a *wh*-question in ASL requires a brow furrow, whereas the same type of question in LSM requires a backward head thrust.

Some writers have suggested that the similarities among sign languages may be partly due to the fact that they are relatively young (it is believed that the oldest sign languages currently in use date to approximately the eighteenth and nineteenth centuries and that the youngest have been created within the last twenty to thirty years). Their histories are thus not long enough to show evidence of significant divergence (Newport and Supalla 2000; Meier 2002; Aronoff, Meir, and Sandler 2005). The similarity across sign languages is true for those that are genetically related, as well as those that are purported to have developed with little or no historical or genetic relationship to other sign languages.

OTHER CONSIDERATIONS FOR THE STUDY OF SIGNED LANGUAGE CONTACT

One must also keep in mind various other points when studying signed language contact. Several sociolinguistic factors make them unique and different from most spoken languages. Whether or not these factors influence the outcomes of signed language contact, they should be considered in discussions of this topic.

As with all sociolinguistic studies of sign languages, one must remember that the vast majority of users were not exposed to signed language as infants or young children. In the United States the likelihood that a deaf child will have deaf parents is roughly 4 to 8 percent (Mitchell and Karchmer 2004), and those are the children who are generally exposed to ASL from birth. Whether similar percentages of native deaf signers exist in other countries with Deaf communities — either emerging or established — is unclear, although Karin Hoyer's chapter in the present volume suggests that it is certainly not the case for Albania.

Another point has to do with the role of education and/or foreign assistance in the development of sign languages. In various Deaf communities throughout the world, the indigenous sign language or visual-gestural system of a community has been influenced by foreigners who, often with the best of intentions, have brought their ability to communicate in sign. Having collected data in Mexico, I know firsthand the challenges of trying to communicate with a user of another sign language without using the one with which I am more comfortable. Regardless of whether one does it intentionally, it is possible that a foreigner will introduce new elements into a sign language. Woll, Sutton-Spence, and Elton (2001) claim that education is a common domain for this type of influence, and they touch upon the influence of Gallaudet University and its students as vessels of such impact. The influence of foreign signing visitors upon a Deaf community is perhaps more common than we imagine, and this is the very type of situation that Hoyer describes in her chapter in this volume.

Karin Hoyer examines the case of Albanian Sign Language and its growth from pre- to post-Communist Albania. She suggests that the Hoxha regime did not allow for the development of a community of deaf people who could create a full-fledged sign language over time. Hoyer suggests, rather, that in predemocratic Albania, deaf people relied heavily on fingerspelling, with a few indigenous signs that may have been influenced largely by the emblematic gestures of the ambient hearing culture. After contact with other Deaf communities through International Sign (and perhaps other sign languages), the sign system of Albanian Deaf people became lexically richer. Hoyer also states that the use of the new signs (now referred to as Albanian Sign Language or AlbSL) occurs mostly within the social spheres of urban males in Albania, while females in rural areas are the least likely to be using AlbSL.

Jean Ann, in collaboration with Wayne H. Smith and Chiangsheng Yu, provides us with another interesting situation in this volume. They show us that, in a specific context, a variety of a sign language can spring up quickly but later disappear if the sociolinguistic environment is not strong enough to support it. Specifically, Ann et al. write about a deaf education setting in Taiwan and the use of Mainland China Sign Language (MCSL) by instructors and students at the Ch'iying School for the Deaf in southern Taiwan. That school has an interesting history: It was established by a deaf man from Mainland China in the 1960s, and the language of instruction for fifteen to twenty years was a variety of MCSL. However, the school closed in the early 2000s. This situation is particularly noteworthy because the Ch'iying signers, upon leaving school after the sixth grade, had to learn Taiwan Sign Language (TSL) in order to interact with other deaf people in Taiwan. One of the authors' goals was to determine whether the MCSL of the Ch'iying signers had any recognizable effects on TSL. In addition to providing the reader with a rich history of the establishment and various facets of the Ch'iying school, Ann et al. present excerpts of Smith's unpublished writings on the Taiwanese school and other historical accounts of TSL.

A FEW FINAL WORDS

There is much to be learned by studying contact in the visual-gestural modality. Although research on certain aspects of this topic has been occurring for years, the present volume adds examples and data from sign language communities around the world that are affected by their interaction with other sign languages. This area of inquiry is ripe for study.

One of the challenges of creating a book-length treatment of this complex topic is that there is a dearth of published materials on which to build. As a result, the reader will notice that various authors throughout this volume rely on information that has been obtained via personal communication with colleagues, other professionals, and members of the Deaf communities in which they work. The reporting of this type of information is vital to the documentation of contact phenomena, and that documentation must begin somewhere. In the future, more systematic reports are needed. My hope is that this book will encourage researchers to undertake some of that investigation.

This volume only scratches the surface of the multifaceted topic of language contact in the signed modality. We can learn much about the human capacity for language by studying this topic, and we do not need to look far to find examples of such contact. Further research in this area will add to the wealth of knowledge that we have already gained by studying languages that are produced without sound.

NOTES

1. This introduction has benefited from the comments of Ceil Lucas and Richard P. Meier. I would like to thank them for their suggestions. Any misinterpretations of the literature and omissions are, of course, my own.

2. Sofinski (2002) also describes contact between ASL and English by addressing the way in which the sign production of interpreters contains features of both languages when they are transliterating. He suggests that signers do not actually shift between languages but rather that mouth and manual-channel articulations guide the user's perception of the production.

3. Cued Speech is a way to make spoken language visible through the use of manual cues articulated by the cue-er's hands.

4. Even a "nonagreement analysis" of verbs in sign languages might suggest that sign language verbs reliably point to their objects more often than to their subjects.

REFERENCES

Akamatsu, C. T. 1985. Fingerspelling formulae: A word is more or less than the sum of its letters. In *SLR '83: Sign language research,* ed. W. Stokoe and V. Volterra, 126–32. Silver Spring, Md.: Linstok.

Ann, J. 2001. Bilingualism and language contact. In *The sociolinguistics of sign language,* ed. C. Lucas, 33–60. New York: Cambridge University Press.

Aronoff, M., I. Meir, and W. Sandler. 2005. The paradox of sign language morphology. *Language* 81(2): 301–44.

Auer, P., ed. 1998. *Code switching in conversation.* New York: Routledge.

Battison, R. 1978. *Lexical borrowing in American Sign Language.* Silver Spring, Md.: Linstok.

———, and I. K. Jordan. 1976. Cross-cultural communication with foreign signers: Fact and fancy. *Sign Language Studies* 10.

Boyes Braem, P. 2001. Functions of the mouthing component in the signing of deaf early and late learners of Swiss German Sign Language. In *Foreign vocabulary in sign languages: A cross-linguistic investigation of word formation,* ed. D. Brentari, 1–47. Mahwah, N.J.: Erlbaum.

Brentari, D., and C. A. Padden. 2001. Native and foreign vocabulary in American Sign Language: A lexicon with multiple origins. In *Foreign vocabulary in sign languages: A cross-linguistic investigation of word formation,* ed. D. Brentari, 87–119. Mahwah, N.J.: Erlbaum.

Brown, P., and S. Levinson. 1987. *Politeness: Some universals in language usage.* New York: Cambridge University Press.

Casey, S. 2003a. "Agreement" in gestures and signed languages: The use of directionality to indicate referents involved in actions. PhD diss., University of California–San Diego.

———. 2003b. Relationships between gestures and signed languages: Indicating participants in action. In *Cross-linguistic perspectives in sign language*

research: Selected papers from TISLR 2000, ed. A. Baker, B. vad den
Bogaerde, and O. Crasborn, 95–117. Hamburg: Signum.

Clyne, M. 2003. *Dynamics of language contact.* New York: Cambridge
University Press.

Cokely, D. 1983. When is a pidgin not a pidgin? *Sign Language Studies* 38:
1–24.

Cormier, K. 2002. Grammaticization of indexic signs: How American Sign
Language expresses numerosity. PhD diss., University of Texas–Austin.

Davis, J. 1989. Distinguishing language contact phenomena in ASL interpretation. In *The sociolinguistics of the deaf community,* ed. C. Lucas, 85–102.
San Diego: Academic Press.

————. 1990. Interpreting in a language contact situation: The case of
English-to-ASL interpretation. PhD diss., University of New Mexico,
Albuquerque.

de Jorio, A. 2000. *Gesture in Naples and classical antiquity.* Bloomington:
Indiana University Press.

Efron, D. 1941. *Gesture and environment.* Morningside Heights, N.Y.: King's
Crown Press.

Ekman, P., and W. V. Friesen. 1969. The repertoire of nonverbal behavioral
categories: Origins, usage, and coding. *Semiotica* 1:49–98.

Eldridge, J. 1996. Code switching in a Turkish secondary school. *English
Language Teaching Journal* 50: 303–11.

Fischer, S. 1996. By the numbers: Language-internal evidence for creolization.
International Review of Sign Linguistics 1–22.

Frishberg, N. 1975. Arbitrariness and iconicity. *Language* 51: 696–715.

Groce, N. E. 1985. *Everyone here spoke sign language.* Cambridge, Mass.:
Harvard University Press.

Guerra Currie, A.-M. P., R. P. Meier, and K. Walters. 2002. A cross-linguistic
examination of the lexicons of four signed languages. In *Modality and
structure in signed and spoken languages,* ed. R. P. Meier, K. Cormier, and
D. Quinto-Pozos, 224–36. New York: Cambridge University Press.

Hauser, P. C. 2000. An analysis of codeswitching: American Sign Language
and Cued English. In *Bilingualism and identity in Deaf communities,* ed.
M. Metzger, 43–78. Washington, D.C.: Gallaudet University Press.

Heine, B., and T. Kuteva. 2005. *Language contact and grammatical change.*
New York: Cambridge University Press.

Hoffmeister, R., and D. Moores. 1987. Code switching in deaf adults.
American Annals of the Deaf (March): 31–34.

Holm, J. 2004. *Languages in contact: The partial restructuring of vernaculars.*
New York: Cambridge University Press.

Janzen, T., and B. Shaffer. 2002. Gesture as the substrate in the process of
ASL grammaticization. In *Modality and structure in signed and spoken*

languages, ed. R. P. Meier, K. Cormier, and D. Quinto-Pozos, 199–223. New York: Cambridge University Press.

Jordan, I. K., and R. Battison. 1976. A referential communication experiment with foreign sign languages. *Sign Language Studies* 5(10): 69–80.

Kachman, W. P. 1991. An investigation of code switching behavior of deaf children. PhD diss., University of Maryland, College Park.

Kendon, A. 1981. Geography of gesture. *Semiotica* 37: 129–63.

———. 1988. How gestures can become like words. In *Cross-cultural perspectives in non-verbal communication*, ed. F. Poyatos, 131–41, Toronto: Hegrefe.

Klima, E., and U. Bellugi. 1979. *The signs of language*. Cambridge, Mass.: Harvard University Press.

Kuntze, M. 2000. Codeswitching in ASL and written English language contact. In *The signs of language revisited: An anthology to honor Ursula Bellugi and Edward Klima*, ed. K. Emmorey and H. Lane, 287–302. Mahwah, N.J.: Erlbaum.

Lane, H., R. Hoffmeister, and B. Bahan. 1996. *A journey into the* DEAF-WORLD. San Diego: DawnSign Press.

Lee, D. 1983. Sources and aspects of code switching in the signing of a deaf adult and her interlocutors. PhD diss., University of Texas–Austin.

Liddell, S. 1996. Spatial representations in discourse: Comparing spoken and signed language. *Lingua* 98: 145–67.

———. 2002. Modality effects and conflicting agendas. In *The study of sign languages: Essays in honor of William C. Stokoe*, ed. D. F. Armstrong, M. A. Karchmer, and J. V. Van Cleve, 53–81. Washington, D.C.: Gallaudet University Press.

———. 2003. *Grammar, gesture, and meaning in American Sign Language*. New York: Cambridge University Press.

———, and M. Metzger. 1998. Gesture in sign language discourse. *Journal of Pragmatics* 30: 657–97.

Lucas, C., and C. Valli. 1988. Contact in the Deaf community: Linguistic change and contact. In *Proceedings of the Sixteenth Annual Conference on New Ways of Analyzing Variation*, 209–15.

———. 1989. Language contact in the American Deaf community. In *The sociolinguistics of the Deaf community*, ed. C. Lucas, 11–40. San Diego: Academic Press.

———. 1991. ASL or contact signing: Issues of judgment. *Language in Society* 20: 201–16.

———. 1992. *Language contact in the American Deaf community*. San Diego: Academic Press.

Mayberry, R. 1978. French Canadian Sign Language: A study of inter-sign-language comprehension. In *Understanding language through sign language research*, ed. P. Siple, 349–72. New York: Academic Press.

McClave, E. Z. 2001. The relationship between spontaneous gestures of the hearing and American Sign Language. *Gesture* 11: 51–72.

McKee, D., and G. Kennedy. 2000. Lexical comparison of signs from American, Australian, British, and New Zealand sign languages. In *The signs of language revisited: An anthology to honor Ursula Bellugi and Edward Klima,* ed. K. Emmorey and H. Lane, 49–76. Mahwah, N.J.: Erlbaum.

McKee, R. L., and J. Napier. 2002. Interpreting into International Sign Pidgin. *Sign Language and Linguistics* 51: 27–54.

McNeill, D. 1992. *Hand and mind.* Chicago: University of Chicago Press.

Meier, R. P. 1982. Icons, analogues, and morphemes: The acquisition of verb agreement in ASL. PhD diss., University of California–San Diego.

———. 2002. Why different, why the same? Explaining effects and non-effects of modality upon linguistic structure in sign and speech. In *Modality and structure in signed and spoken languages,* ed. R. P. Meier, K. Cormier, and D. Quinto-Pozos, 1–25. New York: Cambridge University Press.

Metzger, M. 1995. Constructed dialogue and constructed action in American Sign Language. In *Sociolinguistics in Deaf communities,* ed. C. Lucas, 255–71. Washington, D.C.: Gallaudet University Press.

Miller, C. 2001. The adaptation of loan words in Quebec Sign Language: Multiple sources, multiple processes. In *Foreign vocabulary in sign language: A cross-linguistic investigation of word formation,* ed. D. Brentari, 139–73. Mahwah, N.J.: Erlbaum.

Mitchell, R. E., and M. A. Karchmer. 2004. Chasing the mythical ten percent: Parental hearing status of deaf and hard of hearing students in the United States. *Sign Language Studies* 42: 138–63.

Morford, J., and J. MacFarlane. 2003. Frequency characteristics of American Sign Language. *Sign Language Studies* 32: 213–25.

Mufwene, S. S. 2001. *The ecology of language evolution.* New York: Cambridge University Press.

Myers-Scotton, C. 2002. *Contact linguistics, bilingual encounters, and grammatical outcomes.* New York: Oxford University Press.

Newport, E. L., and R. P. Meier. 1985. The acquisition of American Sign Language. In *The cross-linguistic study of language acquisition,* ed. D. I. Slobin. Vol. 1: *The data,* 881–938. Hillsdale, N.J.: Erlbaum.

Newport, E. L., and T. Supalla. 2000. Sign language research at the millennium. In *The signs of language revisited: An anthology to honor Ursula Bellugi and Edward Klima,* ed. K. Emmorey and H. Lane, 103–14. Mahwah, N.J.: Erlbaum.

Nonaka, A. M. 2004. The forgotten endangered languages: Lessons on the importance of remembering from Thailand's Ban Khor Sign Language. *Language in Society* 33: 737–67.

Padden, C. A. 1983. Interaction of morphology and syntax in American Sign Language. PhD diss., University of California–San Diego.

———. 1998. The ASL lexicon. *Sign Language and Linguistics* 1: 39–60.

Pakir, A. 1989. Linguistic alternants and code selection in Baba Malay. *World Englishes* 8: 379–88.

Parkhurst, S. and D. Parkhurst. 2003. Lexical comparisons of signed languages and the effects of iconicity. Unpublished manuscript.

Pietrosemoli, L. 2001. Politeness in Venezuelan Sign Language. In *Signed languages: Discoveries from international research,* ed. V. Dively, M. Metzger, S. Taub, and A. M. Baer, 163–79. Washington, D.C.: Gallaudet University Press.

Pizzuto, E., and V. Volterra. 2000. Iconicity and transparency in sign languages: A cross-linguistic cross-cultural view. In *The signs of language revisited: An anthology to honor Ursula Bellugi and Edward Klima,* ed. K. Emmorey and H. Lane, 261–86. Mahwah, N.J.: Erlbaum.

Poizner, H., Bellugi, U., and R. D. Tweney. 1981. Processing of formational, semantic, and iconic information in American Sign Language. *Journal of Experimental Psychology: Human Perception and Performance* 7: 1146–1159.

Quinto-Pozos, D. 2002. Contact between Mexican Sign Language and American Sign Language in two Texas border areas. PhD diss., University of Texas–Austin.

———. 2004. Sign frequencies and issues of lexical status: Data from Mexican Sign Language and American Sign Language. Poster presentation at the annual meeting, January 8–11, of the Linguistic Society of America, Boston.

———. 2007. Can constructed action be considered obligatory? *Lingua* 117 (7): 1285–1314.

———. Forthcoming-a. Code switching between sign languages. In *The Cambridge handbook of code switching,* ed. B. Bullock and J. Toribio. New York: Cambridge University Press.

———. Forthcoming-b. Sign language contact and interference: LSM and ASL. *Language in Society.*

Rathmann, C. 2000. Does the presence of a person-agreement marker predict word order in SLs? Paper presented at the Seventh International Conference on Theoretical Issues in Sign Language Research, July 23–27, Amsterdam.

Rosenstock, R. 2004. An investigation of international sign: Analyzing structure and comprehension. PhD diss., Gallaudet University, Washington, D.C.

Schembri, A. 2003. Rethinking "classifiers" in signed languages. In *Perspectives on classifier constructions in sign languages,* ed. K. Emmorey, 3–34. Mahwah, N.J.: Erlbaum.

Schmaling, C. 2001. ASL in northern Nigeria: Will Housa Sign Language survive? In *Signed languages: Discoveries from international research,* ed.

V. Dively, M. Metzger, S. Taub, and A. M. Baer, 180–93. Washington, D.C.: Gallaudet University Press.

Sofinski, B. A. 2002. So, why do I call this English? In *Turn-taking, finger-spelling, and contact in signed languages,* 8th ed., ed. C. Lucas, 27–48. Washington, D.C.: Gallaudet University Press.

Stokoe, W. C., Jr. 1970. Sign language diglossia. *Studies in Linguistics* 21: 27–41.

Supalla, T., and R. Webb. 1995. The grammar of International Sign: A new look at pidgin languages. In *Language, gesture, and space,* ed. K. Emmorey and J. Reilly, 333–52. Mahwah, N.J.: Erlbaum.

Taub, S. 2001. *Language from the body: Iconicity and metaphor in American Sign Language.* New York: Cambridge University Press.

Thomason, S. G. 2001. *Language contact: An introduction.* Edinburgh: Edinburgh University Press.

———, and T. Kaufman. 1988. *Language contact, creolization, and genetic linguistics.* Berkeley: University of California Press.

Wilcox, P. 2002. *Metaphor in American Sign Language.* Washington, D.C.: Gallaudet University Press.

Woll, B. 1984. The comparative study of different sign languages: Preliminary analyses. In *Recent research on European sign languages,* ed. F. Loncke, P. Boyes Braem, and Y. Lebrun, 79–91. Lisse, the Netherlands: Swets and Zeitlinger.

Woll, B., R. Sutton-Spence, and F. Elton. 2001. Multilingualism: The global approach to sign languages. In *Sociolinguistics of sign languages,* ed. C. Lucas. New York: Cambridge University Press.

Woodward, J. 2000. Sign languages and sign language families in Thailand and Viet Nam. In *The signs of language revisited: An anthology to honor Ursula Bellugi and Edward Klima,* ed. K. Emmorey and H. Lane, 23–47. Mahwah, N.J.: Erlbaum.

Woodward, J. C., Jr. 1973a. Implicational lects on the deaf diglossic continuum. PhD diss., Georgetown University, Washington, D.C.

———. 1973b. Some characteristics of Pidgin Sign English. *Sign Language Studies* 3: 39–46.

Part 1 Contact in a Trilingual Setting

Māori Signs: The Construction of Indigenous

Deaf Identity in New Zealand Sign Language

Rachel Locker McKee, David McKee, Kirsten Smiler, and Karen Pointon

The assertion of Deaf cultural identity, minority rights and indigenous self-determination in recent decades has created a platform from which Deaf people of ethnic minority family heritage have begun to voice their multilayered experiences of cultural socialization and identity (Ahmad et al. 1998; Foster and Kinuthia 2003; Humphries 1993; McKay-Cody 1998/1999; Morales-López et al. 2002; Parasnis 1996; Paris and Wood 2002). In those places where an indigenous minority is engaged in cultural revitalization (e.g., Māori in New Zealand, Catalán in Spain, Navajo in North America), a zone of contact exists between the respective empowerment agendas of hearing and Deaf members of that minority. These agendas, in which the validation of a minority language plays both instrumental and symbolic roles, may converge in some respects and compete in others, causing Deaf individuals' sense of allegiance to fluctuate between Deaf and non-Deaf constructions of ethnic identity. Brentari comments from a linguistic point of view that, "(b)ecause cultural identity and empowerment in Deaf communities are primarily expressed through the language, the status of foreign material in sign language becomes very important" (2001a, xii). In a multilingual context, the processes and outcomes of spoken–signed language contact are intertwined with the representation of identity through language use.

Māori Deaf people (hereafter MD)[1] in contemporary New Zealand (NZ) are situated in a context of trilingual, tricultural contact, and some are responding by constructing a distinct indigenous identity within the New Zealand Sign Language (NZSL) community through the development and promotion of Māori signs. Unlike North America or Australia, there is no tradition of manual signs used by hearing Māori people as an alternate or complementary form of verbal communication. "Māori signs" (hereafter MS) that express Māori cultural reference in NZSL have recently developed in response to cultural exchange with non-Deaf Māori and, we contend, have also been appropriated by MD to symbolically enact consciousness of indigenous identity. This chapter describes the processes and outcomes of a contemporary period of borrowing from the Māori language into NZSL and proposes that, from a linguistic perspective, the result is a lexicon within NZSL rather than a separate variety of NZSL, as is sometimes implied by communities of interest in the discourse around MS. We also explore sociopolitical dimensions of ownership of this lexicon and its symbolic role in the mediation of MD identity in a zone of contact between Māori and Deaf decolonization agendas.[2]

METHOD AND DATA

This study is informed by lexical data and interviews that are backgrounded by the researchers' participant-observation in the New Zealand Deaf community over a twenty-year period. The first data source consulted is the lexicographical database of the *Dictionary of New Zealand Sign Language* (Kennedy et al. 1997), which was supplemented in 2003 by authors McKee and McKee through the collection of eight hundred additional signs, including specifically those with Māori reference. This chapter categorizes signs with Māori reference in the NZSL lexicon as established native signs, neologisms, or semantic extensions of existing NZSL signs, according to aspects of their derivation and form.

Second, sociohistorical data were sought through interviews with a focus group of four MD informants, three of whom have led developments in MD identity politics and MS development over the past decade. In addition, three hearing Māori individuals who have been closely involved with MD as interpreters and educators during the same period were interviewed about their perspective on contact between the languages of Māori and NZSL. Data provided by these informants provide the basis for the description of historical developments, and quotes from interviews are used to support our analysis of attitudes and beliefs. Quotes from Deaf participants have been translated into English by authors Pointon and R. McKee from videotaped interviews originally conducted in NZSL. After collection and preliminary analysis of data for this study, Māori authors Pointon and Smiler were present at the 2005 National Māori Deaf Hui conference, which was attended by approximately one hundred MD; at the hui they presented our preliminary analysis for feedback and also observed the use and discussion of MS during the conference, which inform our discussion later in this chapter.

Research in marginalized communities is especially sensitive to the impact of the researchers' identities and sociocultural practices. The authors' identities and relationships with the community of focus in this study constitute a mix of emic and etic lenses through which the data are interpreted (Patton 1990). Mckee and Mckee have been university teachers and researchers in the NZSL community for more than two decades and have been closely involved in the training of interpreters and Deaf NZSL teachers. As a hearing Caucasian New Zealander, Rachel McKee is a second-language interlocutor in hearing Māori and Deaf cultural domains; David McKee, a middle-class American Deaf person fluent in NZSL, has an insider/outsider perspective on the NZ Deaf community. Karen Pointon, MD collaborator and an NZSL teacher, brings personal, historical experience in MD networks and has held national leadership positions in the NZ Deaf community. Kirsten Smiler, a Māori CODA, is the hearing daughter of a Deaf non-Māori parent and a hearing Māori parent and grew up during a period of Māori renaissance and emerging Deaf pride. Smiler completed her 2004 master's thesis on the way in which Māori and Deaf world socialization experiences shape MD individuals' sense of identity. All of the researchers have had previous interaction with some or all of the research participants within Deaf community circles.

We acknowledge that presenting a case study of a recent and small-scale sociolinguistic phenomenon carries a risk of overstating the implications of a situation that is still unfolding (Merriam 1998). On the other hand, a case study can focus attention on a directly observable and current language phenomenon, reveal how these indigenous Deaf people confront specific challenges, and offer a wider understanding of their particular experience (Shaw 1978). Our discussion of the Māori-NZSL contact situation adopts the social constructionist premise that language is used in particular ways "to construct, modify and maintain particular social identities" (Holmes 2003). We contend that MS are evidence of emerging linguistic practices and a consciousness among MD that reflect their desire to address a perceived discontinuity between their linguistic identity as NZSL users and their ethnic identity as Māori. Analysis of the situated use of Māori signs in discourse to demonstrate this process at the microlevel was outside the scope of this study; we aim here to analyze the nature of the signs and the macrosocial factors surrounding their creation and use.

This chapter first outlines certain background factors relevant to the interaction between communities of Māori speakers and NZSL users. The second main section describes the various forms of MS found within NZSL as outcomes of language contact. Finally, the third section focuses on ideological positions around the creation, ownership, and naming of MS. We also briefly discuss Deaf coinages in written Māori that explicitly construct MD identity.

MĀORI REFERENCE IN THE ESTABLISHED NZSL LEXICON

NZSL, the common language of the New Zealand Deaf community, originated in residential school networks, which historically included both Māori and Pākehā (the indigenous term for Caucasian New Zealanders) students. In designing the first comprehensive dictionary of NZSL in the early 1990s, researchers deliberately sought to include all existing signs in NZSL representing Māori referents or concepts (other than place names) by consultation with Māori members of the NZSL community (Kennedy et al. 1997, x). It was considered important to record the extent to which the lexicon of NZSL reflects Māori concepts since they constitute a local feature that distinguishes NZSL from its close relatives, Australian and British Sign Languages (Johnston 2000; McKee and Kennedy 2000). Twenty-five signs with Māori primary glosses (headwords) were recorded in the 1997 dictionary (see Table 1); these signs were apparently in general usage in the Deaf community rather than specific to MD. A follow-up project was undertaken in 2003, at Victoria University of Wellington, to expand the dictionary database, with the aim of documenting signs used by the oldest generation of signers, younger signers (particularly informal or colloquial terms), technical signs, and signs with Māori reference that the researchers believed had increased in number since the dictionary data were collected a decade earlier (the reasons for which are outlined later).

Lexical and stylistic variation in NZSL linked to region and age has been noted in previous research (Collins-Ahlgren 1989; Kennedy et al. 1997; McKee and McKee 2002), but there is no indication that Māori signers' use of NZSL varies systematically from that of non-Māori, whose social networks and domains of language use substantially overlap. However, in order to determine whether patterned variation exists at any level of linguistic structure, a current research project on sociolinguistic variation in NZSL[1] includes Māori ethnicity as a variable.

SOCIOHISTORICAL BACKGROUND OF THE LANGUAGE COMMUNITIES

Māori Population and Ethnic Identity

Māori comprise approximately 15 percent of the overall NZ population (four million) and approximately 35 percent of the population under fifteen years of age (Statistics New Zealand 2007). However, diagnostic data show that 43 percent of the children identified as deaf or hearing impaired in 2005 were Māori (National Audiology Centre 2007). Calculations of the total NZSL community range between 4,500 and 7,700 (Dugdale 2000; Statistics New Zealand 2001); in light of recent reanalysis of deaf demographics in comparable Western countries, it is likely that these estimates are on the high side (cf. Johnston 2004). Currently, no reliable figures on the Māori proportion of the NZSL community are available. While diagnostic data suggest that Māori are overrepresented, the proportion cannot be directly extrapolated since the aggregate figure of 39 percent includes children with mild and moderate hearing impairment who may not necessarily become NZSL users.

Contemporary Māori ethnic identity is a contestable concept. Commentators generally concur that it can be constructed on a range of potential factors that include knowledge of one's tribal genealogy and customs, participation in Māori domains and networks, affiliation with Māori political goals, and speaking Te Reo Māori (TRM) and/or a Māori variety of English (Durie 1997, 2001; Holmes 1997).[3] Recent estimates of the proportion of Māori people who are proficient in TRM range between 20 and 42 percent (Benton 2001, Statistics New Zealand 2002). Native speakers of the older generation are becoming rare, and surveys indicate that the transmission and survival of the language remains precarious despite concerted retention efforts (Benton 2001; Boyce 2005).

1. http://www.vuw.ac.nz/lals/research/deafstudies/DSRU%20site/NZSL%20variation/variation%20project.aspx.

Demographic information shows that more than half of those who identify as ethnic Māori have mixed biological heritage and non-Māori partners (Callister 2004; Chapple 2000). Contemporary Māori ethnicity is thus primarily socially and contextually defined; Māori writer O'Regan (2001, 88), for example, emphasizes that the transmission and expression of indigenous identity is neither straightforward nor static: "The reality is that a person or group may form a web of interwoven identities with corresponding interwoven boundaries. . . . Plural cultural identities are a living reality for many of the world's indigenous populations." This is salient to MD who can potentially claim Māori (and usually Pākehā) biological heritage, as well as Deaf social heritage. By their own account, socialization into Deaf-world identity tends to be the most linguistically and politically accessible to MD (Dugdale 2000; McKee 2001; Smiler 2004).

Māori Cultural Renaissance and the Development of Māori Deaf Pride

In some countries, the legal protection of an indigenous language has created a sociopolitical climate conducive to subsequent recognition of the signed language of a national or regional Deaf community, as for example in Catalonia (Morales-López et al. 2002), Finland (Hoyer 2004), and Ireland (Leeson and Grehan 2004). The past three decades have been a period of cultural renaissance for Māori, during which revitalization of the language has been central to an empowerment agenda known indigenously as *tino rangatiratanga* ("self-determination/sovereignty") (Spolsky 2005). Māori achieved official language status in 1987, while English is the de facto language in most domains of NZ life. We believe that societal acknowledgment of indigenous biculturalism has indirectly supported the emergence of Deaf cultural consciousness and acceptance of NZSL from the mid-1980s, which were spurred by the overseas Deaf Pride movement and linguistic research on sign languages (Dugdale 2001a; McKee 2001). In 2006 NZSL was recognized as an official language in legislation modeled on the Māori Language Act, which grants official status, protection, and the right to use it in legal settings (New Zealand Sign Language Bill; Māori Language Act 1987, 176). The NZSL Act, however, has no resources or enforceable obligations attached to it beyond provision of interpretation in court settings.

Although Māori and Pākehā Deaf are socialized in the same schools, and coparticipate in all other Deaf community domains such as sports, political advocacy, clubs, and marriage, MD perceive that their indigenous identity is not necessarily positively acknowledged within the Deaf community and that their Deaf identity is not understood in the Māori world (AKO Ltd. 1995; Dugdale 2000; Smiler 2004). Generally speaking, MD have had restricted access to the activities and benefits of the Tino Rangatiratanga movement and language regeneration efforts that gained momentum in the 1970s. By the early1990s some hearing Māori in the education and welfare sectors recognized the marginalized position of MD, who had recently begun to articulate their Deaf cultural identity through the use of NZSL interpreters in Māori contexts. A report on the development needs of MD in 1995 observed that "Deaf Māori suffer on two levels because of their dual status of being both Deaf and Māori. To be able to fully exercise their *tino rangatiratanga* there must be acknowledgement of this dual status and changes put in place to enable Deaf Māori to fulfill their aspirations in both the Māori and the Deaf communities where their two cultures will be recognised and validated" (AKO Ltd. 1995, 39).

Acknowledgment of NZSL, opportunities to use it as a medium of education, and the training of some Māori-speaking NZSL interpreters since the mid-1990s have enabled MD to participate more in Māori domains. This contact has stimulated aspirations for stronger Māori consciousness, leadership capacity, and the recognition of Māori identity within the Deaf community (Dugdale 2001; Smiler 2004). Reflecting a wider societal push for political partnership with Māori, Māori participation in national Deaf politics has been strengthened through elected representation and specially created Māori development roles in the Deaf Association of New Zealand (Dugdale 2001a; Jaffe 1992).

According to our informants, intensified contact between TRM and NZSL speakers and the beginning of contemporary MD collective consciousness dates to 1991, when a group of MD formally came together to learn and perform a Māori ceremonial welcome at New Zealand's first "Deaf View" conference. This activity, led by a hearing tutor (who was interviewed for this study) under the auspices of the Kelston Deaf Education Centre in Auckland, progressed into ongoing cultural activities for MD students at the school, in which MD adults also enthusiastically participated. This new site of activity soon involved other hearing Māori and led to an informal network of MD, which has since organized two national hui and regional workshops focused on fostering Māori cultural knowledge and pride.

Another key player in the development of MS has been a Māori adult education institution that began employing MD tutors in 1996 to teach

NZSL to hearing Māori students, who were enrolled mainly to learn TRM. Due to a staff member having a Deaf family member, this institution formed an agenda to engage MD in cultural development activities, develop MS as a bridge between the two cultures, and encourage Māori students to undertake further training as sign language interpreters.

Trilingual interpreters, though few in number, have been important agents of linguistic and political change in MD circles by facilitating participation in Māori cultural settings. The practice of interpreting between TRM and NZSL began on an amateur basis in the early 1990s, and the first Māori-speaking sign language interpreter qualified in 1995 with the generic English-NZSL qualification (no Māori-specific training or qualification is available at present). Currently there are three Māori individuals who are recognized as skilled trilingual interpreters able to work in a full range of Māori contexts, and another three who have undertaken sign language interpreter training but are considered (by our informants) to be novices who are still developing their language and interpretation skills in TRM and/or NZSL. None of these trilingual interpreters have an immediate Deaf family member (i.e., none are native signers), and only one is a native speaker of TRM. The two senior trilingual interpreters whom we interviewed described the motivation of Māori interpreters as a desire to empower and increase opportunities for MD, often motivated by personal links with a Deaf person. From that point, they found a path into the Deaf community and learning NZSL and thus realized the need to further develop whatever TRM skills they had possessed when they started out as interpreters.

Hearing and Deaf Māori engaged in these recent zones of cultural exchange have brought to bear their own goals, understandings of deafness, and cultural resources, all of which have resulted in both synergies and tensions. Language has been at the nexus of these sites of contact, where the fundamental challenge has been to mediate Māori culture — and Deaf people's appropriation of this knowledge — through NZSL. In most instances, Deaf people were immersed in a hearing Māori context, while in some situations, hearing Māori also experienced immersion in Deaf contexts. These dynamics are discussed further in the section on ideologies and ownership of MS.

Contact between Te Reo Māori and New Zealand English

The extent of borrowing of Māori lexical items into New Zealand English (NZE) is relevant background to contact between TRM and

NZSL. It has been said that "the most unmistakably New Zealand part of NZE is its Māori element" (Deverson 1991, 18). Macalister (2005) reports that approximately one thousand Māori words are established loans in NZE (about six out of every thousand words that are written or spoken), of which many are proper nouns. Lexical borrowing in both directions between the two languages has occurred since colonization in the early 1800s. However, as British settlers established political hegemony in the second half of the nineteenth century, cultural assimilation of Māori led to dramatic attrition of the Māori language and a drop in bilingualism (Spolsky 2005).

During the early colonial period, Māori words (primarily nouns) were initially borrowed into NZE to refer to indigenous places, flora, fauna, artifacts, and practices, and, as nationhood progressed, to signify national identity (e.g., christening ships and racehorses with Māori names) (Macalister 2005). Regeneration of the Māori language and the impact of the Tino Rangatiratanga movement since the late 1970s have led to a wider range of Māori loanwords in NZE, particularly to refer to concepts of Māori social culture, as these have gained prominence in the political and social discourse of the contemporary decolonization agenda (ibid.).

The extent to which individual NZE speakers use Māori loans varies, reflecting social dimensions of identity, attitude, audience, as well as situational and contextual factors (Macalister 2003). Between Māori speakers of NZE, code switching is used to signal Māori cultural affiliation; grammatical features (e.g., vernacular verb forms, prosodic aspects) and discourse sequences (e.g., greetings) also mark in-group English used by Māori people (Holmes 1997; Bell 2000).

THEORETICAL CONSIDERATIONS

Language as an Instrument of Ethnolinguistic Identity

The sociolinguistic situation of Māori Deaf and the development of MS are considered here within a poststructuralist framework that views language as a form of symbolic cultural capital (Bourdieu 1991) and as a site of identity construction (Weedon 1987). Language is central to constructing ethnolinguistic identity. The use of a minority language is a vehicle for knowing and participating in the heritage culture; it also performs the affective function of symbolically enacting cultural identity and pride (Fishman 1989). Conscious and unconscious language behavior such as code switching into a minority language encodes aspects of personal identity and social affiliation or distance (Holmes 2001; Milroy 1989).

For Deaf ethnic minority individuals though, the linguistic enactment of plural cultural identity can be problematic in either the Deaf world or the hearing world for several reasons. First, deafness constrains the spontaneous acquisition of a minority spoken language in home and community settings (Gerner de García 1995); thus cultural knowledge encoded in that language is often inaccessible. Moreover, without knowledge of the heritage culture language, the use of code switching as a potential signifier of dual ethnic identity is not an option. The invisibility of minority languages and ethnic role models in deaf education particularly and in mainstream society generally further contributes to Deaf minority individuals' alienation from the heritage culture and language of their hearing family (Aramburo 1989; Davis and Supalla 1995; Dively 2001; Herring-Wright 1999). These factors apply to the situation of MD, who generally have minimal understanding of TRM and superficial access to Māori cultural domains. As Deaf people, they also face potential prejudice with regard to their use of NZSL in both Māori and Pākehā hearing communities. Constructing an ethnolinguistic identity as both Māori and Deaf is thus a challenging journey.

Traditionally, the cultural knowledge underpinning Māori identity is transmitted orally through language arts, including oratory, recitation, and song, which generally exclude Deaf participation. Other contemporary cultural domains such as Māori-dominated sporting codes, Māori television, and TRM-medium schools offer potential new avenues of identity in which MD are participating, although access to meaningful engagement in these is still limited for most Deaf individuals (the main exception being sports). Accomplishment in the manual and performing arts (e.g., wood carving, flax weaving, action songs), which are visually and kinesthetically based, is a source of ethnic pride that is available to some MD. By contrast, the accessibility of NZSL and the common sociopolitical experiences of deafness (i.e., linguistic exclusion, powerlessness, camaraderie with Deaf peers, shared schooling) lead to strong cultural affiliation with the Deaf world. Smiler (2004) reports that MD describe plural, fluid identities, facets of which are foregrounded differently through social interaction in Māori and Deaf cultural environments, respectively. Most participants in that study felt linguistically and socially Deaf but believed that being Māori was also integral to their personal identity, even if their depth of enculturation into the Māori world was limited.

The following excerpt from a MD participant in our study describes her sense of both identification with and exclusion from Māori culture while growing up in a hearing family. Her account is representative of other participants' experiences: "My father, my older brother and his son speak Māori, but my Mum [Pākehā] knew only a little, and my sister and me only a bit. I only know the Māori numbers. I'm not strong with [any] spoken language, but I have a strong feeling of Māori identity. . . . When I was growing up, I didn't know the Māori protocols at the marae, so I learned to watch and copy what people around me were doing, like taking off my shoes before going inside."[4]

This informant, who had mixed parentage, described trying to negotiate an identity while moving between Pākehā, Māori, and Deaf contexts:

My mother is Pākehā, and at home it was different than on the marae. It was confusing! I wasn't frustrated, but I just didn't know why it was different. . . . I had the same communication breakdowns whether people spoke English or Māori. I would think "I am Māori, and I am also Pākehā." But I still couldn't make sense of what I am. I was always mixed up. People used to ask "Are you Māori?" I'd reply "Yes!" and "Can you speak?" I'd say, "No! I don't have to. I've been Deaf all my life." When I moved to a deaf school for one and a half years, I picked up NZSL, and I could communicate easily with everyone. Then I went back to a hearing high school. There was a marae there, and I was amazed to be taught about Māori culture by a hearing person. She would write Māori words and also the English translation on the board. I saw two different languages, but I didn't know what they meant. . . . I accept both Māori and Pākehā sides . . . but spoken language, it's not for me!

Although embracing her dual Māori-Pākehā heritage, this participant's identity is linguistically anchored in being Deaf. She expresses a sense of vulnerability about her identity as defined by others' language criteria in hearing contexts, either Pākehā or Māori. Neither TRM nor English afforded accessible routes to cultural identity for her as a Māori Deaf person, while her NZSL socialization was removed from the Māori aspects of her home background. It is this disjunction between the cultural-linguistic contexts in which they interact that some MD have sought to address by developing new forms of the Māori-NZSL contact language while also invoking a sense of new group membership (cf. Ting-Toomey 1999).

Borrowing as an Outcome of Language Contact

We apply Thomason and Kaufman's (1988, 37) definition of "borrowing" to the development of MS: "The incorporation of foreign features into a group's native language by speakers of that language: the native language is maintained but is changed by the addition of the incorporated features." The native language in this case is NZSL. By "native" we mean endemic to the NZ Deaf community rather than necessarily indigenous since a large proportion of the lexicon is historically related to British Sign Language (McKee and Kennedy 2000). Lexical borrowing generally occurs when speakers in contact with another language perceive a gap or a need for reference to new or foreign concepts in their first language; the outcome is to expand the lexicon or to create substitutes for existing words (Haugen 1938/1972; Thomason and Kaufman 1988). The growth of signs with Māori reference in the NZSL lexicon represents semantic borrowing into NZSL, arising from contact between TRM and NZSL and mediated through signed, spoken, and written modalities.

"Semantic importation" (Haugen 1950/1972a) of spoken lexicon into signed languages exhibits particular features arising from the modality differences; borrowing generally occurs through mechanisms such as fingerspelling, mouthing (unvoiced articulation of a spoken word with or without a manual sign), initialized sign formations, and loan translation (Brentari 2001b). Foreign forms that combine structural elements from two languages may be described as *hybrids*. In NZE, "Māoridom" is an example (Macalister 2005), while initialized signs and the coarticulation of mouthing with a manual sign to specify meaning are forms of hybrid loans commonly found in sign languages, including NZSL (e.g., Boyes Braem 2001; Miller 2001; Machabée 1995).

Haugen (1950/1972b, 75) distinguishes "semantic loans" in which the scope of an existing lexeme is extended to express a foreign meaning (e.g., "flax" in NZE, which has altered its original English sense to now refer to a related but different indigenous New Zealand plant; Macalister 2003) from "loan translations," in which the native morpheme structure is approximated by substituting morphemes from the host language (e.g., "dining hall" in NZE, which approximates the Māori "whare/kai," or in NZSL, the compound loan BABY + SIT, derived from English "baby-sit"). We use the term "semantic loan" to characterize NZSL signs whose semantic scope has been extended to express a Māori meaning due to recent Deaf contact with TRM.

Two social preconditions for borrowing between languages are extended social contact and a degree of bilingualism in speakers (Thomason and Kaufman 1988, 47). In language contact situations, bilingual individuals are instrumental in introducing new usages and coinages from a second language to monolingual speakers who would not otherwise have access to them (Bynon 1977). An important factor in TRM-NZSL contact is the emergence of bilingual individuals and of domains in which the two languages are in use by both Deaf and hearing participants. Māori sign language interpreters and other hearing Māori with NZSL skills have in some instances been key agents of motivating, coining, and disseminating contact forms. Strang (1970, 28) points out that merely exposure to a second language resulting in indirect experience of that language rather than actual bilingualism can be sufficient to prompt lexical borrowing. This describes the circumstances of MD themselves, who have created contact sign forms as a result of indirect exposure to TRM rather than through direct use of it as bilinguals.

Finally, of relevance to this situation is the premise that the "need" to borrow foreign words is not solely about conveying referential meaning but may be equally about the desire to signal shifts in attitude and identity (Poplack et al. 1988). Macalister (2003, 276–79) has identified six possible linguistic and social factors that motivate lexical borrowing from Māori into NZE (from a subordinate to a dominant language): (1) economy of expression; (2) expression of cultural or national identity; (3) displaying empathy with the other language and/or culture; (4) making an impact on an audience; (5) cultural reference to aspects of foreign culture; and (6) clarity and precision of meaning (particularly for abstract concepts). Macalister (ibid., 280) comments that the "operation of these motivations generally needs to be inferred, as definite evidence is unlikely to be available." Our data suggest that these motivations feature in the expansion and use of MS in the NZSL lexicon, as MD have perceived a dual need for linguistic reference to cultural concepts and to signify their cultural identity.

The Established Lexicon

The NZSL lexicon contains a few established signs with Māori reference that are of long-standing use in NZSL. Table 1 lists the twenty-five NZSL signs that encode Māori reference, as recorded in the 1997 *Dictionary of New Zealand Sign Language* (Kennedy et al.).[5] Their derivation can be categorized as (1) "native" (Battison 1978), that is, having an etymology internal to NZSL structure and arising through interaction over time in the NZSL community (the derivation of most of these is motivated by visible aspects of Māori culture, such as appearance, actions, objects; see Figures 1–4); (2) "semantic loan" of an existing NZSL sign meaning by the articulation of a Māori mouth pattern to specify Māori reference, such as *kai*/food and *wharenui*/hall; and (3) "loan translation," that is, structural rendering of the Māori source elements using NZSL morphemes, such as fs-KR for Kōhanga Reo.

We identified three signs for Māori words beginning with *m* that have initialized variants (Māori, marae, and *moko*) coined in the 1980s, when Signed English was used in deaf education with the aim of manually representing each spoken or written word. At this time, a number of hybridized signs (Brentari and Padden 2001) were contrived in Australasian Signed English by adding BSL or ASL fingerspelling handshapes to existing lexemes to represent the first letter of a spoken word equivalent. Initialized signs with Māori reference originating in this period are now

FIGURE 1. MĀORI
(*"indigenous people"*)

FIGURE 2.
PĀKEHĀ
(*"Caucasian"*)

FIGURE 3. HAKA
(*"fierce dance"*)

FIGURE 4. POI
(*"soft balls twirled on string in action songs"*)

TABLE I. Māori Concepts Listed as Headwords in the *Dictionary of New Zealand Sign Language* (Kennedy et al. 1997)

Māori Headword (Number of Variants)	English Translation	Status of Sign N = native NZSL sign SL = semantic loan LT = loan translation SE = Signed English (influence)
haka (3)	fierce rhythmic dance	N, N, N
hāngi (2)	Earth pit oven	N, N
hongi	Māori greeting by touching noses	N
iwi (2)	tribe	SL (1. AREA, 2. GROUP)
kai	food	SL (FOOD)
kaumātua	male elder	N
kina	spiny sea egg	N
kiwi (2)	1. flightless bird 2. New Zealander	N, N
koha	donation, contribution	N
kōhanga reo	Māori language preschool	LT (fs-KR)
kūmara (2)	native sweet potato	N, N
Māori (3)	indigenous people of NZ	N, N, N (SE influence: M handshape)
marae (2)	traditional meeting compound	N, N (SE influence: M handshape)
moko (2)	facial tattoo	N, N (SE influence: M handshape)
Pākehā (3)	non-Māori Caucasian New Zealander	N, N, N
pāua	abalone	N
piupiu	flax skirt	N
poi	soft ball twirled on string in action songs	N
rangatira	chief	N
tangi	Māori funeral	SL (FUNERAL)
tiki	Māori carved pendant/symbol	N
waka	canoe	N
whakairo	Māori carving	N
whānau	family	SL (FAMILY)
wharenui	Māori meeting house	SL (HALL)

rejected by some MD as "hearing" signs, although they are still used in the Deaf community.

Table 1 does not include Māori place names, which tend to be derived according to the NZSL system of name signs rather than being specifically influenced by their Māori origin.

Compared to the number of established Māori loans within NZE, Māori referents established in the NZSL lexicon are few, for the following reasons:

1. Contact between spoken Māori and NZSL is restricted compared to contact between spoken Māori and spoken English since Deaf people do not have aural exposure to Māori words that are familiar to the hearing community. Moreover, it is rare for Deaf people to acquire oracy or literacy in Māori (as a basis for code switching and borrowing) in either community or school settings.

2. Direct or unassimilated borrowing of Māori words into NZSL is unlikely since the language modalities are different and phonological integration is unlikely (except through mouthing, which occurs to some extent).

3. Concepts that are expressed in NZE by Māori loanwords can be independently represented in NZSL by a native form with equivalent meaning (e.g., the bird known in NZE by its Māori name, *tui*, is named in NZSL by descriptive reference to its plumage) or translated by an existing sign (e.g., the concept *tangi* ("Māori wake/funeral") is usually expressed by the NZSL sign meaning "bury/funeral").

4. Deaf NZSL users have less linguistic access to the sociopolitical forces that drive change in contact language behavior in NZE, such as Pākehā speakers using Māori loanwords and accurate pronunciation to encode their bicultural sensitivity or Māori speakers of NZE using code mixing to signal ethnic identity and solidarity.

New Borrowings Motivated by Interaction in Māori Domains

Since the advent of an interpreting service in 1985 and Deaf advocacy over the last two decades in New Zealand, MD have increasingly asserted their right to access Māori contexts (in which TRM and English coexist), such as marae-based community events and the Māori land court (for tribal land claims), as well as other settings such as formal

education and Māori television. Through our involvement in the teaching of NZSL since 1992, we have observed growing interest among hearing Māori in learning NZSL, as also described by our interviewees (one
of whom even suggested a natural affinity between speaking Māori and
NZSL due to their grammatical differences from English and also Māori
familiarity with the use of symbolic hand gestures in performing arts
such as action songs). As MD have entered Māori domains and hearing
Māori have entered Deaf domains seeking a cultural connection, pressure for vocabulary expansion in NZSL has occurred. Discourse in
Māori contexts, whether communication is in TRM or in English with
code mixing, presents a need for signs to represent culturally significant
referents such as proper nouns, abstract cultural concepts, and formulaic
language (such as greetings and elements of formal oratory) not previously used in NZSL discourse domains.

Three main processes have emerged from the Māori-NZSL interface:

1. Deaf-hearing negotiation of vocabulary in which hearing Māori
   with or without knowledge of NZSL have taught Māori cultural
   concepts and practices to MD. Communication in these situations
   has been mediated through a mix of Signed English, gesture, spoken English, spoken Māori used by hearing participants, and
   NZSL with some spoken English used by Deaf participants. As
   MD have encountered new Māori cultural experiences and concepts, sign equivalents have been negotiated. A hearing Māori
   tutor who was the first person to teach aspects of Māori culture to
   the MD group formed in 1991 describes the process that motivated new coinages:

   [A MD man] started talking to me about organizing a hāngi . . .
   and he was going like this [gestures grasping the throat; see Figure
   12], and I said "I don't understand," and it was the sign HANG.
   And I said there was a need to explore *ringa a tohu* [handsigns].
   And I kept really quiet about it right up til then because I wasn't
   comfortable about being able to support a group of people to be
   able to do that because they needed the knowledge, the deep
   meanings of the words of what Māori means and not just to put
   signs to it because it means something. So we spoke about
   kaumātua [male elder] 'cause they were signing "older" but not
   the essence or heart of an elder. So when they talk *kaumātua* now

they basically have two signs for it [see Figure 9]. I explained the meaning of the word, and they'd have a talk about it, and they would develop a sign.

The MD participant mentioned in the preceding account asserted that in this context it was they, the Deaf people, who created signs based on their new understanding: "[The hearing tutor] mainly taught Māori action songs to Deaf children; he did not teach signs. I learnt Māori words and created signs for them."

According to MD participants, the first of these neologisms were KAUMĀTUA (male elder), KUIA ("female elder"), MARAE ("tribal/community meeting compound"), AROHA ("compassion/love"), and IWI ("tribe"). These are core cultural referents in expressing the relatedness of people, places, and emotions within a Māori worldview; they are frequently used in Māori discourse (in either NZE or Māori).

2. Interpreter-mediated communication between Māori, NZSL, and English in which trilingual interpreters use NZSL and MS neologisms to convey Māori meaning within an NZSL frame of reference. A Māori interpreter interviewed in this study commented on the linguistic and conceptual challenges of simultaneously interpreting from TRM into NZSL, particularly in "culturally rich" (Taylor 1993) texts: "How do you talk about 'te ao wairua' [the spiritual world] when they have no concept? It's not 'heaven' . . . we're not talking about any Christian philosophy, and trying to give them an understanding all within the translation period that you've got. . . . All you can do is give a reduced version of the overall ideas."

Our interviewees, both Deaf and hearing, indicated that in this process of cultural mediation, trained Māori interpreters have been conservative about coining new signs or establishing fixed translations, preferring to accept that, for the moment, there will be restrictions on achieving conceptual equivalence, as this interpreter explains: "There's been a need to develop some concepts . . . and they haven't been nutted [worked] out. . . . I mean MD have heard some of those concepts. . . . They use a literal translation, but they still don't have the understanding of the concept. So in the meantime, as interpreters, we just carry on using the literal translation . . . until MD are at a point where *they* develop a sign that's more appropriate."

3. Coinage of neologisms by hearing Māori, with the aim of encoding Māori concepts. This has taken place in learning situations that have involved a minority of Deaf participants and a majority of hearing NZSL learners engaged in Māori-based cultural activities. Neologisms were coined where hearing (and often Deaf) participants perceived a gap in the NZSL vocabulary for rendering Māori concepts into signs (e.g., formulaic phrases in oratory and referents such as deities) or a need to revise NZSL signs that presently convey Māori reference in a form that is conceptually unacceptable to hearing Māori. A Māori interpreter who observed these endeavors during the mid-1990s explained: "[Māori educators] saw the need for Māori hearing who could sign and a need for Māori Deaf to have more conceptually appropriate signs than the ones that were currently being used."

Some hearing-devised signs reveal an assumption that reference in MS (or NZSL generally) should coincide with Māori representations of meaning; a Māori interpreter describes the perspective of a Māori education organization that advocated the development of MS:

The goal was "Māori Sign Language," pretty much to try to get Māori Deaf more of an understanding of Māori signs. Like, the signs that they were using were the English signs. Particularly place names at the time. They were trying to get Māori Deaf to understand what the actual meaning of the word was. . . . Getting Māori Deaf to understand that those place names have a history and they have a meaning, so those signs that you're actually using, even though they're the Deaf signs that you're used to . . . getting them to try and match the history of that word with the [new] sign.

An example is a coinage for the suburb named Papatoetoe, which comprises the morphemes *papa* (earth/area) plus *toetoe* (pampas grass). As both the written word and NZE pronunciation appear to refer to "toe," the established NZSL sign is derived from "visual homonymy" (Miller 2001) as follows: fs-P + TOE TOE (pointing at the signer's feet). This sign follows norms for the structure of NZSL name signs based on elements of description, initials, or semantic translation of an English lip pattern or orthography (McKee and McKee 2000). The contrived MS replacement for Papatoetoe is a loan translation of the two Māori morphemes — a compound of LAND + 2h CL: "bent index fingers" (intended to represent pampas grass). Our informants report that this neologism has not been adopted by the local Deaf community and requires explanation when used.

The idea that signs should coincide with spoken Māori form, as well as meaning, was also evident. Hearing Māori made some attempt to devise a manual code for elements of spoken Māori, which foundered quickly due to Deaf people's distaste for their earlier experience of Signed English in schools, and the outspoken discouragement of Māori trilingual interpreters, one of whom recalls the following:

> [Hearing Māori educators] were looking at sign language following a Māori grammatical word order. . . . They wanted to develop a specific sign for the [causative] prefix *whaka*, so if it was *whakapapa*, then it would be this "developed" sign for *whaka*, and then whatever. *Whakarongo* would no longer just be LISTEN. It would be this *whaka* plus hear. . . . It was the same idea as Signed English: It was based on that same concept that sign language isn't complete, that it's a representation of a spoken language. . . . So there was a lot of debating over that. . . . I battled with them for years!

Hearing-initiated coinages have thus had some influence on the development of MS but have tended to be the most contentious of the neologisms.

Forms of Recent Borrowings

The folk term "Māori signs" refers to signs that have Māori reference, some of which have been coined by MD for use in Māori contexts. Within the signs identified and demonstrated by informants as MS, four types of derivational processes were identified; the number and function of the signs in each of these categories is summarized in Table 2:

1. Established native or other signs in the NZSL lexicon with Māori reference, as previously described and listed in Table 1.
2. Semantic loans (i.e., signs in the established NZSL lexicon that have been appropriated as MS to express Māori reference by the addition of Māori mouthing, as in Figures 5–8). These forms can be described as hybrids in the sense that the "foreign" feature of a Māori lip pattern is added to an existing sign to distinguish a Māori sense from other potential meanings of the manual sign.
   Semantic loans demonstrated to us by MD informants indicated that a Māori meaning and mouth pattern have been con-

FIGURE 5. PŌWHIRI
("welcome")

FIGURE 6. TANGI
("funeral/to bury")

FIGURE 7. WAIATA
("song/to sing")

FIGURE 8. WHĀNAU *("family")*

sciously grafted onto an existing sign as MD have acquired knowledge of TRM vocabulary. One participant, for example, produced the NZSL sign FAMILY + mouthing *whānau* ("family") as an example of a "new" MS for whānau. A similar kind of example is the NZSL sign SEA + mouthing *moana* ("ocean, sea"). This form of borrowing or code switching echoes Boyes Braem's (2001, 111) finding in Swiss German Sign Language that "mouthings are a device for the derivation of related, new lexical items." In this case it is not necessarily the semantic content that is new but the foreign code from which the mouthing feature is borrowed, which in general NZSL usage would be English.

A similar speech-sign contact feature is described for the Swedish Deaf minority in Finland, for whom code switching from Finnish to Swedish mouthing coarticulated with common manual signs encodes Swedish semantic reference, as well as signaling Finnish-Swedish identity (Hoyer 2004). In northern Wales, where Welsh-medium schooling has created a contact environment between spoken/written Welsh and Welsh BSL signers, Welsh mouth patterns are becoming associated with BSL signs as a marker of a Welsh variety of BSL, particularly by younger Deaf people (Julie Watkins, pers. comm., November 15, 2005).

FIGURE 9. KAUMĀTUA
("respected male elder")
Derivation: AROHA +
SENIOR

FIGURE 10. AROHA
("love, compassion")
Derivation: EMOTION +
heart loc

FIGURE 11. IWI
("tribe/tribal area")
Derivation: AREA, as if
on a map

3. Neologisms, which are new signs coined to express Māori cultural concepts, usually fill a lexical gap. In some cases, these are visually motivated, while others recombine existing morphemes of NZSL or a native morpheme with a newly created or contrived element. One interesting example is KAUMĀTUA, which has been recoined as a neologism combining native and contrived morphemes. The sign recorded for this headword in the 1997 dictionary is a semantic extension of the sign meaning "senior" in NZSL, but data collected in 2003 have revealed a new sign, in which the invented morpheme AROHA (love, esteem) (Figure 10) has been prefixed to SENIOR to express a cultural value of esteem for elders. This neologism reflects a refinement of the concept through further exchanges with hearing Māori. Some neologisms are already being displaced by subsequent ones; for example, iwi/tribe (Figure 11) now coexists with another variant observed since collecting the 2003 data reported here.

4. Substitutions are a subgroup of neologisms that have been coined to replace established signs perceived as conceptually inadequate or culturally inappropriate, mainly by hearing Māori learners of NZSL. According to our informants, most of these revised signs are place names that have been constructed from existing NZSL morphemes; some nonnative coinages have been modified by Deaf people within a short period of use, as one MD informant commented: "Over time, the initial signs for Māori concepts were adapted to look and feel more natural to NZSL signers."

Deaf and hearing participants cited HĀNGI ("food cooked in an earth pit oven") as one of the first established NZSL signs to be reevaluated as

FIGURE 12. *old* HĀNGI *Derivation: to hang*

FIGURE 13. *new* HĀNGI *Derivation: pit in the ground*

conceptually inaccurate and deliberately revised. As mentioned in an earlier quote, this was conventionally expressed in NZSL by a visual homonym meaning "to hang by the neck" (see Figure 12), deriving from "hang(i)" in the written form and from the Pākehā pronunciation of the word with a short /a/ vowel, as in "hang." This sign provoked an adverse reaction from hearing Māori learners of NZSL due to its unpleasant and semantically irrelevant connotations. A MD participant explained that at the first hui for MD with hearing Māori cultural tutors in the mid-1990s, there was much discussion about certain signs that seemed conceptually inappropriate from a hearing Māori perspective. HĀNGI was the sign that created awareness among MD about the possibility of revising a conventional form-meaning relationship and rejecting a sign that was patently Deaf, but not Māori, informed in its derivation. A Deaf informant explains: "I think the original sign for 'hāngi' made a huge impact on our thinking. The sign we had always used was based on the mouth pattern of the word 'hāngi,' which was easily recognized by Deaf, but it had the wrong meaning. We decided we needed to modify it to express the Māori concept. There were other Māori words that had signs using the wrong concept."

The new form for "hāngi" depicts a pit in the ground (see Figure 13), which relates transparently to the referent rather than to an English-speaker perspective on the word's form and is thus more acceptable to Māori.

GRAMMATICAL FUNCTIONS OF MS

Like Māori loanwords in NZE, Māori borrowings in NZSL are predominantly nouns. Table 2 summarizes the function of MS in different derivational categories, including signs in the 1997 NZSL dictionary and our 2003 data. Since the collection of the data for this study, we have also observed some additional coinages not recorded here.

TABLE 2. Forms of Māori Borrowings into NZSL

Type of Sign Formation	Number of Signs[1]	Class of Māori Source Word[2]	
Native or established signs of long-standing use in NZSL (Kennedy 1997)	18	common noun verb adjective (Māori/Pākehā)	13 3 2
Semantic loans Extend the meaning of existing signs to Māori reference through Māori mouthing. Most are recent borrowings.	25	common noun verb greeting/phatic	16 6 3
Loan translations Transfer of Māori structure into sign morphemes (e.g., *whare* + *kai* = DINE + HALL, *kōhanga reo* = fs. KR)	6	common noun proper noun	4 2

Neologisms
    New reference: created to fill lexical gaps (Māori-specific concepts)
    Substitutions for existing signs
	23	common noun
		proper noun
		greeting
			10
			12
			1

Totals	72	Common noun Proper noun Verb Adjective Greeting/phatic	43 14 9 2 4

1. Some concepts have competing variants. In all cases, the variants for one concept are of the same derivational type (e.g., semantic loan or neologism). Since our focus is on the extent of semantic borrowing and the possibilities for constructing loans rather than internal variation within this set, Column 2 lists the number of concepts borrowed, rather than the total number of sign variants in existence for these concepts.

2. Some forms that are classed as nouns in Māori have a verblike character in NZSL (e.g., the abstract noun *whānaungatanga* ("collectiveness") in NZSL has a movement that suggests the act or process of connecting. Furthermore, some borrowed terms function as both noun and verb in Māori, which makes this analysis only roughly indicative of the usage borrowed into NZSL rather than a precise description of their grammatical status.

Of the neologisms, the largest number are proper nouns (*iwi* names and substitute place names); six out of ten common nouns are abstract concepts that have no exact equivalence in the existing NZSL lexicon, and these signs have thus been coined to enable cultural reference or to achieve precision of meaning (Macalister 2003). Most of the semantic loans are also common nouns. This breakdown is consistent with Haugen's (1950) early finding that nouns are more frequently imported than other parts of speech (such as function words and verbs). The small number of verbs resulting from TRM and NZSL contact are mostly expressed by the semantic loan of an existing NZSL verb by adding a Māori mouth pattern, or are motivated signs that depict actions mimetically. Given the mimetic nature of many verbs in sign language and the fact that verbs tend to be core concepts across languages, there is intuitively less need for the semantic importation of verbs from a foreign language, except for actions that are highly culture specific (e.g., *haka* or action song/warrior dance).

While neologisms attract the most attention, semantic loan is the most productive process for borrowing Māori concepts into NZSL. This is unsurprising from a linguistic viewpoint but belies folk description and the perception of MS as "new" lexicon or as something other than NZSL. An extension of established signs to express Māori reference simply increases the degree of polysemy already present in NZSL vocabulary and demonstrates mouthing to be a productive mechanism in NZSL for contextualizing and extending the referential meaning of manual signs.

Signed English Influence on MS Forms

When the teaching of Māori culture began in 1991 in a deaf school setting, the use of Australasian Signed English (ASE) was educational policy. This initial cultural exchange within a Signed English context influenced the formation of some of the first signs associated with Māori concepts, which have since been modified. A MD informant referred to the role of Signed English as a transitional contact language that allowed the appropriation of Māori meanings into NZSL: "We [MD group with a hearing tutor] used Signed English as a way to access the meaning of Māori words and concepts. For instance, I learned about the protocol around the correct place and time to stand and speak in a formal Māori setting. Signed English gave me access to understanding the protocol and the meaning behind it. But signs used for Māori concepts at this time were sometimes not natural — didn't feel right — so we would modify the signs."

An example of this process was the translation of the Māori word "kai" as the Signed English form of FOOD in early contact between Deaf and hearing Māori. The Signed English form is articulated with closed fingers (baby O) circling the mouth (the circular movement being a modification for the pedagogical purpose of allowing lipreading of the spoken word). Although this sign is a contrived and marked form in NZSL, it was readily adopted as the fixed translation for "kai" by MD who otherwise used the established NZSL sign, in which the hand moves toward the mouth, for reference to food or eating. There are two possible reasons for this alternation between the conventional NZSL sign and the "Māori"/TC sign: First, the translation was originally made by a hearing Māori tutor who at that time had learned Signed English but not NZSL; in addition, this sign was demonstrated as being a "Māori sign" on the basis that it was different from the established NZSL (i.e., "English") sign for food and was distinguishable as having Māori meaning (i.e., its different form marked its foreign status). Currently, the traditional NZSL sign FOOD appears to have regained favor among our informants as the translation for "kai" in a Māori context. This change probably reflects a maturing understanding of the relationship between spoken and sign languages (i.e., the realization that signs and words do not need to exist in a one-to-one form/meaning correspondence), as well as a changing political sensitivity in the Deaf community about the different symbolic capital of Signed English versus NZSL, as hearing versus Deaf-controlled codes.

Another usage that originated in the Signed English context and has subsequently undergone phonological modification is a neologism for the phrase *tena koutou* ("greetings to you [plural]), which is a conventional acknowledgement uttered in Māori welcome and closing sequences. The original sign coined for this was formed with the G handshape of the two-handed manual alphabet (Figure 14) derived from the first letter of the English translation, "greetings." The G handshape is moved in neutral space toward the addressees. This form/meaning pairing was twice removed from the Māori source since the G handshape was a manual representation of an English translation of a Māori phrase. Moreover, the combination of a fingerspelling handshape with another morpheme is a relatively rare derivation in NZSL, as the manual alphabet was not widely known prior to the introduction of Signed English in 1979. The original sign has been modified through usage to a noninitialized formation with a flat base hand (Figure 15), and its etymology in

FIGURE 14. TENA
KOUTOU 1 *Derivation:*
initialized g(reetings)

FIGURE 15. TENA
KOUTOU 2 *Derivation:*
modified form of 1

FIGURE 16. TENA
KOUTOU 3 *Derivation:*
semantic loan HELLO

ASE is now opaque. Neither the original nor the modified form of tena koutou had any semantic or formal relationship to conceptually equivalent signs of greeting in NZSL and are thus clearly distinguished by form and meaning as new MS. Some MD stated that a native NZSL sign (HELLO) (as in Figure 16) or another sign of acknowledgement (HONOR) with tena koutou mouthing is a more meaningful way of borrowing this formal greeting into NZSL.

The evolution of a sign equivalent for tena koutou illustrates the idea, current at the time it was coined, that sign language is a code for spoken — and specifically English — words. Borrowing Māori lexicon into NZSL via the representation of an English equivalent was an attempt to negotiate between Māori and Deaf reference by using English as an intermediary contact language, resulting in some borrowings that reflect "artificial influences" on the language (Battison 1978, 96). Moreover, confusion around the "need" to coin MS to correspond with Māori word forms for concepts already in the NZSL lexicon, such as "food," point to the "tyranny of glossing" (Slobin 2006), that is, the hazards of representing the vocabulary of a sign language through the medium of a dominant spoken language, as is conventional (albeit often unavoidable) in sign language research and dictionaries. Glossing not only creates a potentially false or restrictive sense of natural association between the forms and semantics of the two language but, in this case, also apparently supports a Māori perception that NZSL is culturally synonymous with the dominant spoken language.

Acceptability of Contact Forms

New coinages and usages are potentially contestable, especially when they are considered to be linked to sociopolitical goals or particular parties, as with MS. New MS that fill lexical gaps in Māori discourse domains appear to have been the most readily adopted. Substitutions for signs that are patently offensive to Māori — and where the new coinage has a transparent origin (e.g., hāngi) — also seem to be readily accepted. However, signs coined with the aim of supplanting established NZSL signs (particularly place names) are generally contentious; this mirrors the resistance of hearing Māori to many TRM neologisms coined and promoted by the Māori Language Commission (Keegan 2005).

Responses to revised Māori suburb names in Auckland illustrate cases of dubious acceptability. The MD informants discussed recent changes to the sign for Mangere, the airport suburb of Auckland, which Deaf Aucklanders traditionally refer to as AIRPLANE + mouth: MANGERE, in a descriptive name sign. They also reported that two new coinages were initiated through interaction with hearing Māori: The first was a semantic translation of the Māori word LAZY, which has gained some currency in the Auckland community, and the second was a complex, polymorphemic sign referring to a historical aspect of the area that is opaque without knowledge of the story. Our group of informants disagreed about the naturalness and relevance of the two introduced name signs: While some had adopted the neologisms, one participant felt that they were meaningless from a Deaf perspective, compared to the relevance of the original sign AIRPLANE, which is an iconic feature of the area. This participant self-identified as ethnically Māori but was not active within the MD network; she was openly skeptical about out-group intervention in the creation of signs. Based on our interaction in the Deaf community, we believe this attitude is probably reflective of other MD who have not been involved in the development of MS through joint activity with hearing Māori.

Deaf participants described situations in which new signs or translations were being coined, where hearing Māori were arguing among themselves about the precise meaning of Māori concepts and the acceptability of new sign coinages. Some hearing participants (such as elders or cultural "experts") were concerned with the accurate representation of cultural meaning from a Māori perspective, while others (usually trilingual interpreters) argued from a linguistically informed perspective about respecting the integrity of meaning and structures within NZSL. A Deaf informant explains:

A wānanga [workshop] took place in a marae for the MD community, and one session was about 'Māori Sign Language'. There was friction between the hearing Māori who felt that MD did not understand Māori concepts. MD wanted to create a Māori sign if a Māori concept was clear to us, but the hearing Māori didn't always agree with our signs. Sometimes the Māori concept of a word has a deeper meaning that MD don't fully grasp. . . . If there was a clear instant definition, MD could come up with a sign relevant to the meaning of the Māori concept, then it would be shown to hearing Māori, as we think it is adequate in the MD community.

An interpreter recalls the same event:

The hearing people got upset because they were the ones that had developed the signs, and they thought that we [interpreters and Deaf] were being offensive by saying the sign was inappropriate. And the Kuia was getting upset because [the meaning of a Deaf-derived sign was inaccurate]. And the Deaf were getting frustrated. . . . So it ended up being quite a heated hui, that one! . . . And in the end, [a Deaf leader] got up and said, "No, we won't take these signs." Because we'd been developing signs back at Kelston [Deaf Education Centre] . . . with MD students. So he got up and showed the signs that they had already developed, which were different.

In the situation just described, the MD refused to accept the determination of new language items from outside their group. Commenting on similar issues around coinages in spoken Māori, Benton (2001, 43) observes that "there seems to be a perennial conflict between the 'owners' of a concept . . . and various speakers and semi-speakers with equally varied claims or pretensions to ownership or control of the language through which the concept is to be expressed." Contested boundaries between hearing and Deaf cultural expertise, as well as the ownership of language creation, are evident, even within a superficially shared frame of ethnic empowerment.

New MS for iwi names and aspects of marae protocol appear to have been readily adopted because they have functionality and relevance for MD who wish to participate in Māori domains. Iwi names, for example, are essential to establishing one's identity as Māori because a formulaic introduction in Māori settings includes, at a minimum, identifying one's tribal affiliation and lineage, as well as tribal geographical landmarks. To express Māori identity by adopting customary forms of interaction, MD need new language.

Participants reported a number of iwi names that have recently been coined. As happens with personal name signs, an iwi might be identified by a particular sign by its members but teasingly referred to by an alternative sign by nonmembers, usually highlighting a notorious trait of that iwi (mirroring similar jokes among hearing Māori). Teasing through MS about iwi identity shows that Māori cultural knowledge has been appropriated by Deaf people, and is being used to generate in-group humor, which constructs and reinforces MD ethnicity. The flipside is that claiming iwi versus Deaf community or collective MD affiliation introduces a source of new identity tension, as this interpreter's anecdote illustrates:

> At a meeting recently, Māori Deaf were debating amongst themselves over what iwi they were, saying, only Ngati Kahungunu MD can have these T-shirts that they wanted to get printed. And when we sat down and talked about it, there was only one actually from Ngati Kahungunu. All the rest were from Ngati Porou, and then this realization that how they all *connect* is through this fact that they're all Deaf! . . . But they debated. It was those two cultures clashing about "Who are we? How is it that we are all here in this one room together, but we are all from different iwi?" . . . And they were fighting about who could be part of this group. It wasn't 'til somebody said that "We're all Deaf" that they kind of went, "Yeah, we are, aren't we!" . . . And it's progress. . . . It's how these people are starting to reidentify themselves . . . reinvent themselves.

Diffusion of New Contact Forms

Theoretical accounts of borrowing posit that two language communities in contact may remain essentially monolingual, but a small subset of bilinguals can become the vehicle for introducing borrowed elements. In Strang's (1970) account, the borrowers do not have to be bilingual but must simply have enough exposure to the other language and the social motivation to introduce new forms to the host language. Figure 17 represents this scenario, in which the agents of contact (hearing and deaf Māori) and diffusion are not necessarily fully bilingual (with the exception of trilingual Māori interpreters).

Transmission of MS between MD is potentially hindered by the fact that their participation in Māori events is often in the context of hearing kin groups, more often with an interpreter than with other Deaf people. Māori interpreters are thus potentially key agents of MS diffusion, as this

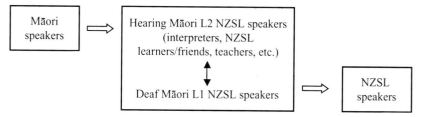

FIGURE 17. *Contact and diffusion between Māori and NZSL. Adapted from Macalister 2003.*

interpreter explains: "We're going to be the vehicle of getting the language out to other MD. . . . We shift from one region to another; the signs go with us, and so other MD or other Deaf become exposed to these new signs and concepts."

Diffusion will be determined by the capacity to maintain Māori Deaf social networks and to sustain Deaf-dominant domains where MS serve a communicative purpose. A small marae established at Kelston Deaf Education Centre in Auckland, named Ruamoko, is currently regarded as a habitat for nurturing MD language and ways. An interpreter refers to the importance of this place, which follows Māori principles but is firmly in Deaf territory:

You see MD *tikanga* [customs] being used at the marae, and I think if other Deaf came in, they may not straight away pick up what the sign is, but in the context they would. Because it is still the development of NZSL, so it's not these *created* signs from people who have no idea what Deaf culture and sign language is about. These are all signs that have been developed by MD who have been out there to *pōwhiri* and been at *tangi* and gotten an idea of what's going on now, and they've developed those signs. And they're being used a lot.

In a final stage in the transfer of words between languages, idiosyncratic borrowings become habitualized and generalized to other users (Haugen 1950, 87). The extent to which MS have become habitualized as loans in wider NZSL usage has not yet been empirically measured. At a national Māori Deaf hui in November 2005, the topic of MS was a key focus, and we observed from this interaction that many neologisms and usages under discussion were unfamiliar to those outside a small network of politically active MD, indicating that contact forms (and indeed participation in Māori domains) are still of limited diffusion in the wider community. It was apparent that many MS are conceptually new to the majority of MD, who have had little exposure to TRM; uptake of these forms will require mastering form and meaning correspondences between Māori and NZSL. There was debate over the merits of competing variants of some neologisms, some of which have not yet moved from individual (or localized) lexicons to the generalized community lexicon. If loanwords are defined as lexical items integrated into another language in the sense of being regularly used by monolinguals (see Boyes Braem 2001, 121, for example), it is more accurate to characterize most MS as borrowings or even code switches rather than established loans at this stage.

As already indicated, some signs that were motivated by hearing Māori have achieved limited diffusion, as they are either redundant (Deaf people have established ways of referring to these meanings) or perceived to be artificial in their formation (e.g., Papatoetoe and Mangere [suburb names]). Some neologisms express culturally significant meanings from a Māori perspective but are so infrequently used by MD that they have little currency (e.g., names for deities or the lineage of tribal chiefs), as this Māori interpreter commented: "As wonderful as these signs are, and the development of more concepts, it's not *relevant* to the everyday use of the language. . . . How often would you get up and sign all the different *atua* [deities]?"

These outcomes indicate that individuals, hearing or Deaf, who are marginal members of the MD/NZSL community "may be useful points of contact between language communities, but they do not necessarily influence the speech of those communities" (Macalister 2003, 285). While interpreters and hearing signers have been actively involved with initiating borrowing from TRM into NZSL, the acceptance of new usages is ultimately determined by processes within the networks of MD who use them frequently and in effect screen their acceptability according to intuitive (but not necessarily unanimous) criteria before disseminating them into the wider NZSL community.

IDEOLOGIES AND OWNERSHIP OF MS

Ideologies about languages are "always socially situated and tied to questions of identity and power in societies" (Blackledge and Pavlenko 2001, 246). The goals of Deaf and hearing people involved in the development of MS overlap but do not completely converge, as each group brings its own historical experience of language-power relations and contemporary agendas of identity politics to the interaction. This section considers hearing and Deaf ideas and aspirations relating to MS.

Hearing Agendas

The first hearing Māori person to tutor MD in 1991 described an intense exchange in which both parties recognized themselves as learners and teachers of culture and language:

> As soon as the MD community knew that I was teaching at KDEC my privacy went right out the door. They came every night, and they wouldn't go home till midnight. They'd just sit there and just throw this knowledge out — more and more and more. They immersed me. Everywhere I went, people were just coming with me. It was their way of trying to open a door that hadn't been open to them in their schooling experience.

Because this activity was situated in a school for deaf students, Deaf people were in the majority in relation to the Māori tutor, and reverse immersion experiences in each other's territory ensued. He refers to MD "immersing" him, while he was simultaneously enabling a "closed door" to be opened for them. This sociocultural exchange is where the spark for MS was lit.

Hearing Māori arriving as nonsigners or NZSL learners to intercultural encounters have generally wanted MD to gain access to the Māori cultural capital, which is encoded in knowledge of TRM, as a route to connecting with the benefits of Māori ethnic solidarity. From a hearing perspective, the dual goals of encoding cultural knowledge through MS are for MD to adopt behavior and values consistent with Māori cultural norms and to build self-worth through stronger connection and identity with Māori. All of our hearing participants used the metaphor of "opening a door" into the Māori world.

Hearing Māori have also gained from this contact the experience of learning NZSL and in some cases status, expertise, and career opportunities linked to "supporting the needs" of Deaf people. A Māori interpreting student quoted in a 2003 article expresses such motives: "I would love people to learn Māori signs, so we can better communicate as a Māori culture. We need to help MD understand the true meaning of what is being said and done on a marae. Sign language interpreting helps bridge those communication gaps" (quoted in West 2003, 4).

An experienced trilingual Māori interpreter interviewed in this study reflects more critically on the hearing agenda:

It all started out with really good intentions . . . a group of Māori who had a connection to the Deaf community through a *whānau* [family] member who was profoundly deaf, and what they saw from a non-Deaf community member's point of view was a language that didn't accommodate for te reo Māori and didn't accommodate for access to tikanga. And so that's where the concept was born — that we need to develop a language that would accommodate for tikanga.

Several participants mentioned hearing Māori perceptions of NZSL as an English- or Pākehā-based language and a feeling that the development of "Māori Sign Language" is a step toward liberation from the hegemony of a language identified with the dominant culture. This perception is built on several factors: first, the fact that NZSL users frequently use English mouthing with signs, due to a natural and pedagogical situation of language contact with English, which supports the misapprehension that Deaf sign languages derive from spoken languages; second, the idea that, since English is the dominant language of the educational system and sign language is acquired mainly in school settings, NZSL would therefore be derivative of that language; third, Māori NZSL users, when asked, may be unable to produce a lexical NZSL equivalent for a given Māori word either because the Māori word or concept is unfamiliar or they are not used to the process of finding equivalence between languages giving the impression of untranslatability.

Underlying a perception of NZSL as Pākehā is an element of "social evaluation" (Horvath and Vaughan 1991): Seen through the lens of a decolonizing agenda, the majority of the Deaf community are Pākehā, and so NZSL is "naturally" aligned with the identity and culture of that colonizing majority. Hearing Māori who encounter the Deaf community tend to readily empathize with their historical experience of linguistic oppression in the school system and find resonance between the Deaf struggle for empowerment and the Tino Rangatiratanga movement. Since hearing Māori ethnicity and cultural empowerment are powerfully signaled by speaking TRM, the parallel assumption is often made that MD identity would also be marked — and indeed advanced — by a distinct sign language variety (MSL). This kind of parallelism is also observed as a factor in Catalonian Deaf attitudes toward Spanish and Catalonian sign and speech varieties (Morales-López et al. 2002). A Māori interpreter explained this belief: "They [hearing Māori in contact with MD] didn't know that NZSL was an independent language: They saw English and NZSL as the same language, just that one's visual. So hence, 'We need to develop Māori Sign Language because they've got English, and we need one for Māori.' So that's where you started getting this grammatical 'Signed Māori' thing happening."

The Māori Language Commission, which is responsible for the maintenance and promotion of TRM, was reportedly approached by more than one hearing Māori organization with Deaf participants for assistance to develop Māori Sign Language, although the commission has no relationship to the Deaf community. This is an example of a perception of signs as a potential manual extension of TRM, and MD as potential beneficiaries of access to TRM via contrived means.

Trilingual interpreters are positioned slightly differently from other hearing parties in relation to MD and MS (and also perhaps differently from non-Māori interpreters in relation to the Deaf community generally). Their definition of their role as interpreters is framed by the contemporary political ethic of self-determination for Māori through strengthening cultural identity and also by the strong traditional Māori value of seeking connectedness (known as *whānaungatanga* ["familyness/ relatedness"]). The trilingual interpreter's role is sensitive to a Māori social framework, which values the collective over the individual and where process and maintenance of relationships may be more important than outcomes. Accordingly, Māori participants in intercultural situations tend to see the interpreter as having a supportive role as a participant in the activity rather than an outside or a neutral role (Napier et al. 2006). Trilingual interpreters are thus positioned between two communities (Deaf and Māori) in which participation and personal connection are highly valued and where boundaries between professional and social relationships are more relaxed. Our interviewees, Deaf and hearing, recognized the Māori interpreters' primary function of language mediation but also saw them as holding extended roles as allies in the larger *kauapapa* or agenda for MD empowerment, which includes the development of NZSL to express Māori concepts.

As a generalization, hearing agendas around MS reflect an integrationist desire to afford a marginalized group access to its (hearing) culture and empowerment strategies, grounded in the assumption that its goals and intentions will align since both groups have experienced cultural domination. While parallel ethnic agendas have certainly opened new paths for MD, some of our participants also noted the risk of assuming too much common ground. An interpreter reflected, "There's a risk that MS could still be captured by hearing people to some degree . . . because we are a people that [feel] 'What's yours is mine. You don't have to carry this on your own. We'll help!' And that's the way we approach everything. . . . It's a very strong connection there [between Deaf power and tino rangatiratanga], so people do get quite passionate about it."

This is not a new or unique scenario for Deaf people, according to Humphries:

> Solidarity, or the stressing of the same in the same-but-different approach to intercultural contact, may threaten the modern Deaf self. . . . In intercultural interactions, there is sometimes a natural tendency for one party to break down differences, to assert sameness, to assume that despite cultural differences, underneath the skin, we are all the same. It is this assertion of sameness that is threatening to the Deaf self because most Deaf people are still struggling with or can remember what it was like to be totally dominated and defined by others. (1996, 358)

In this case, some hearing people involved in the contact were more aware than others of the subtle differences between Deaf and hearing solidarity agendas, according to their insight into the hegemony of spoken over signed language and the difference between their own and MD people's positioning in relation to Māori culture and identity.

Deaf Agendas

MD share with hearing Māori an aspiration to create contact language forms that symbolize their indigenous ethnicity and enable them to participate more easily in Māori domains. However, their accounts of how this process has unfolded suggest that their agenda differs fundamentally from that of hearing participants. MD enter the cultural contact process as members of a "community of solidarity" in the Deaf world (Johnson 1991), which is not always apparent to hearing people who see themselves as natural cultural allies within a Māori community of solidarity. Echoing Humphries, MD participants described paternalism in hearing-Deaf interactions and their desire to maintain an autonomous Deaf self, hinging on ownership of sign language:

> Hearing Māori tend to control us when we discuss things in Māori settings, like following Māori protocols appropriately or doing things

Māori the right way when it involves language and behavior. For example, from the perspective of Māori protocol, I could be displaying inappropriate cultural conduct when I'm actually communicating effectively in my language. . . . When hearing Māori come, we conceal our language because we want to protect our *natural* language. . . . Sign language belongs to us.

In Smiler's 2004 study, a MD NZSL teacher (who also has some knowledge of spoken TRM) expressed resistance to hearing intervention in language change and questioned the construct of MS or MSL as promoted by individuals who lacked sociohistorical and metalinguistic insight into the NZSL community:

Some Māori hearing people set up Māori education training establishments, and they teach what they call "Māori Sign." I reject that. I mean, how do they know? They haven't seen the research on Deaf studies, nor do they know about Deaf history or what it is like to grow up Deaf. . . . You can't set up "Māori Sign Language" because Māori Deaf people don't have a history of being socialized in the Māori world. They don't know what the concepts in the Māori world mean. And Māori hearing don't know about Deaf history. They don't know about Deaf oppression. They don't know any of these things! So I can't see how Māori hearing think that they can take the ownership of sign language away from us. . . . They need to have Māori Deaf in there being involved and giving regular input, and Māori Deaf should not be pushed aside so that they can claim the fame! I believe there should be a focus on the Deaf way, and the Māori Deaf community as a whole need to use their own initiatives to make claims to their own sign language that represents them as a collective community. But the thing is that Māori hearing people tell us that we are wrong and we need to understand the traditional concepts, and I agree with that. So I say to them, if you want me to understand the *wairua* [spirituality] of Te Reo Māori or you want Māori Deaf to understand about *whakapapa* [history] . . . then you need to understand our perspective as Deaf so that we can work alongside one another. (Smiler 2004, 123)

This informant also commented that men have had a dominant role in coining MS, motivated by the public speaking roles assigned to males in formal Māori contexts, which entail the use of formulaic language.

This gender dynamic in motivating borrowing was not explored in this study but points to the complex interplay of social factors in the process of language contact and change.

MD informants believe that hearing allies, particularly trilingual interpreters, are indispensable to their goals; one stated that in Māori-speaking contexts "TRM is inaccessible to us, which is why a trilingual interpreter is vital to facilitate the communication process — so we can understand. Māori trilingual interpreters are desperately needed for MD to advance in their learning and sharing of information with hearing Māori."

Yet the same informant also commented that hearing mediation of cultural contact can inhibit a sense of autonomy:

A trilingual interpreter is helpful for us to access Māori concepts or teach us the appropriate way of doing things Māori. Naturally, hearing Māori trilingual interpreters who have extensive knowledge of Māori customs might feel that Māori Deaf are not mindful of cultural protocols. That can make us feel incapable or inferior. They'll tell us what we should or shouldn't do, but we strongly feel as Deaf people, we can advance. Our language wouldn't have been disrupted if hearing Māori allowed us to develop ourselves and our language. Many times since 1991 our ambition to develop and increase Māori signs has been suppressed by hearing Māori, when our language should have been expanded more.

The MD informants made it clear that their agenda in developing and using MS is not primarily about integrating into the hearing Māori world. For them, acquiring knowledge of Māori culture and expressing this via new contact language forms in NZSL is a route to constructing MD identity on their own terms.

The importance participants attached to having their own marae (Ruamoko) represents a desire to build their own community foundations (Jankowski 1995), though the creation of both physical place and a MD cultural space (Gulliver 2005), as this participant implies: "We are fortunate and thankful to be able to develop our own *tūrangawaewae* in our marae, a place where we stand strong and create our language of Māori concepts."[6] The phrase "our language of Māori concepts" implies that sign language is the natural medium for MD expression of Māori culture; a "place to stand strong" asserts that MD are the guardians of their own process of cultural development. Vis-à-vis the modern redefining of the Deaf self in relation to hearing society, Humphries (1996, 358) observes that "Although hearing people may think that Deaf people's goal is to be included in society, it is more likely that Deaf people's goal is one of maintenance of boundaries between cultures and a search for accommodation that allows the Deaf person to remain true to the self."

The sense of ownership of MS that Deaf participants expressed indicates their ambition to adopt Māori concepts and cultural forms in ways that are meaningful to them — through a Deaf lens, effectively constructing a "MD culture" rather than simply transposing Māori culture into a Deaf context or assimilating themselves into a Māori context. The divergence in goals that Humphries describes was evident in this case study of intercultural situations between Deaf and hearing Māori.

INVOKING ETHNIC IDENTITY THROUGH THE USE OF MS

Borrowing the idea that the use of fingerspelled items in ASL assigns both foreign meaning and foreign status to certain words (Padden and Gunsauls 2003), we contend that the use of MS has a dual function of expressing foreign (in this case indigenous but foreign to NZSL) referential content, as well as signifying the signers' personal sphere of cultural reference. In this sense, the acts of coining, using, and labeling certain signs as "MS" function symbolically to enact ethnic identity as MD and to alter the situational frame (Goffman 1974) from "Deaf" to "Māori Deaf."

At the 2005 National MD Hui, debate over the semantics and form of MS revealed a desire for MS to be distinct in form, as well as in cultural reference, from other NZSL signs. For example, discussion arose over two variants for the concept *pōwhiri*, for which the most commonly used translation is the sign WELCOME + mouth: pōwhiri. An alternative form exists that mimetically depicts the action of two hands waving bunches of leaves in a ritual movement performed by women as they welcome visitors onto a marae. It was mooted that this variant is a more indigenous form since it consists of a visually iconic description (i.e., Deaf perspective) of a culturally symbolic detail (Māori perspective) of the event; moreover, it is distinct from the NZSL sign WELCOME, which is usually associated with an English gloss. Debates like these are less motivated by issues of semantic equivalence or articulation preferences and more by considerations of how the packaging of meaning (such as the "foreignness" or uniqueness of the sign form) indexes both a Deaf and a Māori worldview.

MS or MSL? Naming the Signs

Speakers of community languages and linguists often disagree about what constitutes a separate language, dialect, or variety; speakers may emphasize the social significance of distinctions in usage that linguists regard as empirically minimal (Horvath and Vaughan 1991). From a linguistic point of view, this category of new forms and meanings in NZSL can be described as "contact signs" since they arise in interactional contexts of Māori-NZSL contact, but ultimately they are NZSL signs. As an expansion of the NZSL lexicon, semantic imports from TRM enable communication in new content domains and utilize known mechanisms for borrowing or creating lexicon. As such, they are like the contact forms resulting from other contexts that NZSL users have recently entered, where academic, technical, or other foreign vocabulary is necessary to the interaction and influences the actual form of the equivalent signs coined.

However, social perspectives on how users choose to characterize such language developments are complex. Some participants in this study felt that the term MSL, which implies a distinct language variety and/or a derivative relationship to spoken Māori, is a misnomer. A Māori interpreter stated, "A conversation in 'Māori Sign Language,' it's NZSL with some Māori signs that have been developed."

Some Deaf and hearing individuals use the term "MSL" loosely in MD circles, while using MS with uninformed outsiders, who may incorrectly assume that "MSL" means a historical sign language indigenous to Māori, a manual equivalent of spoken Māori, or a distinct sociolect of NZSL. On the other hand, some deliberately or indiscriminately use the term MSL to promote recognition of their dual identity. Politically, this has had some effect in attracting Māori attention and resources even though the goals are often confused by the terminology. For example, a headline in a professional teachers' journal reads "Signing in Te Reo" above an article about a government initiative to support training of NZSL interpreters who can also speak Māori (West 2003). Māori tertiary education institutions have even advertised "Māori Sign Language" courses; in some cases MD tutors have supported this mislabeling of what are actually NZSL courses taught by MD, while others have challenged the inaccuracy of the term (Karen Pointon, pers. comm., November 2005).

Connecting MD with TRM sits well with the Māori agenda of cultural regeneration and also with a governmental imperative to address the inclusion of Māori with disabilities; the ambiguous term "MSL" creates the impression of a vehicle for achieving such goals. A Deaf representative of the government agency who drafted the NZSL Act told MD at the 2005 hui that the loose use of the term "MSL" has already prompted some confusion and misplaced concern among policy makers about recognizing NZSL as an official language of the Deaf community if Māori Deaf language rights might be marginalized by this, which is patently not the case.

The terms "MS" or "MSL" are used (often interchangeably) with different intent by different parties — as a label for a category of signs with Māori reference and/or as a tool of identity politics that distinguishes Māori within the NZSL community and simultaneously increases solidarity between MD and hearing Māori. This echoes the conclusion of Morales-López et al. (2002, 143) that Deaf Catalonians' characterization of their regional sign variety as a distinct language (LSC) is an attempt to constitute both a political reality and an identity motivated by a larger nationalist movement. We contend that for MD, using the terms "MSL" and "MS" invokes a framework of cultural alliance (Goffman 1981) and indexes an indigenous identity that previously had no linguistic means of symbolic expression.

It remains to be seen how this development will be perceived within the wider NZSL community. There is functional value to all NZSL users in having a lexicon to express Māori reference, yet it is also possible that use of MS as emblems of MD identity and the assertion of proprietary rights over change in NZSL might be perceived as a shift in cultural allegiance that potentially threatens community solidarity — a phenomenon described in international contexts of shifting language-ethnic boundaries in which the "one language, one people" formula is disputed (Blackledge and Pavlenko 2001). As Humphries (1996) observes of the Deaf culture revolution, control of language is a mechanism for creating distance and shifting the balance of power in defining self and others. Just as the New Zealand Deaf collective has promoted the recognition of NZSL as a route to articulating a culturally distinct voice within NZ society, MD may be simultaneously using the development of MS as a means of "distancing of wills, self-images, and voice" (ibid., 361) from the majority Deaf community and thus diversifying its image.

Construction of MD Identity in Written and Spoken Māori

Deaf contact with the discourse of tino rangatiratanga has also manifested in some interesting Deaf contact forms in written Māori. An everyday example is MD people's use of Māori greetings and sign-offs in text messaging and emails, reflective of hearing Māori usage. Unique to MD are two Māori terms that challenge hearing Māori definitions of their identity. The first of these is *Ngati Turi,* roughly meaning "tribe of Deaf people." "Ngati" is a conventional prefix in tribal names, meaning "descendants/people of," and Turi means "deaf."[7] The term "Ngati" is applied in contemporary New Zealand to other communities of interest not originating in the Māori world, often humorously, such as *Ngati Cappuccino,* a hybrid term for professional, urban Māori (Macalister 2005) and *Ngati Pākehā* (the tribe of non-Māori). By invoking indigenous reference to kinship, the coinage Ngati Turi boldly constructs Deaf people as a historically continuous collective with common purpose, culture, and kin-like bonds.

A second coinage is *tino rangatira-turi-tanga*, a Deaf appropriation of the Māori slogan of political self-determination (*tino* = self or ultimate; *rangatiratanga* = sovereignty). By inserting the segment *turi* ("deaf"), this morphologically unconventional form invokes solidarity between MD and hearing Māori in their struggle for empowerment and cultural acknowledgment. By deliberately adapting a phrase that is recognizable yet somewhat challenging to a Māori understanding of Deaf people, MD are invoking a convergence of agendas that hearing Māori will intuitively support. This echoes the rhetorical strategy of the "Deaf President Now" movement at Gallaudet University of borrowing Martin Luther King's slogan "We have a dream" to evoke a frame of civil rights struggle. Interestingly, the written term "tino rangatiraturitanga" has no signed equivalent yet, suggesting that its impact is aimed at a non-Deaf audience; a sign translation (or rather its meaning) was discussed inconclusively at the 2005 MD hui. To date, we have not been able to identify an NZSL form that represents this written coinage.

CONCLUSIONS

Over the last decade, Deaf-hearing interaction in Māori domains has generated more contact between the languages, cultures, and sociopolitical agendas of Deaf and Māori communities, motivating both spontaneous and deliberate coining of NZSL forms known locally as "Māori signs" or "Māori Sign Language." This development follows the increasing use of Māori borrowings and code switching by hearing speakers of NZE for the purposes of signaling cultural reference, identity, and political solidarity.

The development of MS appears to be a case of borrowing non-basic lexical items in a situation of "minimum cultural pressure" (Thomason and Kaufman 1988, 77), where foreign meanings are imported through loan shifts in the form of neologisms, loan translations, and the semantic extension of existing signs through mouthing. The forms identified in this study are still in the process of becoming naturalized borrowings and are used mainly within the idiolects of those MD engaged in ethnic identification and interaction with the Māori world and their immediate networks. In the NZSL community generally, recent MS, including neologisms and semantic extensions of native signs, remain mostly in the foreign category and thus are unfamiliar to most and restricted to certain domains of use (such as ceremonial Māori welcome). However, social indicators such as the increasing profile of Māori leaders in the Deaf community, as well as the incorporation of Māori cultural elements into Deaf events and symbols of national Deaf identity, indicate a likely shift toward the naturalization of MS in the lexicon. Further analysis of sociolinguistic variation in NZSL may determine whether Māori usage of NZSL exhibits consistent distinctions in the lexicon and other structures.

Naming is important to the perception of a language and the group boundaries it defines. Our analysis is that "Māori signs" — although frequently referred to as "Māori Sign Language" — constitute neither a sign language indigenous to Māori nor a manual equivalent of spoken Māori nor, at this time, a distinct sociolect of NZSL. Māori signs are a set of lexical items arising from contact between TRM and NZSL, created by existing sign language mechanisms for borrowing semantic reference into NZSL.

Deaf and hearing Māori have jointly engaged in processes of contact language creation, each bringing their respective linguistic knowledge, cultural agendas, and preferred ways of constructing Māori and Deaf identity. This study shows how traditional hearing-Deaf power dynamics may be replicated in intercultural interactions within an apparently shared minority empowerment agenda. In this case, limited attempts to devise Signed Māori and to revise existing NZSL signs exemplify a familiar Deaf experience of linguistic paternalism, framed by benevolent but unexamined integrationist aspirations for the advancement of Deaf people. On the other hand, collaboration with hearing allies who have deferred to a Deaf perspective has been instrumental to the process of MD claiming and constructing — through linguistic and social means — their own place to stand.

Jankowski (1995, 309) identifies three strategies in cultural diversity movements: "creation of a sense of self worth, establishment of an internal foundation for community building, and participation in public life." Māori contact signs have arisen in contexts in which Deaf and hearing people have jointly focused on the first of these goals: strengthening of self-worth through exploration of cultural heritage. The creation of MS obviously performs a communicative function of allowing MD to engage with Māori cultural heritage in both external (hearing) and internal (Deaf) contexts. The development of MS is also seen as a tool for facilitating participation in public (Māori) life, a goal that is prioritized more strongly by hearing Māori than by MD. Future study of how MS are used in discourse will offer a further window on MD as an emerging "community of practice" (Wenger 1998), in the sense of a group who are engaged in a particular endeavor and are characterized by distinctive beliefs, values, and ways of talking and doing (Eckert and McConnell-Ginet 1992).

Regardless of how the lexicon currently known as MS develops within NZSL, the activity surrounding its creation and dissemination constitutes a politicizing process that potentially reconstructs power relations and a sense of cultural affinity among Māori Deaf, hearing Māori, and Pākehā Deaf. Linguistic responses to contact between the Māori language/culture and NZSL users show the potential complexity and multiplicity of the construct of "Deaf identity" and the role that foreign language borrowing may play in constituting it.

ACKNOWLEDGMENTS

We thank the participants who shared their knowledge and perspectives for this study, in particular, Deaf members of Te Komiti o Ruamoko at Kelston Deaf Education Centre for their support of the research. This analysis is our interpretation of the language and experiences of the people who informed the study; we accept responsibility for any potential errors of commission or omission in our representation and acknowledge that there may be alternative perspectives on the events and motives described here. Deaf artist Shaun Fahey created the sign illustrations, and Karen Pointon is the model in Figures 14–16. Comments from two reviewers were helpful in improving an earlier draft of the chapter.

NOTES

1. A word on labels: In New Zealand, the word "Māori" is used in contemporary Māori and English discourse as a plural noun to refer collectively to Māori people; in fact, this form is often preferred by Māori speakers over the full English phrase "Māori people," in which "Māori" functions as an adjective or a secondary characteristic. "Deaf" is similarly used as a collective noun both in NZSL discourse and often in Deaf people's spoken and written English. Within both of these usages, the characteristic of humanness is assumed. While we acknowledge that it may differ from current conventions in terminology that refers to people who have disabilities or other minority statuses, we have chosen to use MD as an abbreviation for collective reference to "Māori Deaf" (people) as a close reflection of how our informants label themselves and their intent in doing so.

2. By decolonization, we refer to the processes through which a subordinated or colonized group tries to reverse the negative psychological and material impacts of political and cultural domination (cf. Tuhiwai-Smith 1999). The decolonization agendas of Deaf and of Māori communities both manifest in activities such as deconstructing historical accounts of the group, political consciousness raising, advocacy for political (and territorial) sovereignty, building collective identity and pride, and revitalizing the culture and language.

3. Te Reo Māori is the indigenous, formal term for the Māori language. Although the language is also commonly referred to in New Zealand as "Māori" and also as "Te Reo," we use the abbreviation TRM to distinguish reference to the language from other uses of the word "Māori."

4. A *marae* is a traditional venue where community events such as meetings, funerals, workshops, and community celebrations are hosted. The marae comprises an enclosed area of ground where the initial formalities between hosts and visitors are exchanged, a large meeting house used for discussion and sleeping, a dining hall, and sometimes other dwellings. The location, structures, traditions, and protocols of a marae all have ancestral significance.

5. Eighteen more Māori words also appear in the NZSL dictionary as possible synonyms or translations listed under an English headword (the primary gloss). These Māori translations were included because they are familiar as equivalents to hearing speakers of NZE, but these signs do not have exclusively

Māori reference (e.g., *kawa* is listed along with "protocol" as a secondary synonym under the headword/sign "way").

6. Tūrangawaewae means "home ground" or a "place to stand."

7. Williams (1971, 459) lists "obstinate" as a related, secondary meaning of "turi," and the causative prefix "whakatuturi" gives the meaning "to turn a deaf ear to, be obstinate, be unyielding." This parallels English metaphors of deafness as intentional uncooperative or inattentive behavior, suggesting some common ground in Māori/Pakeha relations with Deaf people.

REFERENCES

Ahmad, W., A. Darr, L. Jones, and G. Nisar. 1998. *Deafness and ethnicity: Services, policy, and politics*. Bristol, UK: Policy Press.

AKO Ltd. 1995. Tautoko Tāngata Turi [Support Deaf Māori]: A report for the Deaf Association of New Zealand. Te Puni Kokiri and the Auckland Deaf Association.

Anderson, G. B. 2002. The impact of sign language research on black Deaf communities. In *The study of signed languages: Essays in honor of William C. Stokoe*, ed. D. F. Armstrong, M. A. Karchmer, and J. V. Van Cleve, 161–71. Washington, D.C.: Gallaudet University Press.

Aramburo, A. J. 1989. Sociolinguistic aspects of the black Deaf community. In *The sociolinguistics of the Deaf community*, ed. C. Lucas 103–119. New York: Academic Press.

Battison, R. 1978. *Lexical borrowing in American Sign Language*. Silver Spring, Md.: Linstok.

Bell, A. 2000. Māori and Pākehā English: A case study. In *New Zealand English*, ed. A. Bell and K. Kuiper, 221–48. Wellington, New Zealand: Victoria University Press.

Benton, R. 2001. Whose language? Ownership and control of Te Reo Māori in the third millennium. *New Zealand Sociology* 16: 35–54.

Blackledge, A., and A. Pavlenko. 2001. Negotiation of identities in multilingual contexts. *International Journal of Bilingualism* (September) 5: 243–57.

Bourdieu, P. 1991. *Language and symbolic power*. Cambridge, UK: Polity.

Boyce, M. 2005. Attitudes to Māori. In *Languages of New Zealand*, ed. A. Bell, R. Harlow, and D. Starks, 86–110. Wellington, New Zealand: Victoria University Press.

Boyes Braem, P. 2001. Functions of the mouthings in the signing of deaf early and late learners of Swiss German Sign language (DSGS). In *The hands are the head of the mouth as articulator in sign languages*, ed. P. Boyes Braem and R. Sutton-Spence, 99–131. Hamburg: Signum.

Branson, J., and D. Miller. 2004. The cultural construction of linguistic incompetence through schooling: Deaf education and the transformation of the linguistic environment in Bali, Indonesia. *Sign Language Studies* 5: 6–38.

Brentari, D. 2001a. Borrowed elements in sign languages: A window on word formation. In *Foreign vocabulary in sign languages: A cross-linguistic investigation of word formation*, ed. D. Brentari, ix–xx. Mahwah, N.J.: Erlbaum.

———. ed. 2001b. *Foreign vocabulary in sign languages: A cross-linguistic investigation of word formation*. Mahwah, N.J.: Erlbaum.

Brentari, D. and C. Padden. 2001. Native and foreign vocabulary in American Sign Language: a lexicon with multiple origins. In *Foreign vocabulary in sign languages: A cross-linguistic investigation of word formation*, ed. D. Brentari, 87–119. Mahwah, N.J.: Erlbaum.

Bynon, T. 1977. *Historical linguistics*. New York: Cambridge University Press.

Callister, P. 2004. Māori/non-Māori ethnic intermarriage. *New Zealand Population Review* 29: 89–105.

Chapple, S. 2000. Māori socio-economic disparity. *Political Science* 52: 101–15.

Collins-Ahlgren, M. 1989. Aspects of New Zealand Sign Language. PhD diss., Victoria University of Wellington, New Zealand.

Davis, J., and S. Supalla. 1995. Language use in a Navajo family. In *The sociolinguistics of the Deaf community*, ed. C Lucas, 77–106. Washington, D.C.: Gallaudet University Press.

Deverson, T. 1991. New Zealand lexis: The Māori dimension. *English Today* 26: 18–25.

Dively, V. L. 2001. Contemporary native Deaf experience: Overdue smoke rising. In *Deaf world: A historical reader and primary sourcebook*, ed. L. Bragg, 390–405. New York: New York University Press.

Dugdale, P. O. 2000. Being Deaf in New Zealand: A case study of the Wellington Deaf community. PhD diss., Victoria University of Wellington, New Zealand.

———. 2001. *Talking hands, listening eyes: The history of the Deaf Association of New Zealand*. Auckland: Deaf Association of New Zealand.

Durie, A. 1997. Te aka matua: Keeping Māori identity. In Te Whaiti, P., McCarthy, M., and Durie, A. (Eds.) *Mai i Rangiatea:Māori wellbeing and development*. Auckland: Auckland University Press. Bridget Williams Books.

Durie, M. 2001. *Te mana, te kawanatanga: The politics of Māori self-determination*. New York: Oxford University Press.

Eckert, P., and S. McConnell-Ginet. 1992. Think practically and look locally: Language and gender as community-based practice. *Annual Review of Anthropology* 21: 461–90.

Fishman, J. A. 1989. *Language and ethnicity in minority sociolinguistic perspective*. Philadelphia: Multilingual Matters.

Foster, S., and W. Kinuthia. 2003. Deaf persons of Asian American, Hispanic American, and African American backgrounds: A study of intraindividual diversity and identity. *Journal of Deaf studies and Deaf Education* 8 (3):271–290.

Gerner de García, B. 1995. Communication and language use in Spanish-speaking families with deaf children. In *The sociolinguistics of the Deaf community*, ed. C. Lucas, 221–254. Washington, D.C.: Gallaudet University Press.

Goffman, E. 1974. *Frame analysis*. New York: Harper and Row.

———. 1981. *Forms of talk*. Philadelphia: University of Pennsylvania Press.

Gulliver, M. 2005. Deafscapes: The landscape and heritage of the Deaf world. Paper presented at the Annual Conference Institute of British Geographers. London, September 2.

Haugen, E. 1938/1972. Language and immigration. In *The ecology of language: Essays by Einar Haugen*, ed. E. Haugen, 1–36. Stanford, Calif.: Stanford University Press.

———. 1950/1972a. The analysis of linguistic borrowing. In *The ecology of language: Essays by Einar Haugen*, ed. E. Haugen, 79–109. Stanford, Calif.: Stanford University Press.

———. 1950/1972b. Problems of bilingualism. In *The ecology of language: Essays by Einar Haugen*, ed. E. Haugen, 59–78. Stanford, Calif.: Stanford University Press.

Herring-Wright, M. 1999. *Sounds like home: Growing up black and Deaf in the South*. Washington, D.C.: Gallaudet University Press.

Holmes, J. 1997. Māori and Pākehā English: Some New Zealand social dialect data. *Language in Society* 26: 65–101.

———. 2001. *Introduction to sociolinguistics*, 2d ed. New York: Longman.

———. 2003. Social constructionism. In *International encyclopedia of linguistics*, 2d ed., ed. W. J. Frawley, 88–91. New York: Oxford University Press.

Horvath, B., and P. Vaughan. 1991. Sociolinguistic profiles: A guide for multicultural policymakers. In *Community languages: A handbook*, ed. B. Horvath and P. Vaughan, 1–17. Philadelphia: Multilingual Matters.

Hoyer, K. 2004. The sociolinguistic situation of Finland-Swedish Deaf people and their language, Finland-Swedish Sign Language. In *To the lexicon and beyond: Sociolinguistics in European Deaf communities*, ed. M. Van Herreweghe and M. Vermeerbergen, 3–23. Washington, D.C.: Gallaudet University Press.

Hudson, R. A. 1980. *Sociolinguistics*. New York: Cambridge University Press.

Humphries, T. 1993. Deaf culture and cultures. In *Multicultural issues in deafness*, ed. K. M. Christensen and G. L. Delgado, 3–15. White Plains, N.Y.: Longman.

———. 1996. Of Deaf-mutes: The strange and the modern Deaf self. In *Deaf world: A historical reader and primary source book*, ed. L. Bragg, 348–64. New York: New York University Press.

Jaffe, R. 1992. *Toward the creation of a consumer-based organisation: A review of the New Zealand Association of the Deaf*. Auckland: Deaf Association of New Zealand.

Jankowski, K. 1995. Empowerment from within: The Deaf social movement; Providing a framework for a multicultural society. In *The sociolinguistics of the Deaf community*, ed. C. Lucas, 307–329. Washington, D.C.: Gallaudet University Press.

Johnson, R. 1991. Sign language, culture, and community in a traditional Yucatec Maya village. *Sign Language Studies* 73: 461–74.

Johnston, T. 2000. BSL, Auslan, and NZSL: Three signed languages or one? Paper presented at the Seventh International Conference on Theoretical Issues in Sign Language Research (TISLR), Amsterdam, July.

———. 2004. W(h)ither the Deaf community? Population, genetics, and the future of Australian Sign Language. *American Annals of the Deaf* 148(5): 358–75.

Keegan, P. 2005. The development of Māori vocabulary. In *Languages of New Zealand*, ed. A. Bell, R. Harlow, and D. Starks, 131–48. Wellington, New Zealand: Victoria University Press.

Kennedy, G., R. Arnold, P. Dugdale, S. Fahey, and D. Moskovitz. 1997. *A dictionary of New Zealand Sign Language*. Auckland: Auckland University Press with Bridget Williams Books.

Leeson, L., and C. Grehan. 2004. To the lexicon and beyond: The effect of gender on variation in Irish Sign Language. In *To the lexicon and beyond: Sociolinguistics in European Deaf communities*, ed. M. Van Herreweghe and M. Vermeerbergen, 39–73. Washington, D.C.: Gallaudet University Press.

Macalister, J. 2003. The presence of Māori words in New Zealand English. PhD diss. in Applied Linguistics, Victoria University of Wellington, New Zealand.

———. 2005. *A dictionary of Māori words in New Zealand English*. New York: Oxford University Press.

Machabée, D. 1995. Description and status of initialized signs in Quebec Sign Language. In *Sociolinguistics in Deaf communities*, ed. C. Lucas, 29–61. Washington, D.C.: Gallaudet University Press.

Māori Language Act. 1987. http://www.tetaurawhiri.govt.nz/act87/title.shtml.

McKay-Cody, M. 1998/1999. The well-hidden people in Deaf and native communities. Deaf American Monograph Series. Silver Spring, Md.: NAD.

McKee, D., and G. Kennedy. 2000. A lexical comparison of signs from American, Australian, British, and New Zealand sign languages. In *The signs of language revisited*, ed. K. Emmorey and H. Lane, 49–76. Mahwah, N.J.: Erlbaum.

McKee, R. 2001. *People of the eye: Stories from the Deaf world.* Wellington, New Zealand: Bridget Williams Books.

McKee, R., and D. McKee. 2000. Name signs and identity in New Zealand Sign Language. In *Bilingualism and identities in Deaf communities,* ed. E. Winston, 3–42. Washington, D.C.: Gallaudet University Press.

———. 2002. New Zealand Sign Language grammar: A guide for learners. Deaf Studies Research Unit, Occasional Paper 3, Victoria University of Wellington, New Zealand.

Merriam, S. B. 1998. *Qualitative research and case study applications in education.* San Francisco: Jossey-Bass.

Metge, J. 1976. *The Māoris of New Zealand: Rautahi,* rev. ed. London: Routledge and Kegan Paul.

Miller, C. 2001. The adaptation of loan words in Quebec Sign Language: Multiple sources, multiple processes. In *Foreign vocabulary in sign languages: A cross-linguistic investigation of word formation,* ed. D. Brentari, 139–74. Mahwah, N.J.: Erlbaum.

Milroy, J. 1989. The concept of prestige in sociolinguistic argumentation. *York Papers in Linguistics* 13: 215–26.

Morales-López, E., D. Aliaga-Emetrio, J. A. Alonso- Rodríguez, R. M. Boldu-Menasanch, J. Garrusta-Ribes, and V. Gras-Ferrer. 2002. Deaf people in bilingual-speaking communities: The case of Deaf people in Barcelona. In *Turn-taking, fingerspelling, and contact in signed languages,* ed. C. Lucas, 107–155 Washington, D.C.: Gallaudet University Press.

Napier, J., R. McKee, and D. Goswell. 2006. *Sign language interpreting: Theory and practice in Australia and New Zealand.* Sydney: Federation Press.

National Audiology Centre. 2007. New Zealand deafness notification database, January–December 2005. Auckland, New Zealand.

New Zealand Sign Language Bill. http://www.odi.govt.nz/documents/nzds/nzsl-bill.doc.

O'Regan, H. 2001. *Ko Tahu, ko au: Kai Tahu tribal identity.* Christchurch, New Zealand: Horomaka.

Padden, C., and D. C. Gunsauls. 2003. How the alphabet came to be used in sign language. *Sign Language Studies* 4: 10–33.

Parasnis, I. 1996. *Cultural and language diversity and the Deaf experience.* New York: Cambridge University Press.

Paris, D. G., and S. K. Wood. 2002. *Step into the circle: The heartbeat of American Indian, Alaska Native, and First Nations Deaf communities.* Salem, Ore.: AGO.

Patton, M. Q. 1990. *Qualitative evaluation and research methods*. London: Sage.

Poplack, S., D. Sankoff, and C. Miller. 1988. The social correlates and linguistic processes of lexical borrowing and assimilation. *Linguistics* 26: 47–104.

Shaw, K. E. 1978. Understanding the curriculum: The approach through case studies. *Journal of Curriculum Studies* 10: 1–17.

Slobin, D. 2006. Breaking the molds: Signed languages and the nature of human language. Keynote address at Revolutions in Sign Language Studies: Linguistics, Literature, and Literacy conference. Gallaudet University, Washington, D.C., March 22.

Smiler, K. 2004. Māori Deaf: Perceptions of cultural and linguistic identity of Māori members of the New Zealand Deaf community. Master's thesis in Applied Linguistics, Victoria University of Wellington, New Zealand.

Spolsky, B. 2005. Māori lost and regained. In *Languages of New Zealand*, ed. A. Bell, R. Harlow, and D. Starks, 67–85. Wellington, New Zealand: Victoria University Press.

Statistics New Zealand. 2007. Quick stats about Māori. Retrieved electronically June 8, 2007, at http://www.stats.govt.nz/2006-census-data/quickstats-about-maori.

Statistics New Zealand. 2001. New Zealand disability survey snapshot 6: Sensory disabilities. Wellington, New Zealand.

Statistics New Zealand. 2002. New Zealand population and dwelling statistics. Wellington, New Zealand.

Strang, B. 1970. *A History of English*. London: Methuen.

Taylor, M. 1993. *Interpretation skills: English to American Sign Language*. Edmonton, Canada: Interpreting Consolidated.

Thomason, S. G., and T. Kaufman. 1988. *Language contact, creolization, and genetic linguistics*. Berkeley: University of California Press.

Ting-Toomey, S. 1999. *Communicating across cultures*. New York: Guilford.

Tuhiwai-Smith, L. 1999. *Decolonisation methodologies: Research and indigenous peoples*. Otago, New Zealand: Otago University Press.

Weedon, C. 1987. *Feminist practice and post-structuralist theory*. New York: Blackwell.

Wenger, E. 1998. *Communities of practice*. New York: Cambridge University Press.

West, E. 2003. Signing in Te Reo. *New Zealand Education Gazette, Tukutuku Korero* 28 (June 2): 3–5.

Williams, H.W. 1971. *A Dictionary of the Maori Language*. Seventh Edition. Wellington: Government Printer Books.

Part 2   Lexical Comparisons

North American Indian Signed Language

Varieties: A Comparative Historical

Linguistic Assessment

Jeffrey Davis

As an alternative to spoken language, signed language has been observed and documented for certain North American Indian groups (e.g., Davis 2005, 2006; Davis and Supalla 1995; Mallery 1880, 1881; McKay-Cody 1997; Taylor 1978, 1997; Tomkins 1926; Umiker-Sebeok and Sebeok 1978).[1] The North American continent was once an area of extreme linguistic and cultural diversity, with hundreds of distinct and mutually unintelligible languages spoken by the native populations. For example, Mithun (1999, 1) points out that "while the languages of Europe are classified into just three families, Indo-European, Finno-Ugric, and Basque, those of North America constitute over 50."

The major published research on the languages of native North America (reported in Campbell 2000 and Mithun 1999), early anthropological linguistic fieldwork and descriptions (Kroeber 1958; Voegelin 1958; West 1960), and a survey of documentary materials from archival sources (Davis 2006) indicate that signed language was used in varying degrees as an independent communication system within most of the language families indigenous to North America. For many generations, signed language emerged as a way to make communication possible between individuals and groups speaking many distinct and mutually unintelligible languages.

This chapter is a continuation of an earlier study reported in volume 12 of this series. I would like to acknowledge the support of the National Anthropological Archives, the Smithsonian Institution, and a National Endowment for the Humanities and National Science Foundation Documenting Endangered Languages fellowship (FN-50002-06). The results of the study reported here do not necessarily reflect those of the Smithsonian Institution, National Endowment for the Humanities, or National Science Foundation.

This was documented in numerous historical accounts, including the field-work of nineteenth-century ethnologists and anthropologists, most notably Boas (1890) and Mallery (1880, 1881), who were among the first scholars to do fieldwork among American Indian groups.

This chapter focuses on previously collected lexical descriptions from written, illustrated, and filmed sources of conventionalized signs that were used among North American Indian groups for a variety of discourse purposes (reported in Davis 2006). The chief aims of the present study are (1) to provide a preliminary assessment of historical relatedness, language variation, and dialect differences based on lexical comparisons of signs used among North American Indians of the Great Plains; (2) to compare the signs documented for North American Indians with lexical descriptions and illustrations of American Sign Language (ASL) from comparable historical periods; and (3) to point others to the corpus of North American Indian signed language so that various linguistic levels — from the phonological to the grammatical — can be further studied and described. Documenting and describing a language are enormous undertakings that are rendered urgent by the endangered status of these signed language varieties. The study of indigenous signed languages helps broaden our understanding of the cognitive and social bases of human language and raises historical linguistic and sociolinguistic questions (e.g., about language origins, spread, attitude, contact, change).

PREVIOUS STUDIES

I have previously reported on the documented cases of historical and contemporary signed language use among North American Indian groups, and some of these findings are summarized in the following sections (see Davis 2006 for further descriptions).[2] The previously collected historical linguistic and ethnographic documentation from archival sources indicates that signed language was used across the major American Indian cultural areas (e.g., the Southeast, Gulf Coast, Southwest, Great Plains, Plateau/Great Basin, Northeast, Subarctic, and Mesoamerican geographic areas; Campbell 2000; Davis 2005, 2006; Mithun 1999). A number of volumes have been published on the traditional use of signed language among American Indians (most notably, Clark 1885; Mallery 1881; Tomkins 1926; Umiker-Sebeok and Sebeok

1978), and more recently, several publications have described both the historical and contemporary use of signed language among Indian groups (Davis 2005, 2006; Davis and Supalla 1995; Farnell 1995; Kelly 2004; Kelly and McGregor 2003; McKay-Cody 1997).

In the research literature, the historical varieties of indigenous signed language specific to North America are sometimes collectively referred to as "North American Indian Sign Language" (see Wurtzburg and Campbell 1995). Historically, these varieties of signed language were named in various ways: Plains Indian Sign Language (PISL), Indian Sign Language, the Sign Language, and Indian Language of Signs. "Hand talk" was the way that some American Indian groups commonly referred to sign language (Tomkins 1926). In this chapter these terms are used interchangeably depending on the historical context and sources that are cited.

Early Anthropological Linguistic Fieldwork

The first works to describe the distinctive features of conventionalized signed language among American Indians were published by researchers (Kroeber 1958; Voegelin 1958; West 1960), who helped establish the discipline of anthropological linguistics. Based on these findings and other historical accounts reported in the literature (cf. Campbell 2000; Davis 2005, 2006; Mithun 1999), linguistic variation was observed within and between different North American Indian groups that used signed language (e.g., not all of the members of the group may have signed, and those who did sign may not have been equally fluent). Reportedly, the more nomadic groups were the best signers; dialect differences were evident but did not seriously hinder communication; and signing was not limited to intertribal ceremonial occasions but was also used in storytelling and conversation within groups speaking the same language. Moreover, signing occurred both with and without speech as an alternative to spoken language for Indians who were hearing and as a primary language for those who were deaf. For further descriptions see Davis (2005, 2006).

Contemporary Documentation and Description

Davis (2005, 2006), Davis and Supalla (1995), Farnell (1995), Gordon (2005), Kelly (2004), Kelly and McGregor (2003), and McKay-Cody (1997) have reported that the traditional ways of signing are currently known primarily by hearing elders and some deaf members of several different American Indian language groups. The number of signers is unknown at this time, but due to a variety of sociocultural and historical factors reported in these studies, traditional sign language use among hearing Indians has been replaced by spoken English. Most of the deaf members of these groups attend schools for deaf students and learn ASL as a primary language. Thus, fewer hearing and deaf Indians are learning the traditional ways of signing, suggesting that these varieties of sign language are currently endangered. Although greatly diminished from once having been used among dozens of distinct Native American cultural groups, contemporary sign language use has been reported (see Davis 2006) within seven distinct spoken language groups, representing four major spoken native language families:[3] Algonquian (Blackfoot = Piegan, Northern Cheyenne), Athabaskan (Navajo = Diné), Siouan (Assiniboine, Crow, Sioux = Lak(h)ota = Dakota = Nakota), and New Mexican Pueblo Isolates (Keresan = Keres). It has been reported (Davis and Supalla 1995; Kelly and McGregor 2003) that some members of the Navajo/Diné and Keresan groups use a signed language variety that is distinct from those used by Plains cultural group members, primarily of Algonquian and Siouan descent (Farnell 1995; Mithun 1999; McKay-Cody 1997; West 1960).

Primary and Alternate Sign Language

Davis and Supalla (1995) and McKay-Cody (1997) studied the similarities and differences between deaf and hearing Indian signers and between signing that occurs with or without speech. For example, the "alternate sign systems" used by hearing Indians became a "primary sign language" when acquired natively by deaf Indians. The linguistic evidence suggests that alternate signs are used to varying degrees of proficiency, ranging from those that accompany speech, to signing without speech, to signing that functions similarly to a primary sign language. Davis and Supalla (1995, 83–85) have proposed that (1) *primary signed languages* have evolved within specific historical, social, and cultural contexts and have been used across generations of signers (e.g., ASL, French Sign Language, British Sign Language) and that (2) *alternate sign systems* have been developed and used by individuals who are already competent in spoken language (e.g., the highly elaborated and complex sign system used historically by the Plains Indians of North America).

McKay-Cody (1997) has described what happened when the alternate sign language traditionally used by hearing members of the Plains cultural groups was acquired as a primary sign language by members of the group who are deaf. The deaf members of these native groups "seem to gain a higher level of proficiency" when compared to members who are hearing (ibid., 50). These findings suggest that the alternate sign language becomes linguistically enriched when learned as a primary language by members of these native communities who are deaf. Further historical (diachronic) and contemporary (synchronic) comparative linguistic analyses are needed to clarify these similarities and differences and to assess the historical relatedness or unrelatedness among these signed language varieties.

Plains Indian Sign Language

Previous anthropological linguistic field research showed that sign language was used in varying degrees within most of the spoken language families of Native North America and that the best-documented cases involved members of the Plains Indian cultural and linguistic groups (Kroeber 1958; Voegelin 1958; West 1960). Historically, the Great Plains cultural area was centrally located on the North American continent and spanned approximately one million square miles. Intensive language and cultural contact occurred between the native peoples inhabiting these areas (cf. Campbell 2000; Mithun 1999). It should be pointed out that these cultural-linguistic boundaries are based on numerous sociocultural, linguistic, and historical variables and do not imply the existence of only a few sharply distinct ways of life on the continent (e.g., Washburn, in the *Handbook of North American Indians* [1988, viii], states that "in reality, each group exhibits a unique combination of particular cultural features, while all neighboring peoples are always similar in some ways and dissimilar in others").[4]

Traditionally, Plains Indian Sign Language (PISL) is used within the Plains cultural and linguistic groups of the United States and Canada (Gordon 2005). Documentary materials on PISL are the primary source of the lexical comparisons presented in this chapter. Davis (2006, 8) reports that "historic and contemporary uses of signed language have been documented in at least one dozen distinct North American language families (phyla)" and that "the archived data reveal that regardless of hearing status, signing was used by members from approximately thirty-seven distinct American Indian spoken language groups." Although greatly diminished from its former widespread use across the Great Plains, PISL has not vanished. Gordon (2005) classifies PISL as a language that is distinct from ASL. Today PISL is used within some native groups in storytelling, rituals, legends, and prayers, as well as by American Indians who are deaf (Davis 2005, 2006; Davis and Supalla 1995; Farnell 1995; Gordon 2005; Kelly 2004; Kelly and McGregor 2003; McKay-Cody 1997).

Origins and Spread

The origins of North American Indian signed language varieties remain uncertain. From the sixteenth through the nineteenth centuries, numerous descriptive accounts of the signing of American Indians were written by early European explorers who spent years in the area and colonizers who settled in North America (Mithun 1999). In their historical study of "North American Indian Sign Language," Wurtzburg and Campbell (1995, 160) have defined "sign language" as "a conventionalized gesture language of the sort later attested among the Plains and neighboring areas." Goddard (1979) and Wurtzburg and Campbell (1995) have made compelling cases for a preexistent, well-developed indigenous sign language that was used across the Gulf Coast–Texas–northern Mexico area before European contact, and these scholars have also discussed the pidgins, trade languages, and mixed systems used by native groups. The generally accepted hypothesis among scholars (see also Campbell 2000; Mithun 1999) is that North American Indian Sign Language (Wurtzburg and Campbell's designation) originated and spread from the Gulf Coast, became the intertribal lingua franca of the Great Plains, and spread throughout the Northwest Territories of the United States and Canada.[5] Along these lines, Taylor (1997, 275) proposes that "trade may have been an important stimulus in the development of sign language, and it was certainly an important factor in its diffusion after the rise of horse nomadism."

Evidence of a Historical Signed Lingua Franca

During the nineteenth and early twentieth centuries, signed language use among native groups was so widespread that scholars of this period considered it to be a lingua franca. In other words, signing was used between indigenous groups who did not otherwise share a common spoken language (Clark 1885; Scott 1931; Mallery 1880; Tomkins 1926). Previously, documentation was made by some of the philologists and ethnologists who worked at the Smithsonian Institution's Bureau of Ethnology and were among the first scholars to do fieldwork with American Indian groups (most notably Boas 1890 and Mallery 1880).

The previous documentation occurred before the decline in the use of indigenous sign language due in large part to its replacement by English as a lingua franca (Davis 2005, 2006). Following Mallery's seminal research on this subject at the Smithsonian Institution (1880–1900), a fifty-year time period elapsed before additional peer-reviewed studies of Indian Sign Language were resumed and published by qualified and recognized researchers (e.g., Kroeber 1958; West 1960; Voegelin 1958).[6] These early scholars laid the groundwork for the consideration of Indian Sign Language as a preexistent, full-fledged language (Davis 2006).

Kroeber (1958) and Voegelin (1958) published the first scholarly works describing the conventionalized signs used by American Indians in terms of distinctive features similar to the sounds of spoken language. This was followed by a two-volume doctoral dissertation written by LaMont West, one of Carl Voegelin's students (1960). Kroeber, Voegelin, and West developed an elaborate transcription system and phonemic-like inventory for Indian Sign Language of the Great Plains cultural area and were the first scholars known to describe the distinctive phonetic features of a sign language in terms of handshape, place of articulation, and movement. For example, handshape features were described as open, closed, fingers extended, straight, curved, and so on; different points on the body were considered places of articulation; and the movement patterns of the hands were described in detail (e.g., up, down, left, right, repeated, straight lines, curves, circles) and included one hand acting alone, as well as one stationary and the other active, with both hands moving in parallel or interacting.

The published research on Indian Sign Language helped inform and was cited in the seminal work of some of the first signed language linguists (e.g., Stokoe 1960, 1972; Battison 1978/2003). However, the same biases that delayed the recognition and academic acceptance of ASL as a distinct language also appear to have contributed to the oversight and neglected study of sign language among American Indian groups (Baynton 2002). There has been a general lack of understanding about the nature and structure of indigenous sign language even though it has been observed and reported since the 1500s (Davis 2005, 2006). Perhaps this area of sign language studies has been neglected for the past several decades due to the understandable need to provide linguistic descriptions of the primary sign languages of Deaf communities. A review of the previous linguistic and ethnohistorical studies of indigenous sign language will bridge some of the gaps in the research, encourage further studies of this subject, and draw attention to this little-known and often over-looked part of Native American heritage and sign language studies.

West's Studies

One of the major contributions of West's (1960) research was the observation that signed language use exhibited the same duality of patterning as spoken language. In addition to the structural properties and production of sign language, West and his colleagues carefully examined the lexicon, semantics, and possible origins of the system.[7] During the late 1950s West conducted extensive anthropological linguistic fieldwork among Plains tribal groups over a period of several years and reported that a number of Native American groups used different varieties and dialects of sign language. His study of more than one hundred American Indian informants reported that 87 percent were fluent in sign language (1960, 2, 62–68). Mithun (1999, 293) writes that "when La Mont West visited Plains communities in 1956 he found signing still practiced, particularly on intertribal ceremonial occasions but also in storytelling and conversation, even among speakers of the same language."

Taylor (1997, 276) points out that West's findings show that, by the 1950s, sign language was known primarily by the elders (77 percent of West's informants were older than sixty years of age, including 18 percent who were past eighty) and that the shift away from the use of sign language as an alternate to spoken language was due largely to its replacement by English as a lingua franca (55 percent of West's informants were fluent in English, whereas only 18 percent knew more than one of the Indian languages). See West (1960, 2, 62–68) for a summary of these findings.

West's fieldwork focused primarily on groups of the northern Plains cultural area, but he reported that dialect groups also lived beyond this geographic area. West identified a major dialect split between the Northern Plains and native communities beyond this region: (1) a North Central Plains dialect referred to as Plains Standard and (2) a Far Northern Plains dialect referred to as Far Northern or Storytelling dialect, which was used mainly in the Canadian provinces of Alberta, Saskatchewan, Manitoba, and British Columbia. More recent studies (e.g., Davis 2006; Mithun 1999; McKay-Cody 1997) have also suggested that different varieties and dialects of sign language were used among Indian groups and that these were distinct from the variety of ASL used in North American Deaf communities.

THE PRESENT STUDY

Comparative historical linguistic analyses are necessary before we can reach conclusions about historical relatedness and the outcomes of language contact between the signed language varieties used by American Indians and individuals who are deaf. To determine whether these varieties are historically related, this chapter presents a long-overdue comparative assessment of the sign lexicon used by North American Indians; it also compares North American Indian signs with lexical descriptions and illustrations of ASL from comparable historical periods. The study of lexical similarity can help us assess historical relatedness, and there are several important terminological and methodological considerations for the present work.

Terminology and Methodology

Linguistic researchers who are concerned with the historical (i.e., diachronic) relationship between languages commonly carry out studies of lexical similarity. This approach is useful in determining whether language varieties share the same historical roots or can be traced to a common parent language or lineage. Historical linguistic researchers distinguish two main types of historical relatedness (cf. Campbell 2004; Parkhurst and Parkhurst 2003). First, genetically related languages have developed from a common ancestor and are classified as members of the same language family. A second type of historical relationship is lexical similarity due to language contact and lexical borrowing. In other words, two languages may have borrowed from each other over time, but their origins can be traced to two distinct original languages (cf. Campbell 2004).

The study of lexical similarity and cognates offers important insights into historical relatedness. As defined by Fromkin, Rodman, and Hyams (2007, 480) "*cognates* are words in related languages that developed from the same ancestral root, such as English *horn* and Latin *cornu*," and, as they point out, "Cognates often, but not always, have the same meaning in different languages." For example, "it is possible that at one time two words may have been historically very similar, but with the natural changes that occur over time the two words have evolved into forms that are so distinct as not to be easily recognizable" (Parkhurst and Parkhurst 2003, 1). Another example of this principle comes from Campbell (2004), who points out that the English word *eight* and the Spanish equivalent *ocho* do not look or sound at all alike, yet both words can be traced to the Latin word *octo*. Monolingual English or Spanish speakers are unlikely to recognize that such words are historically related.

When comparing two languages to determine historical relatedness, one must take great care to sort out instances in which the lexical similarity between words may be coincidental rather than due to historical relatedness (Guerra Currie, Meier, and Walters 2002; Parkhurst and Parkhurst 2003). In comparing sign languages, Guerra Currie et al. (2002, 224) distinguish two historical causes of lexical similarity (i.e., a genetic relationship and lexical borrowing) and two factors that are non-historical (i.e., chance and shared symbolism). To illustrate this distinction between spoken languages, Parkhurst and Parkhurst (2003, 2) use the example of *madre* in Spanish and *mae* in Thai. Both words share the same meaning and appear to be similar lexically (a natural sound change could have deleted the intermediate consonants). In this case, the lexical similarity is based on *chance* or *coincidence* and not historical relatedness or lexical borrowing (Campbell 2004). This distinction "does not deny that the words for *mother* and *father* around the world tend to use those sounds first articulated by infants, nor does it deny that the reason for chance similarity in sign languages is primarily based on iconicity" (Parkhurst and Parkhurst (2003, 2).

Researchers in the field of historical linguistics recognize that these terms and distinctions may be difficult to define or apply in practice. According to Campbell (2000, 7), a *language family* "is a group of genetically related languages, ones that share a linguistic kinship by virtue of having developed from a common earlier ancestor." The term *dialect* "means only a variety (regional or social) of a language mutually intelligible (however difficult this concept may be to define or apply in practice) with other dialects/varieties of the same language" (ibid.). Simply defined, *mutual intelligibility* means that speakers or signers of different dialects and varieties understand each other. Clearly these terms are far from unambiguous.

As Hoyer (2004, 7) points out, "one problem is that sometimes mutually intelligible varieties are defined as different languages for historical or political reasons." For example, Swedish, Norwegian, and Danish are considered different languages, although they are generally mutually intelligible among native speakers. Conversely, in many instances, a speaker of a standard language does not understand a dialect of the same language (e.g., varieties of English spoken in the southern United States or northern United Kingdom). Hoyer (ibid., 8) also cites other problems with the criterion of mutual intelligibility, such as the methods used to assess the degree of mutual understanding (via written or spoken language modalities), and reminds us "that these notions are not purely linguistic; they are also influenced by political and cultural factors."

Campbell, Parkhurst and Parkhurst, and other researchers sometimes use the terms *historically related* and *genetically related* synonymously to mean *two languages that can be traced to the same parent language.* However, a review of the research literature indicates that there are two main types of historical relationship between languages: (1) genetic relatedness (i.e., coming from the same parent language), and (2) lexical similarity or relatedness due to borrowing (i.e., *historically* two languages may have borrowed from each other, but their origins can be traced to two distinct original languages). The study of lexical similarity is considered a major way to distinguish and elucidate these differences.

Methodologies Considered and Employed in the Present Study

Several researchers have compared sign languages to determine whether they are historically related (e.g., Guerra Currie, Meier, and Walters 2002; Kyle and Woll 1985; McKee and Kennedy 2000; Parkhurst and Parkhurst 2003; West 1960; Woodward 1978). It is recognized that iconicity and indexicality features may potentially skew the results of lexical similarity studies of sign languages, and this is a major theoretical issue that signed language researchers continue to deal with in various ways. For example, to control for iconicity effects, some researchers use word lists with a lower potential for iconicity. In the research studies cited here, signed language researchers have proposed that a relatively high base level of lexical similarity — generally 80 percent — is necessary to determine that two lexical items can be considered to be cognates of genetically or historically related sign languages.

Woll, Sutton-Spence, and Elton (2001, 22) note that the following standards are generally applied to determine whether languages are separate languages or dialects of the same language: "If 80 percent or more of the words or signs are similar, then the variants are dialects of the same language. If 36 percent to 80 percent of the words or signs are similar, then the two languages belong to the same family. If the similarity is 12 percent to 35 percent, then the languages belong to families of the same stock. If it is under 12 percent then they are unrelated."

However, when Kyle and Woll (1985) compared four European sign languages that they believed were not related to each other, they found that 40 percent of the signs in the four languages were quite similar or identical. Woll et al. (2001, 23) suggest that a higher level of lexical similarity between unrelated sign languages is "caused by the presence of visually motivated (iconic) signs in the languages which exhibited similarity independently of historical links" and that "this feature of sign language will always cause problems for the classification of sign languages, unless such examples can be factored out."

Along similar lines, in a study to determine probable historical relatedness, Parkhurst and Parkhurst (2003) first compared four European sign languages that are not known to be related to each other (i.e., those of Spain, Northern Ireland, Finland, and Bulgaria); they then compared a second sample of sign language dialects from five major Spanish cities: Madrid, La Coruña, Granada, Valencia, and Barcelona. They found that comparing lexical items chosen for "low potential of iconicity" resulted in significantly lower similarity scores among unrelated languages than did word lists of basic vocabulary of "highly iconic signs." Parkhurst and Parkhurst (ibid., 3) point out that *iconic signs* look or act like the thing they represent," thus skewing the results of cognate studies, but acknowledge that "the vast majority of signs in a sign language have some iconic reference." They propose that cognate studies use word lists that comprise signs that are "low in iconicity."[8] Considering the highly visual-gestural nature of sign language, sorting out the iconic from the noniconic may be a somewhat arbitrary or subjective endeavor, and overcompensating for potential visual symbolism might also skew the results. Woll et al. (2001) have also reported that the results of lexical similarity studies may be skewed by limiting the comparisons to small vocabulary lists of signs (e.g., fifty to one hundred items) and stress "the need to recognize that some dialects of different sign languages may be more similar to each other than other dialects" (23), thus the need to take language variation into account. Moreover, like other language phenomena, the feature of iconicity is perhaps best considered along a continuum.

Parkhurst and Parkhurst (2003) have proposed that a higher standard is needed to determine the number of cognates in historically related sign languages; they have also suggested that the thresholds may need to be raised an additional 5 to 10 percentage points (i.e., 91 percent similarity indicates the same language) to account for the iconicity factor. They also state that such adjustments may not be necessary if lexical comparisons are limited to noniconic vocabulary. In other words, if highly iconic words are avoided, 81 to 90 percent similarity likely indicates that the languages are genetically and historically related. In their cognate studies of sign languages, Parkhurst and Parkhurst (2003) set the following thresholds:

0–40 percent similarity means separate languages
41–60 percent similarity means separate languages in the same family
61–70 percent similarity means inconclusive (likely to be different languages)
71–80 percent similarity means inconclusive (likely to be the same language)
81 percent similarity means they are the same language

Parkhurst and Parkhurst (12) use the "inconclusive" categories to indicate that the "similarity shows inconclusive results and other testing is necessary" to determine whether the sign languages in question are genetically related (i.e., the same language or different ones). That is, larger data sets should be studied. Again, a relatively high baseline is needed to determine the degree of similarity and is congruent with lexical similarity studies reported by the other signed language linguists cited throughout this section.

Due to the greater potential for shared symbolism (i.e., iconicity) among unrelated sign languages, other researchers (e.g., Guerra Currie, Meier, and Walters 2002, 233) have also suggested the need to follow a relatively high baseline level of similarity and cite Woll and Kyle's (1985) 80 percent baseline. In their study of Mexican Sign Language (la Lengua de Señas Mexicana, or LSM), Guerra Currie et al. (ibid.) focused on LSM tokens that are proper nouns but did not exclude some signs that might be considered to have shared symbolism.[9] With this approach, signs that may be considered somewhat iconic are not excluded but are simply coded as having "shared symbolism." See Guerra Currie et al. (2002), Parkhurst and Parkhurst (2003), Woll and Kyle (1985), and Woll et al. (2001) for more discussion of methods of comparing historically related and unrelated sign languages.

In short, the results of lexical similarity comparisons may be useful in assessing degrees of genetic relatedness; however, such scores alone are not adequate to determine historical relatedness. Other major factors to consider include historical change, language contact, and lexical borrowing. A sizeable linguistic corpus is also needed to ensure greater accuracy of comparisons. Most lexical similarity studies of sign languages have used relatively small vocabulary lists (e.g., groups of fifty to two hundred words). The largest-known published study of lexical similarity to date (i.e., Guerra Currie et al. 2002) examined 915 sign tokens from Mexican Sign Language that generated 367 pairwise comparisons with three other sign languages (French Sign Language, Spanish Sign Language, and Japanese Sign Language). Guerra Currie et al. (ibid., 228) write that, "in analyzing only signs with approximately identical meanings and similar forms, we ultimately provide a conservative estimate of the strength and nature of similarities between the languages examined, especially those 38 percent lexical similarity between LSM and French Sign Language (with known historical contact and lexical borrowing) and 23 percent lexical similarity between LSM and Japanese Sign Language (with no known historical contact or lexical borrowing).

A Corpus of Lexical Descriptions

The language corpus (more than 8,000 lexical descriptions and illustrations of American Indian signs) that is the focus of this chapter offers a unique opportunity to provide a linguistic assessment of the signed language varieties that were historically used by American Indian groups and Deaf communities (see also Davis 2006). The sources for the lexical descriptions used here are highlighted in Table 1. For the purpose of this study, 1,500 American Indian and ASL signs were examined:

- One thousand previously collected lexical descriptions and illustrations of American Indian signs from five time periods (1800s, 1820s, 1920s, 1930s, and 2000s) were examined; the comparison of American Indian signs from these five historical periods with ASL of the early 1900s generated 797 pairwise comparisons.
- Five hundred previously photographed ASL signs (Long 1918) were also examined and compared with contemporary ASL (2000) to establish a baseline of lexical similarity and historical relatedness.

Thus, the present study generated 1,297 pairwise comparisons of PISL and ASL from a sign vocabulary base of 1,500 items.

TABLE 1. Data Sources for the Lexical Comparisons

Sources	Date	Number of Lexical Descriptions	Format
Dunbar	1801	50	written
S. H. Long	1823	104	written
J. S. Long	1918	500	written and photographed
Tomkins	1926	500	written and illustrated
Sanderville	1934	200	filmed
Weatherwax	2002	150	filmed

It should be noted that Stephen H. Long and John S. Long are two different individuals from different historical periods and are not known to be related. Stephen H. Long (1823) provided one of the first compilations of written descriptions of Indian signs in the early nineteenth century, and John S. Long (1918) published the first dictionary of ASL with written descriptions and photographic illustrations in the early twentieth century.

Standards

The following standards and procedures were adhered to in the present study:

- Signs in the language corpus with greater potential for lexical transparency (i.e., iconic or indexic) were not used for lexical comparisons (e.g., personal pronouns and numbers).
- Signs that were specific to the historical-cultural context during the time of the original documentation were also excluded (e.g., sign names for various Indian nations and the tools, weaponry, and animals that were hunted during the time period in which the descriptions were made, for example, bison, turkey, white tail deer, and dung fowl).
- The original lexical descriptions that are the focus of this study were collected from archival sources over a fifteen-year period (1990–2005). To ensure that the highest standards have been followed throughout the collection and digitization processes, I was assisted by archivists and researchers at the National Archives and the Smithsonian Institution and collaborated with fellow researchers (e.g., Sam Supalla and Melanie McKay-Cody).

- During subsequent stages of data collection, digitization, classification, verification, and translation (2002–2005), I was assisted by several deaf graduate and undergraduate students.
- In the process of selecting, digitally capturing, and coding the lexical descriptions (2004–2005), I was assisted by a deaf graduate student.
- A threshold of 80 percent similarity or greater between signs was used to determine whether the variants are dialects of the same language (i.e., genetically and historically related). This reflects the higher thresholds of similarity that are necessary when comparing sign languages.
- The standard followed is that, if less than 80 percent of the sign comparisons are similar or identical, then the two languages are considered separate (i.e., not genetically related).
- Lexical descriptions considered to be gestures have also been excluded in these comparisons; this determination is based on published criteria to distinguish gestures from signs (cf. McNeil 1992, 2000).[10]

Sample Illustrations and Summary of Coding Procedures

The coding procedures followed in this study are based on similar criteria set forth by Guerra Currie et al. (2002, 227). Signs were coded as *similarly articulated* if they shared approximately the same meaning and differed according to only one major sign language parameter (e.g., handshape, movement, place of articulation). This designation also included signs that were articulated similarly or identically with regard to all three major parameters. Although signs coded as similarly articulated exhibited some differences in orientation, orientation was not considered a major formational parameter (cf. ibid., 228).

Moreover, the use of photographs, illustrations, and written descriptions to compare sign languages entails certain limitations. However, these are the only data sources for lexical comparisons of nineteenth- and early twentieth-century sign languages. Digitized motion picture films from the 1930s obtained from archival sources (cf. Figure 4) were also considered in this study. The Sanderville and Weatherwax comparisons were based on filmed and videotaped lexical data.

Digitized samples of original pen-and-ink illustrations of Indian signs from the Garrick Mallery files (ca. 1880, MS 2372) in the National Anthropological Archives at the Smithsonian Institution illustrate the

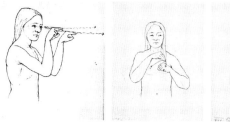

FIGURE 1 *Illustrations of PSL signs coded as similar to ASL.* [SEE, ON, ENTER, CHILD][1]

conventionalized signs used by North American Indians and demonstrate how the coding procedures were applied in this study. To the best of my knowledge, the rare and fragile pen-and-ink illustrations shown in these figures have not been previously published. To help determine lexical similarity based on written descriptions, more than one written source was consulted and also compared with illustrated, photographed, and filmed sources. Figure 1 shows illustrations of Indian signs that were coded as similar to ASL.

SAMPLE WRITTEN DESCRIPTIONS

For the lexical comparisons in this study, written descriptions were also examined. For example:

SEE. "Bring right 2 hand to opposite eyes, and the two fingers should point in the direction one is looking" (Tomkins 1926, 51).

ENTERING (a house or lodge). "The left hand is held with the back upward, and the right hand also with the back up, is passed in a curvilinear direction, down under the other, so as to rub against its palm, then up on the other side of it. The left hand here represents the low door of the skin lodge, and the right, the man stooping down to pass in" (Long 1823, 158).

EXAMPLES OF SIGNS CODED AS LEXICALLY DIFFERENT FROM ASL

Indian signs that differed in more than one major parameter were considered to be distinct from ASL. Samples of these signs are presented in Figure 2.

1. Generally, arrows indicate the direction of movement; X marks the end point of articulation; and shaded handshapes show transitional movements (although this may vary somewhat between illustrations).

FIGURE 2 *PSL signs coded as lexically different from ASL* [GOOD, LONG-TIME, BROTHERSISTER, KNOW-NOT][2]

The following written descriptions are examples of signs coded as lexically different:

Indian sign for GOOD: "Hold the flat right hand, back up, in front of and close to left breast, pointing to left; move hand briskly well out to front and right, keeping it in a horizontal plane" (Tomkins 1926, 31).

ASL sign for GOOD: "Place the end of the palm against the mouth; then bring it down against the open left hand so the back of the right hand rests on the palm of the left. In common use the latter part of the sign is omitted and the hand is simply thrown forward from the mouth" (Long 1918, 107).

Although GOOD is coded as lexically different (in location and movement), the PISL sign for GOOD is comparable to the two-handed ASL sign for NICE, CLEAN, PURE: "Place the right open hand upon the open left, crosswise and palm to palm, and letting the right hand rest near the ball of the thumb; pass the right hand along the length of the left" (ibid., 121).

In ASL, LONG-TIME is a compound sign: LONG: "placing the forefinger of the right 'G' hand lengthwise near the wrist of the extended left arm, draw it up the full length of the arm to the shoulder" (ibid., 109); TIME: "crook the forefinger of the right 'G' hand and with the tip end tap the back of the left 'S' hand" (ibid., 126). BROTHER and SISTER are also ASL compound signs (BOY + same and GIRL + same). In ASL, KNOW, which is "tap the forehead with the end of the hand" (ibid., 56), can be negated (NOT-KNOW) if the sign is produced with a movement toward, then away from the forehead.

2. Note the similarity between the sign glossed GOOD and the ASL sign for NICE (although these were coded as different); KNOW-NOT could also be glossed as SPEAK-NOT.

The Indian sign for KNOW-NOT in Figure 2 is a compound sign (SPEAK + NOT). The Indian sign for KNOW is more commonly described as "hold right hand, back up, close to breast; sweep hand outwards and slightly upwards, turning hand by wrist action until palm nearly up; thumb and index extended, other fingers closed, thumb and index horizontal, index pointing nearly to left, thumb pointing to front" (Tomkins 1926, 37). These examples demonstrate the issue of following written lexical descriptions alone from a single source. In this study, illustrations, photographs, and films from multiple sources were used to make lexical comparisons.

Description of Historical Sources for the Lexical Comparisons

I first examined 50 descriptions of Indian signs originally published by William Dunbar (1801) and 104 Indian sign descriptions from Stephen H. Long's (1823) account of an official expedition to the Rocky Mountains. Subsequent to their original printings, both previously published historical accounts (Dunbar and Long) were reprinted collectively (with the omission of approximately ten descriptions that the editor considered redundant) as the "Indian Language of Signs" in the *American Annals of the Deaf and Dumb* (Gallaudet 1852). These historical publications present descriptions of the signs reportedly used by American Indian groups of the early 1800s. They also provide discussion of some similarities with the signs used by deaf people of that historical period. In the present study, lexical comparisons are made between descriptions and illustrations of signed language varieties reportedly used by deaf people of several different historical periods (1800s–2000). Table 1 lists the lexical descriptions and data sources used in this study.

The earliest known descriptions and illustrations of signs used by American Indians were made in the early 1800s, during the first official expeditions to the western territories of what is now the United States. They formed the basis of a paper titled "Sign Language of the Indian Nations to the West of the Mississippi River," which was presented by Thomas Jefferson, president of the American Philosophical Society (Dunbar 1801). Descriptions were given for more than fifty signs used by members of the Indian nations. Jefferson made this presentation in January 1801, one month prior to his presidential inaugural address. The title and content of his lecture reflect the fact that Jefferson had an enthusiastic interest in the subject and realized the relevance of the sign language used by the Indian nations. Although previously published in the

1800s, the address has long been out of print. The original copy of Dunbar's (1801) paper and original pen-and-ink drawings are from the Garrick Mallery files in the National Anthropological Archives at the Smithsonian Institution (ca. 1880, MS 2372).

The Natural Language of Signs

The next official U.S. expedition following that by Lewis and Clark was led in 1819 by Maj. Stephen H. Long of Pittsburgh, Pennsylvania, and went as far as the Rocky Mountains (Davis 2005, 2006). The vital communication role that Indian Sign Language played is described in the published account of the expedition (Long 1823, 378–94), which included more than one hundred descriptions of Indian signs. Thomas H. Gallaudet, cofounder of the first school for deaf students in the United States in 1817, used these early descriptive accounts of Indian signs to make a case for "the Natural Language of Signs" for teaching and communicating with people who are deaf.

Gallaudet's first published papers advocated the use of the natural language of signs to teach children who were deaf. In 1848, he published an essay that included detailed descriptions of some of the signs used by the "aboriginal Indians" taken from Long's (1823) account. It is clear from his writings that Gallaudet considered Indian Sign Language, like the sign language of deaf people, to be a natural occurrence. Historical records indicate that frequent contact occurred between signing Native American and deaf groups (Mallery 1880; McKay-Cody 1997). Gallaudet's attention to Indian Sign Language in these early publications and the dissemination of descriptions of Indian signs to educators of deaf people through the *American Annals for the Deaf and Dumb* (1823–1890, vols. 1–35) make it plausible that during this period American Indian signs were introduced to people who were deaf. However, such claims remain speculative at this point. See Nover (2000) for more discussion of nineteenth-century authors (e.g., Fay 1874, 1890; Rae 1852; Tylor 1878; Mallery 1882) who provided detailed descriptions and comparisons of ASL signs and the "Indian Language of Signs."

Early Descriptions of American Sign Language

In 1910, J. Schuyler Long, long-time principal at the Iowa School for the Deaf, published one of the earliest-known compilations of ASL lexical descriptions, which also included 500 photographic illustrations. Long's "manual of signs" was first published in its entirety in 1910 and included 1,063 *root signs;* in 1918, after Long's death, it was republished by Gallaudet College. By 1963, his work, titled *The Sign Language: A Manual of Signs* (and subtitled *Being a descriptive vocabulary of signs used by the Deaf of the United States and Canada*), had been reprinted nine times.

Reference to Indian Sign Language is noticeably absent from J. S. Long's manual. However, it is known that he corresponded with both Mallery and Scott, the preeminent scholars of Indian Sign Language of the time. Long and Scott apparently held very different perspectives on sign language, as is evident from an article reprinted in the *Kentucky Standard* (ca. 1930) that had originally appeared in the *Iowa Hawkeye*. In this newspaper article, Hugh Scott (ca. 1930, 4) proposed that Indian Sign Language be used as a form of *international communication.* Scott described its role: "Before the coming of the white man, [it served as] the arbiter between peace and war and the means of spreading intertribal culture." He also wrote that Indian Sign Language was "subject to all the general laws of linguistic science save those of sound and differs from vocal speech mainly in that it makes appeal to the human brain through the eye rather than the ear" (ibid.). In the 1930 *Kentucky Standard* newspaper article, Scott responded to J. S. Long: "You know we have invented some 300 artificial languages like Esperanto etc., for international communication, not one of which has been successful because the people will not use them."

Hugh Scott was one of the progenitors of PISL as learned internationally by the Boy Scouts. Long sent Scott a copy of his *Sign Language* (1910) and wrote to convince him of the "value of the sign language of the deaf as a universal language." Scott believed that the sign language of deaf people would not capture the interest of the Boy Scouts as would the sign language of the Indians. Concerning this, J. S. Long listed several "disadvantages of the Indian sign language as compared with that of the deaf":

Romantic interest evidently blinds the judgment in this case. How the language of a primitive of civilization can become a universal language is hard to understand. Science, literature, commerce and religion are all foreign to the Indian's experience. What signs can he have to express the thoughts of a cultivated people in connection with them? As a universal language the Indian signs may serve the boy minds of scouts, but as a universal language it will go the way of

Esperanto and its kind [reprinted from the *Iowa Hawkeye* in the *Kentucky Standard* (4, ca. 1930).

Clearly, Scott and Long held vastly different positions on this subject. Central to these differences were issues of language status, universality, and the iconicity of sign language. They were men of their times, and their writings reflect certain biases. Scott believed that others would not be interested in learning the sign language of deaf people. Long advocated that the sign language of those who are deaf was superior to the alternate sign language of the American Indians, a language he considered to be the consequence of a "primitive civilization."

RESULTS

Establishing a Baseline of Lexical Similarity for Historical Relatedness

The focus of this chapter is not a diachronic study of ASL; however, John S. Long's (1918) *Sign Language* is a useful starting point for making lexical comparisons with the earliest-known descriptions of Indian sign lexicon (i.e., Dunbar 1801; Stephen Long 1823). Comprising 1,000 written descriptions and 500 photographs of ASL signs, J. S. Long's easily accessible *Sign Language* is the earliest-known such compilation. In order to establish a baseline of lexical similarity, I first compared his photographs and descriptions with contemporary ASL. Following the coding procedures and criteria established for this study, I was able to code 465 of the 500 photographs and descriptions (93 percent) as similar or identical to contemporary ASL signs. These results are summarized in Table 2.

Ninety-three percent is a very high rate of lexical similarity and is congruent with lexical comparisons of the same language (i.e., historically and genetically related). Frishberg (1975) and Woodward (1978), among

TABLE 2. Summary of Similarly Articulated Signs for ASL (Long 1918) and Contemporary ASL

Pairwise Comparison	Total Sign Pairs	Similarly Articulated Signs and Similarity Percentages
ASL (Long 1918) compared with contemporary ASL	500	465 (93 percent)

others, have described language-internal historical change in ASL. The comparison of lexical similarity presented in Table 2 also takes into account historical changes that have occurred in ASL (cf. Valli and Lucas 2000, 170–72).

Historically, some two-handed ASL signs have become one-handed signs and vice versa. The following examples of historical change appear in J. S. Long (1918). In that work, FATHER and MOTHER are described and photographed as two-handed signs: "With the fingers closed and thumb extended, place thumb at the right side of the forehead [at the right cheek for MOTHER] and at right angles to it; with a slightly twisting motion, bring hand away, opening fingers and turning palm upward; at the same time bring the left hand up similarly and place parallel to the right as if lifting up a babe" (ibid., 36–37). Assimilation (i.e., over time, the handshape of one hand comes to resemble that of another) is also evident in the data (e.g., the dominant hand becomes the same as the passive hand in SON, DAUGHTER, BROTHER, SISTER, HUSBAND, WIFE, and HOPE).

Changes in the location of a sign also commonly occur over time (e.g., for HOME, the initial place of articulation has shifted from the mouth to the cheek; DON'T CARE was formerly articulated at the forehead instead of the nose; HONOR is now produced in the neutral space in front of the body instead of at the forehead; for PICTURE, the initial contact is in front of the face instead of at the side of the face).

Comparisons of the Earliest Indian Sign Descriptions and ASL

Next I examined the earliest-known descriptions of Indian signs from Dunbar (1801) and Long (1823), which were also compiled into one list and published as the "Indian Language of Signs" in the *American Annals of the Deaf and Dumb* (Gallaudet 1852). The combined descriptions from Dunbar and Long covered 154 different signs. After the exclusion of the signs mentioned in the methodology section, eighty-five different sign pairs were available for comparison. Of the fifty-three sign pairs from S. Long's (1823) descriptions, twenty-nine (55 percent) were coded as similar or identical to ASL. Of the thirty-two from Dunbar (1801), twelve (38 percent) were coded as similar or identical to ASL. Taken together, the Indian and ASL signs showed a similarity of 48 percent (41 out of 85). The results of these pairwise comparisons are summarized in Table 3.

The percentages of similarity in these pairwise comparisons indicate separate languages (i.e., unlikely to be genetically related). However,

TABLE 3. Summary of Similarly Articulated Signs between the Dunbar/Long
Corpus and ASL

Pairwise Comparison	Total Sign Pairs	Similarly Articulated Signs and Similarity Percentages
S. Long (1823) corpus compared with ASL (J. Long 1918)	53	29 (55 percent)
Dunbar (1801) corpus compared with ASL (J. Long 1918)	32	12 (38 percent)
S. Long (1823); Dunbar (1801); ASL (1918)	85	41 (48 percent)

55 percent is a relatively high degree of lexical similarity and suggests possible contact and borrowing between the languages (cf. Parkhurst and Parkhurst 2003 12; Woll et al. 2001, 22). Because the 170 comparisons in Table 3 represent a small language sample, more sign-pair comparisons are needed before firmer conclusions can be drawn. Based on the historical evidence, however, it is highly probable that lexical borrowing occurred as a consequence of language contact between native groups of American Indians and individuals who were deaf, especially in view of the fact that, during this period, the original descriptions of Indian signs were distributed to educators of deaf people around the country through the *American Annals of the Deaf* (1848, vol. 1, through 1890, vol. 35). The illustrations in Figure 3 (ALIKE, YES, EXCHANGE, SUN) are examples of PISL signs that are lexically similar to ASL signs.

As the original pen-and-ink illustrations in Figure 3 show, certain Indian signs are lexically similar to ASL, such as ALIKE (also used to mean "married"), YES (also used to indicate 'truth"), and EXCHANGE. The Indian sign for "sun" is comparable to ASL SUNRISE/SUNSET and OVERSLEEP. The following written descriptions are from Dunbar (1801) and S. Long (1823):

"SAME or SIMILAR (to what went before) — Place the two fore fingers parallel to each other and push them forward a little" (Dunbar 1801, 1).

"TRUTH — The fore finger passed, in the attitude of pointing, from the mouth forward in a line curving a little upward, the other fingers being carefully closed;" and "LIE — The fore finger and middle fingers extended, passed two or three times from the mouth forward: they are

FIGURE 3 *Additional PSL signs lexically similar to ASL signs* [ALIKE, YES, EX-CHANGE, SUN]

joined at the mouth, but separate as they depart from it, indicating that the words go in different directions" (S. Long 1823, 160).

"SUN — The fore finger and thumb are brought together at [the] tips, so as to form a circle, and held up toward the sun's track. To indicate any particular time of the day, the hand with the sign of the sun, is stretched out toward the east horizon, and then gradually elevated, to show the ascent of that luminary, until the hand arrives in the proper directions, to indicate the part of the heaven in which the sun will be at the given time" (ibid., 157).

"EXCHANGE — The two fore fingers are extended perpendicularly, and the hands are then passed by each other transversely in front of the breast, so as nearly to exchange positions" (ibid., 160).

COMPARISON OF WRITTEN DESCRIPTIONS OF LEXICALLY SIMILAR SIGNS

Indian sign: "NOW (or at present) — The two hands forming each a hollow and brought near each other and put into a tremulous motion upwards and downwards" (Dunbar 1801, 7).

ASL sign: "NOW, PRESENT — Place the open hands pointing outward, palms up, in front, about the waist line; drop them a little and rather quickly" (J. Long 1918, 129).

Indian sign: "DONE, FINISHED — The hands placed edge up and down parallel to each other, the right hand without, which later is drawn back as cutting something" (Dunbar 1801, 8).

ASL sign: "COMPLETE, FINISH (bring an end to anything) — Place right 'B' hand with lower edge at right angles across the top edge of left 'B' near the wrist; push it along the edge of the hand till it reaches the end, then 'chop' it off" (J. Long 1918, 92).

PISL/ASL Comparisons of Early Twentieth-Century Descriptions

William Tomkins (1926) published a dictionary titled *Universal Indian Sign Language of the Plains Indians of North America* with more than five hundred illustrations. This publication had nine editions and was widely used by the Boy Scouts International as a "universal" means of communication. Despite the questionable use of the term "universal," the renowned anthropological linguist Albert Kroeber (1958) considered Tomkins's dictionary to be a very reliable source for Indian Sign Language.

In the late 1800s, Tomkins grew up "on the edge of the Sioux Indian Reservation in Dakota Territory," where he first learned sign language as a boy (1926, 7). He studied the published works of Mallery (1880, 1881) and Clark (1880) and maintained his studies of Indian Sign Language through frequent interaction with Blackfoot, Cheyenne, and Arapahoe signers. His primary informant was J. L. Clark, a Blackfoot Indian sculptor from Glacier Park, Montana, who was deaf.[11]

For the present study, I made 306 sign pair comparisons between ASL and the PISL descriptions and illustrations from Tomkins (1926). Of these, 150 of 306 (49 percent) Indian signs were coded as similar or identical to ASL. This is consistent with the pairwise comparisons made between earlier descriptions of Indian signs (Dunbar 1801; S. Long 1823) and ASL, in which 48 percent similarity was evident (see Table 3). According to the standards of historical linguistics and the thresholds of lexical similarity (discussed in the literature section), this percentage of similarity indicates separate languages. The relatively high percentage of similarity (49 percent) warrants further investigation and suggests that language contact and lexical borrowing took place between ASL and PISL. These results are presented in Table 4.

TABLE 4. Summary of Similarly Articulated Signs for PISL/ASL Lexical Comparisons

Pairwise Comparison	Total Sign Pairs	Similarly Articulated Signs and Similarity Percentages
PISL (Tomkins 1926) ASL (J. Long 1918)	306	150 (49 percent)

LEXICAL COMPARISONS FOR DUNBAR/LONG (EARLY 1800s) AND TOMKINS (EARLY 1900s)

When I compared the Dunbar (1801) and Long (1823) descriptions with Tomkins's (1926) descriptions and illustrations, the percentage of similarity was higher. This time fifty-two of sixty-one (85 percent) descriptions from Long and twenty-two of twenty-seven (81 percent) from Dunbar were similar or identical to those by Tomkins. The combined total indicates that, between Long-Dunbar and Tomkins, seventy-four of eighty-eight (84 percent) sign pairs were similar. Following the standards described earlier, these findings suggest that the sign varieties represented in this sample, with a historical range from 1801 to 1926 (125 years), appear to be genetically related (i.e., from the same language origins). These results are summarized in Table 5.

Indian Sign Language Film Dictionary (1930s)

The motion pictures that were produced by Hugh Scott (with support from a 1930 Act of the U.S. Congress) constitute one of the richest sources of PISL data. These films documented chieftains and elders from thirteen distinct spoken language groups who were communicating with each other through sign language. During the historic three-day Indian Sign Language Council (September 4–6, 1930), several discussions were signed, including the telling of anecdotes and stories. These documentary films show the Indian participants engaging in several types of discourse (e.g., making introductions and showing name signs for each of the tribes represented; signing traditional cultural and medicine stories; making metaphorical comparisons; see Davis 2006).

TABLE 5. Summary of Similarly Articulated Signs for the Dunbar/Long-Tomkins Sign Pairs

Pairwise Comparison	Total Sign Pairs	Similarly Articulated Signs and Similarity Percentages
S. Long (1823) and Tomkins (1926)	61	52 (85 percent)
Dunbar (1801) and Tomkins (1926)	27	22 (81 percent)
Dunbar/Long and Tomkins	88	74 (84 percent)

One of Scott's primary consultants was Richard Sanderville, a Blackfeet tribal elder and interpreter. In 1934, Sanderville traveled to the Smithsonian Institution in Washington, D.C., to complete the Indian Sign Language film dictionary started by Scott, who died before finishing the project. Scott's contribution (i.e., 358 proper noun signs for tribes and geographic locations) were included with the 1930s' films. While working at the National Archives in 2002, I located Sanderville's contribution to Scott's "dictionary," which was filmed at the Smithsonian in 1934. Unfortunately, the only preservation copies available were either poorly processed or produced in an outmoded format. After three years of analysis to decipher what remains of Sanderville's film contribution, I examined approximately 347 signs and idioms in a variety of lexical categories including abstract nouns, classifier predicates, and noun and verb modifiers. Some PISL sign examples from Sanderville are the following:

SPOTTED	FAMOUS
HORSE DISMOUNT	FEW
LAKE (WATER ROUND)	QUARRELSOME
GALAXY/MILKY WAY	TRADITIONAL
GLAD	WANT
ANXIOUS	CHOLERA
BEAUTIFUL	

Along with Sanderville's original translations, examples of what he called "idioms" are the following:

Signed Expression	Sanderville's Translation
BREAK MY TALK	disobey
GRASS CUT THREE TIMES	alfalfa
PRAIRIE THINK	believe without cause
PRAIRIE KILLING	accidental killing
PRAIRIE DO TO ME	not my fault
TINY BIT RECOVER	saved by the skin of one's teeth
TO CARRY OR HAVE A PIPE	to be a leader
PUT BLANKET OVER THE HEAD	to suppress
SOLDIER DO IT	to effect tribal decision
HIDE TALK	whisper

COMPARISONS OF SANDERVILLE AND WEATHERWAX

Sanderville's (1934) contribution may be considered a type of Rosetta stone. That is, the lexical inventories documented in these films, combined with the basic written and voice-over translations provided by Sanderville and Scott (1931–1934), are the keys to deciphering what the original participants at the council were signing. Figure 4 provides digitized movie stills from the 1930s' Council of Indian Sign Language. In that figure, Short Face of the Piegan tribal group signs NOW to mark his turn to sign. Bitter Root Jim, representing the Flathead (Salashian) people, uses the tribal sign PIEGAN, the sign for SAME-AS, and the traditional sign for INDIAN.

In the next analysis I compared Tomkins's early twentieth-century descriptions with 150 examples of Indian signs that were contemporarily signed and videotaped in 2002 by Martin Weatherwax, chair of Blackfeet Studies at Blackfeet Community College in Browning, Montana (near the original site of the 1930s' Indian Sign Language Council). Weatherwax (pers. comm., May 2002) reported that he learned Indian Sign Language natively from his Blackfoot grandfather.

The comparisons of sign tokens from the Sanderville-Weatherwax corpus involved the following. First, in the Sanderville-Tomkins comparison of 100 pairs, 90 percent were coded as similarly articulated. Second, the comparison of eighty sign pairs between Weatherwax and Tomkins showed that sixty-four pairs (80 percent) were similarly articulated. Third, the comparison of fifty sign pairs between Weatherwax and Sanderville revealed that 92 percent were similarly articulated. Table 6 summarizes these results.

Nevertheless, 230 sign pairs constitute a relatively small sample, and additional pairwise comparisons are needed before definitive conclusions

FIGURE 4 *Movie stills from 1930s Council of Indian Sign Language* [NOW, PIEGAN, SAMEAS, INDIAN] *(Source: Scott 1934, Courtesy of the National Archives, Washington, DC)*

TABLE 6. Summary of Similarly Articulated Signs for the Sanderville-Tomkins-Weatherwax Lexical Comparisons

Pairwise Comparison	Total Sign Pairs	Similarly Articulated Signs and Similarity Percentages
Sanderville-Tomkins	100	90 (90 percent)
Weatherwax-Tomkins	80	64 (80 percent)
Sanderville-Weatherwax	50	46 (92 percent)

can be reached. Still, these preliminary findings (a 90–92 percent range of similarity between Sanderville and Tomkins and between Sanderville and Weatherwax, respectively) is a strong indication that the PISL sign varieties used by Sanderville, Tomkins, and Weatherwax are genetically and historically related. Tomkins had reportedly been signing since 1884, and the descriptions and illustrations used in those sign-pair comparisons were compiled in the early 1920s. Sanderville had been signing all of his life and was filmed in 1934, when he was in his late seventies. Weatherwax, who was filmed in 2002, had also been signing his entire life (having learned it from his Blackfoot grandfather in the early 1950s). Thus, these sign models had been signing throughout their lives, and these data thus span a 200-year time period, from the nineteenth to the early twenty-first century.

SUMMARY AND CONCLUSIONS

The PISL corpus considered for this study was collected from several generations of signers (i.e., from the early 1800s to the early 2000s). More than 8,000 descriptions of Indian signs were identified from previously collected written, illustrated, and filmed sources (Davis 2006). Given the richness and potential number of comparisons offered by this corpus, there is an evident need for expanded historical (diachronic) and contemporary (synchronic) comparative analyses of language change, shared symbolism, lexical borrowing, and historical relatedness among these signed language varieties. For the present study, 1,500 lexical signs were selected from the sources mentioned. This resulted in 1,297 pairwise comparisons between PISL and ASL historical antecedents. The analyses of the admittedly small data sets led to several conclusions.

Due to the greater potential for shared symbolism (i.e., iconicity) among unrelated sign languages, researchers (cf. Guerra Currie et al.

2002; Parkhurst and Parkhurst 2003; Woll et al. 2001) have proposed that a relatively high baseline of percentage of lexical similarity is needed to determine whether sign languages are historically related. While researchers vary to some degree in the standard or method applied to determine lexical similarity and historical relatedness, they generally agree that a base level of at least 80 percent similarity is needed to determine whether two sign languages are historically or genetically related. Because iconicity and indexicality features may potentially skew the results of lexical similarity studies of sign languages, signed language researchers continue to deal with this major theoretical issue in various ways (e.g., establishing high thresholds to determine lexical similarity and using word lists with a low potential for iconicity).

The present study has followed the methods and standards established in previous lexical similarity and cognate studies; two main causes of historical relatedness have been considered: genetic and lexical borrowing as a result of language contact. Genetically related languages develop from a common ancestor and are classified as members of the same language family (cf. Campbell 2000, 2004). Lexical similarity or relatedness may also be caused by historical language contact and borrowing (i.e., two languages may have borrowed from each other over time, but their origins can be traced to two distinct original languages). The 80–90 percent range of lexical similarity among the PISL sign varieties compared in this study indicates that these varieties were dialects of the same language. These findings are congruent with West's (1960) earlier findings that PISL of the North Central Plains area was the standard dialect and that different dialects of PISL were used by Native American groups beyond this geographic area. Although the best-documented cases are of the PISL variety used among the more nomadic groups of the Great Plains region, different sign varieties have been observed among the tribes of northwestern Canada and the southwestern region of the United States (see Davis 2006). Further studies are needed to clarify the similarities and differences between these signed language varieties.

The percentages of lexical similarity (in the 50-percent range) in the pairwise comparisons between historical varieties of ASL and PISL indicate that they are separate languages (i.e., unlikely to be genetically related). However, this is a relatively high range of lexical similarity and indicates possible lexical borrowing between the languages. Based on this evidence, it is highly probable that lexical borrowing occurred as a consequence of language contact between native groups of American Indians and individuals who were deaf. Supporting this conclusion is the fact that, during the eighteenth and early nineteenth centuries, the original descriptions of Indian signs were published and distributed to educators at schools for deaf children around the country; moreover, there are also several historical accounts of American Indians visiting residential schools for deaf students during the nineteenth century (e.g., Mallery 1880). I maintain that a need exists for additional studies of larger data sets and of historical sign language contact between individuals from the American Indian and the Deaf communities.

The historical analysis of lexical similarity discussed here offers a relatively limited picture of the numerous sociolinguistic factors at the interface of language and culture. Nonetheless, as signed language researchers employ new and better methods of data collection and analysis, particularly in the fields of sociolinguistics and historical linguistics, the accuracy of cross-linguistic sign language studies will be enhanced and provide a better picture of the relationship between signed languages. Further research of naturally occurring discourse that characterizes other linguistic levels (e.g., the phonological to the grammatical) is also needed. I hope that the preliminary findings reported here will inform future studies of historical and contemporary sign language use among North American Indians and encourage additional language revitalization, preservation, data collection, descriptions, and ethnographic fieldwork.

NOTES

1. Various terms are used in the literature to refer to the aboriginal peoples of the Americas. Members of these cultural groups generally call themselves Indians. The term "North American Indian" is sometimes necessary to distinguish the indigenous peoples of North America from those of Central and South America. Specific tribal affiliations and cultural-linguistic groups are acknowledged whenever possible (e.g., Assiniboine, Blackfeet, Lakota, Northern Cheyenne; cf. Campbell 2000; Davis 2006; Mithun 1999).

2. I offer readers a link to a prototype online digital archive of documentary materials and continue to expand this open-access online linguistic corpus to include translations, linguistic analyses, and descriptions. Readers may view samples of the historical documentary films and illustrations documenting tradi-

tional signed language used by some Indian groups at the following website: http://sunsite.utk.edu/plainssignlanguage/. The development and maintenance of this archive is supported by a 2006–2007 fellowship for Documenting Endangered Languages from the National Endowment of the Humanities and National Science Foundation, with the endorsement of the Smithsonian Institution and support from the University of Tennessee's Digital Library, Office of the Chancellor and Dean of Graduate Studies.

3. Linguistic families are capitalized and the "equals" sign (=) indicates dialects of the same language (Campbell 2000; Mithun 1999).

4. Generally, twelve major geographic cultural areas of Native North America have been identified in the literature, with the Plains cultural area centrally located to all of these. Waldman (2000 32–33) explains that these cultural areas were "not finite and absolute boundaries" and "that tribal territories were often vague and changing, with great movement among the tribes and the passing of cultural traits from one area to the next; and that people of the same language family sometimes lived in different cultural areas, even in some instances at opposite ends of the continent."

5. Wurtzburg and Campbell (1995, 154–55) report that the earliest-known descriptions of the Indians signing come from the 1527 Spanish expedition to Florida and were written by Álvar Núñez Cabeza de Vaca, who described numerous occasions during which Indian groups communicated with each other in signs. According to the historical record, Cabeza de Vaca "also clearly distinguished which groups spoke the same language, which spoke different languages but understood others, and which groups did not understand others at all, except through the use of sign language" (ibid., 155). Pedro de Castañeda made similar descriptions during the Coronado expedition of 1541–1542, and subsequent reports continued into the eighteenth century (see Wurtzburg and Campbell 1995 for further descriptions).

6. It is noteworthy that Franz Boas and Garrick Mallery helped establish and served terms as presidents of learned societies during the late 1800s and early 1900s (e.g., the Linguistic Society of America, the American Philosophical Society, and the American Anthropological Society). Mallery was credited as one of the first scholars of his time to use the term "semiotics" (Umiker-Sebeok and Sebeok 1978). During the mid-1900s Albert Kroeber and Charles Voegelin each also served terms as president of the Linguistic Society of America and were considered pioneers in the emergent field of anthropological linguistics; the two developed the most widely used classification systems for Native American languages that are still in use today.

7. Since West's two-volume dissertation, there has been only one published linguistic analysis of American Indian Sign Language (i.e., Newell's analyses of morphosyntactic structures, which supported Kroeber's [1958] earlier observation

that, "whereas writing systems such as Chinese or Hieroglyphics are alternate expression systems of a single communication system, sign language is an independent communication system in its own right" [1981, 1989]).

8. Parkhurst and Parkhurst (2003) recommend using sign vocabulary lists that comprise primarily common nouns (e.g., family members, animals, foods, clothing), wh-questions (who, what, where, how), calendar terms (days of the week, months, year), basic color terms (white, black, blue, green), and a limited number of adjectives (poor, sweet, young, dirty, afraid) and verbs (to begin, to lie, to play). They provide a single example of a highly iconic sign (BOOK) and do not describe the process of elimination for highly iconic vocabulary from the "Parkhurst word lists" (their term for their basic 50-word short lists and 100-word long lists).

9. For example, Guerra Currie, Meier, and Walters (2002) compared sign pairs between Mexican Sign Language (la Lengua de Señas Mexicana, or LSM) and Japanese Sign Language (Nihon Syuwa, or NS) that share no known historical or cultural links and found that 23 percent of the signs compared were similarly articulated. As Guerra Currie et al (2002, 229) describe this, "the forms of these signs appear to be drawing from similar imagistic sources, such as shared visual icons in such sign pairs as FIRE, BIRD, and HOUSE." Such visual imagery is reflected in the signs for the fire's "flame"; bird's "beak"; and house's "roof."

10. McNeill (1992, 6) identified four types of gestures that should be considered along a continuum of "gesticulation," "pantomime," "emblem," and "sign language." McNeill (2000, 6) has proposed that "gesticulation accompanies speech" and "is non-conventionalized" and distinguished this from the signs in a signed language that, "like words in speech, are conventionalized, segmented, and analytic, and possessed of language properties, while they are obligatorily not performed with speech." McNeill correlated the presence or absence of speech with gesture and with the absence or presence of conventional linguistic properties and concluded that "emblems are at an intermediate position . . . partly like gesticulations, partly like signs." McNeill (1992, 6) emphasized "the nonlinguistic character of these gestures: the lack of a fully contrastive system and the lack of syntactic potential."

11. Tomkins (1926, 9) claimed that "every sign in this work is a true Indian sign. . . . Nothing has been borrowed from the deaf or from other sources." That is, he did not include the ASL signs of schools for deaf children or the Deaf community. Although his primary consultant was a deaf Blackfoot, it was common during this time period for American Indians who were deaf to remain on the ancestral lands or Indian reservations with little or no contact with ASL-signing Anglo Deaf community members. Following traditional ways, it was common for some deaf American Indians not to attend state residential schools for deaf children (see Davis and Supalla 1995 for further descriptions).

REFERENCES

Battison, R. 1978/2003. *Lexical borrowing in American Sign Language*. Silver Spring, Md.: Linstok.

Baynton, D. 2002. The curious death of sign language studies in the nineteenth century. In *The study of signed languages: Essays in honor of William C. Stokoe*, ed. D. Armstrong, M. A. Karchmer, and J. V. Van Cleve, 13–34. Washington, D.C.: Gallaudet University Press.

Boas, F. 1890/1978. Sign language. In *Aboriginal sign language of the Americas and Australia*. Vol. 2, ed. D. J. Umiker-Sebeok and T. A. Sebeok, 19–20. New York: Plenum. Reprinted from the *Report of the sixtieth meeting of the British Association for the Advancement of Science* (1890), 638–41. London: John Murray.

Campbell, L. 2000. *American Indian languages*. New York: Oxford University Press.

———. 2004. *Historical linguistics: An introduction*, 2nd edition. Cambridge: MIT Press.

Clark, W. P. 1885. *The Indian sign language*. Philadelphia: Hamersly.

Crystal, D. 2000. *Language death*. New York: Cambridge University Press.

Davis, J. E. 2005. Evidence of a historical signed lingua franca among North American Indians. *Deaf Worlds* 21(3): 47–72.

———. 2006. A historical linguistic account of sign language among North American Indian groups. In *Multilingualism and sign languages*, ed. C. Lucas, 3–35. Sociolinguistics of the Deaf Community series, vol. 12, Washington, D.C.: Gallaudet University Press.

———. In press. *Hand talk: Sign Language among American Indian Nations*. Cambridge: Cambridge University Press.

Davis, J. E., and S. Supalla. 1995. A sociolinguistic description of sign language use in a Navajo family. In *Sociolinguistics in Deaf communities*. ed. C. Lucas, 77–106. Sociolinguistics of the Deaf Community series, vol. 1. Washington, D.C.: Gallaudet University Press.

Dunbar, W. 1801. On the Language of Signs among certain North American Indians. *Transactions of the American Philosophical Society*, 6 (1): 1–8.

Farnell, B. M. 1995. *Do you see what I mean? Plains Indian sign talk and the embodiment of action*. Austin: University of Texas Press.

Frishberg, N. 1975. Arbitrariness and iconicity: Historical change in American Sign Language. *Language* 51, 696–719.

Fromkin, V., R. Rodman, and N. Hyams. 2007. *An introduction to language*, 8th ed. Boston: Thomson Wordsworth.

Gallaudet, T. H. 1848. On the natural language of signs; and its value and uses in the instruction of the deaf and dumb. *American Annals of the Deaf and Dumb* 1: 55–60.

―――. 1852. Indian language of signs. *American Annals of the Deaf and Dumb* 4: 157–71.

Goddard, I. 1979. The languages of South Texas and the lower Rio Grande. In *The languages of native America: Historical and comparative assessment*, ed. L. Campbell and M. Mithun, 70–132. Austin: University of Texas Press.

Gordon, R. G., Jr., ed. 2005. *Ethnologue: Languages of the world*, 15th ed. Dallas: SIL International. http://www.ethnologue.com/.

Groce, N. E. 1985. *Everyone here spoke sign language: Hereditary deafness on Martha's Vineyard*. Cambridge, Mass.: Harvard University Press.

Guerra Currie, A.-M., R. P. Meier, and K. Walters. 2002. A cross-linguistic examination of the lexicons of four signed languages. In *Modality and structure in signed and spoken languages*, ed. R. Meier, K. Cormier, and D. Quinto-Pozos, 224–36. New York: Cambridge University Press.

Hoyer, K. 2004. The sociolinguistic situation of Finland-Swedish deaf people and their language: Finland-Swedish Sign Language. In *To the lexicon and beyond: Sociolinguistics in European Deaf communities*, ed. M. Van Herreweghe and M. Vermeerbergen, 3–23. Sociolinguistics in Deaf Communities series, vol. 10. Washington, D.C.: Gallaudet University Press.

Karttunen, F. 1994. *Between worlds: Interpreters, guides, and survivors*. New Brunswick, N.J.: Rutgers University Press.

Kelly, W. P. 2004. History of the American Indian Deaf. In *Deaf studies today! A kaleidoscope of knowledge, learning, and understanding*, ed. B. K. Eldredge, D. Stringham, and M. M. Wilding-Díaz, 217–23. Orem: Utah Valley State College.

―――, and T. L. McGregor. 2003. Keresan Pueblo Indian Sign Language. In *Nurturing native languages*, ed. J. Reyhner, O. Trujillo, R. L. Carrasco, and L. Lockard, 141–48. Flagstaff: Northern Arizona University.

Kendon, A. 1988. *Sign languages of aboriginal Australia: Cultural, semiotic, and communicative perspectives*. New York: Cambridge University Press.

Kroeber, A. L. 1958. Sign language inquiry. *International Journal of American Linguistics* 24: 1–19.

Kyle, J. G., and B. Woll. 1985. *Sign language: The study of deaf people and their language*. New York: Cambridge University Press.

Long, J. S. 1908–1910. The sign language: A manual of signs. *American Annals of the Deaf* 53–55(1): (230–49); 2: (438–48); 3: (23–37); 4: (140–60); 5: (213–81); 6: (239–47); 7: (420–38); 8: (142–55).

―――. 1918. *The sign language: A manual of signs; being a descriptive vocabulary of signs used by the deaf of the United States and Canada* (reprint of 2d ed.). Washington, D.C.: Gallaudet College (Professional Printing).

Long, S. H. 1823. *Account of an expedition from Pittsburgh to the Rocky Mountains*. Philadelphia: Edwin James.

Lucas, C. 2001. *The sociolinguistics of sign languages*. New York: Cambridge University Press.

Mallery, G. 1880. A collection of gesture-signs and signals of the North American Indians with some comparisons. In *Aboriginal sign languages of the Americas and Australia*. Vol. 1, ed. D. J. Umiker-Sebeok and T. A. Sebeok, 77–406. New York: Plenum.

———. 1881. Sign language among North American Indians. In *First annual report of the Bureau of Ethnology of the Smithsonian Institution for 1879–1880*, ed. J. W. Powell, 263–552. Washington, D.C.: USGPO. Reprint, New York: Dover, 2001.

McKay-Cody, M. 1997. Plains Indian Sign Language: A comparative study of alternate and primary signers. Master's thesis, University of Arizona.

McKee, D., and G. Kennedy. 2000. Lexical comparison of signs from American, Australian, British, and New Zealand sign languages. In *The signs of language revisited: An anthology to honor Ursula Bellugi and Edward Klima*, ed. K. Emmorey and H. Lane, 49–76. Mahwah, N.J.: Erlbaum.

McNeill, D. 1992. *Hand and mind: What gestures reveal about thought*. Chicago: Chicago University Press.

———. 2000. *Language and gesture*. New York: Cambridge University Press.

Mithun, M. 1999. *The languages of native North America*. New York: Cambridge University Press.

Morford, J. 1996. Insights to language from the study of gesture: A review of research on the gestural communication of non-signing deaf people. *Language and Communication* 16: 165–78.

Newell, L. E. 1981. A stratificational description of Plains Indian Sign Language. *Forum Linguisticum* 5: 189–212.

Nover, S. M. 2000. History of language planning in deaf education: The 19th century. PhD diss., University of Arizona.

Parkhurst, S., and D. Parkhurst. 2003. Lexical comparisons of signed languages and the effects of iconicity. In *Working papers of the Summer Institute of Linguistics, University of North Dakota session*. Vol. 47. http://www.und.edu/dept/linguistics/wp/2003ParkhurstParkhurstPDF.

Pritchard, E. T. 2002. *Native New Yorkers: The legacy of the Algonquin people of New York*. San Francisco: Council Oak Books.

Scott, H. L. ca. 1930. Indian Sign Language. *Kentucky Standard* (reprinted from the *Iowa Hawkeye*).

———. 1931–1934. *Film dictionary of the North American Indian Sign Language*. Washington, D.C.: National Archives.

Stokoe, W. C. 1960. Sign language structure: An outline of the visual communication systems of the American deaf. *Studies in Linguistics Occasional Papers* 8. Rev. 1978, Silver Spring, Md.: Linstok.

─────. 1972. *Semiotics and human sign languages.* The Hague: Mouton.

Supalla, T. 1978. Structure and acquisition of verbs of motion and location in American Sign Language. Ph.D. dissertation, University of California, San Diego.

Taylor, A. R. 1978. Nonverbal communication in aboriginal North America: The Plains Sign Language. In *Aboriginal sign languages of the Americas and Australia.* Vol. 2, ed. D. J. Umiker-Sebeok and T. A. Sebeok, 223–44. New York: Plenum.

─────. 1997. Nonspeech communication systems. In *Handbook of the North American Indian.* Vol. 17, *Languages,* ed. I. Goddard, 275–89. Washington, D.C.: Smithsonian Institution Press.

Tomkins, W. 1926. *Universal Indian Sign Language of the Plains Indians of North America.* Reprint, New York: Dover, 1969.

Umiker-Sebeok, J., and T. A. Sebeok, eds. 1978. *Aboriginal sign languages of the Americas and Australia.* Vols. 1 and 2. New York: Plenum.

Valli, C., and C. Lucas. 2005. *Linguistics of American Sign Language,* 4th ed. Washington, D.C.: Gallaudet University Press.

Voegelin, C. F. 1958. Sign language analysis: On one lever or two? *International Journal of American Linguistics* 24: 71–77.

Waldman, C. 2000. *Atlas of the North American Indian.* New York: Facts on File.

Washburn, W. E., ed. 1988. *Handbook of North American Indians.* Vol. 4: *History of Indian-white relations.* Washington, D.C.: Smithsonian Institution.

Weatherwax, M. 2002. *Indian Sign Language.* Videotape. Department of Blackfeet Studies, Blackfeet Community College, Browning, Montana.

West, L. 1960. The sign language: An analysis. Vols. 1 and 2. Ph.D. diss., Indiana University, Bloomington, Indiana.

Woll, B., R. Sutton-Spence, and F. Elton. 2001. Multilingualism: The global approach to sign languages. In *The sociolinguistics of sign languages,* ed. C. Lucas, 8–32. New York: Cambridge University Press.

Woodward, J. 1978. Historical bases of American sign languages. In *Understanding language through sign language research,* ed. P. Siple, 333–48. New York: Academic Press.

Wurtzburg, S., and L. Campbell. 1995. North American Indian Sign Language: Evidence of its existence before European contact. *International Journal of American Linguistics* 61: 153–67.

The Lexicons of Japanese Sign Language and

Taiwan Sign Language: A Preliminary

Comparative Study of Handshape Differences

Daisuke Sasaki

It is often said that sign languages in Taiwan and Korea are quite similar to Japanese Sign Language (JSL) (e.g., Smith 1989, 1990). Yasuhiro Ichida, a hearing signer and researcher of JSL, made a trip to Korea in the spring of 2002 and reports on the similarity between JSL and Korean Sign Language (KSL): "First of all, the overall impression was that the difference between Korean Sign Language (KSL) and Japanese Sign Language (JSL) could be regarded as a dialectal difference.¹ Many of the basic vocabulary items are similar. Of course, there are completely different vocabulary items, and some identically articulated forms have

This study is based on my qualifying paper for Ph.D. candidacy submitted to the Department of Linguistics at the University of Texas at Austin (Sasaki 2003). My research at the University of Texas at Austin was made possible by the Fulbright Program, jointly funded by the Japanese and the U.S. governments, and this study was partially funded by a grant from Hokusei Gakuen University and a Grant-in-Aid for Young Scientists (B) (no. 18720109) from the Ministry of Education, Culture, Sports, Science, and Technology (MEXT), Japan. Part of the study was presented at the Seventh Annual International Conference of the Japanese Society for Language Sciences (Sophia University, Tokyo, Japan, June 25–26, 2005), the thirty-second conference of the Japanese Association of Sign Linguistics (Chiba University, Chiba, Japan, July 16–17, 2005), and the ninth conference on Theoretical Issues in Sign Language Research (Universidade Federal de Santa Catarina, Florianópolis, Brazil, December 6–9, 2006). I am greatly indebted to the readers of my qualifying paper, Richard P. Meier and Nora C. England, as well as two anonymous reviewers of this volume and the editor David Quinto-Pozos, for their valuable comments and encouragement. All remaining errors are, of course, my own.

different meanings, but the mutual intelligibility is fairly high since both languages are also very similar to each other in terms of grammar" (Ichida 2002, translated from Japanese by D.S.).[2]

The same things seem to be true of Taiwan Sign Language (TSL). Osugi (1995) reports that, in conversation with a Taiwanese deaf person who had graduated from a school for the deaf in the southern part of Taiwan, he used the western dialect of JSL and the Taiwanese deaf individual used TSL, yet they could make themselves understood well. I had a similar experience with deaf people from Taiwan. When I conversed with them, I used JSL, and they used TSL. Although we sometimes needed to check the meaning of some of the signs, our communication was smooth enough for us to understand each other.

When linguists discuss the similarity of lexical items between languages, they are focusing on similarity in both form (i.e., sound or articulation patterns) and meaning. In spoken languages, that similarity may or may not be the realization of some historical relationship between given languages. For "sound-meaning similarities" or "sound-meaning resemblances," Greenberg (1953, 1957) posits four possible classes of causes or explanations. Two of them, genetic relationship and borrowing, involve historical factors, whereas the other two, chance and symbolism, do not. If we follow Guerra Currie, Meier, and Walters (2002, 224), "symbolism," as used by Greenberg, can be paraphrased as "shared symbolism," which refers to a situation in which "a pair of words happens to share the same motivation, whether iconic or indexic."

In the case of TSL in relation to JSL, it seems likely that some historical factors played an important role in the fairly high intelligibility between the two languages. Ichida (2000) explains that "[I]n Asia, due to the colonial occupation, signs in Taiwan and Korea have a strong influence from Japanese Sign Language" (original text in Japanese, translated by D.S.). In addition, Nakamura (2002) claims that "[T]he national sign languages in Taiwan and Korea apparently have incorporated some JSL signs and forms from the colonial occupation of these countries by Japan prior to World War II."[3]

The objectives of this study include the comparison of the lexicons of the sign languages of East Asia and, in particular, a focus on JSL and TSL. Similar studies have been conducted on many other sign languages, but none has compared the lexicons of sign languages in East Asia. Therefore, this work will at least help to illustrate the relationship between JSL and TSL. Furthermore, it pursues phonological explanations for differences, both synchronic and diachronic, among "phonologically similarly articulated" signs in the sign languages in question. Such explanations have been absent from most of the previous research on the comparison of the lexicons of sign languages.

In the following section, I briefly discuss the history of deaf education in Taiwan, TSL, and previous studies of lexical comparisons. Then I compare lexical items of JSL and TSL using three different vocabulary lists. Finally, I explain "phonologically similarly articulated" signs in which a difference occurs only in the handshape parameter. In that section, I maintain that the handshapes used in TSL signs are more difficult to articulate than those in the corresponding JSL signs.

HISTORICAL BACKGROUND OF DEAF EDUCATION IN TAIWAN

According to Smith (1976) and Modern Classics Cultural Enterprises Ltd., Division of Sign Language Books, Research and Compilation Committee (MCCE 1999), although deaf education in mainland China began during the Qing dynasty in 1888, it was not until 1915 that deaf education in the island of Taiwan was initiated. In Tainan, a major city in southern Taiwan, the English Presbyterian Mission in 1890 established a school for the blind, which was supervised by the Rev. William Campbell. After the Japanese colonial occupation of Taiwan began in 1895, the school accepted deaf students for the first time in 1915 and changed its name to the Tainan School for the Blind and the Mute.[4] In the meantime, in Taipei, Kingo Kimura, head of the Taipei Gastroenterology Hospital, asked the Japanese government to grant him the permission to establish a school for the blind. Parents of deaf children in Taiwan then urged him to also accept their children for his school. Their request was honored, and in 1917, he opened the Kimura Education Center for the Blind and the Mute in his own home.

After 1945, at the end of both World War II and the Japanese occupation of Taiwan, the island was returned to China. At this time, two more schools for the deaf were founded in Taiwan. In 1956, the third school for the deaf was established in Fengyuan as a branch of the Tainan school. After the Fengyuan school became independent in 1960, it moved to Taichung, a major midwestern city, in 1979 and was renamed the Taiwan Provincial Taichung School for the Deaf.[5] The fourth school for the deaf, the Private Chi-Ying School for the Deaf, is in

Kaohsiung, a southern seaport. It offers only a six-year elementary program, and its graduates usually continue their studies at the other schools for the deaf.

According to MCCE (1999) both the Tainan and the Taipei schools adopted a teaching methodology using sign language. After the Tainan school began accepting deaf pupils, its principal was Katsukuma Hamazaki, who was sent from the Department of Teacher Training at the Tokyo School for the Deaf. He was an advocate of deaf education using sign communication, and it is claimed that it was he who introduced Japanese Sign Language to southern Taiwan. In Taipei, too, sign language was used in the classrooms. You may wonder why sign language was still used at schools for the deaf in Taiwan even in the 1910s, however. In other words, long after the Milan Conference (the Second International Congress on Education of the Deaf) of 1880, where it was decided that schools for the deaf should ban the use of sign language and adopt an oral approach,[6] why did sign language continue to be used as a medium of instruction in Taiwanese schools for the deaf? To answer this question, let us consider the situation of deaf education in Japan at that time.

According to Smith (1976) and Seino (1997), when the first school for the deaf in Japan, the Kyoto Institute for the Blind and the Mute, was established in 1878, Toshiro Furukawa, who was its first principal and is also known as the "father of Japanese Deaf education," employed "gestures, mime signs, pronunciation, speech, dictation, speaking, writing and composition" (Smith 1976, 1). Moreover, the Tokyo School for the Blind and the Mute,[7] the second school for the deaf established in 1880,[8] also adopted Furukawa's educational methods. It seems that both schools tried to use every possible method in teaching deaf students but, due to a lack of success with oral training, eventually dropped their oral programs. Neither a lecture by Alexander Graham Bell at the Tokyo School for the Blind and the Mute in November 1898 nor a visit by John Dutton Wright, an American oral educator, to Japan in 1919 bolstered the popularity of oral education. Smith (1976, 2) explains that "[T]he manual method reigned in the schools for the deaf in Japan until about 1920 as the oral method was considered too difficult for use in the schools." In fact, Shimpachi Konishi, principal at the Tokyo school (1896–1925), was reluctant to adopt the oral approach, and it was not until 1925 that oral classes were reopened (Seino 1997).

However, the situation changed quickly. In 1920, August Karl Reischauer (1879–1971) and his wife[9] founded the Tokyo Oral School for the Deaf. In 1924, Unosuke Kawamoto (1890–1960)[10] became a teacher for the Department of Teacher Training at the Tokyo School for the Deaf as well as a teacher at the school itself, after his twenty-month stay overseas as a researcher for the Ministry of Education, and established the Japan Association to Promote Speech for the Deaf in 1925. He was joined in this endeavor by Tokuichi Hashimoto (1879–1968), principal of the Nagoya Municipal School for the Blind and the Mute, Kichinosuke Nishikawa (1874–1940), father of a deaf daughter and the founder of the Shiga Prefectural Oral School for the Deaf, and others. The association published a journal called *Deaf Education in the Oral Method*. Kawamoto also conducted a workshop at the Tokyo School for the Deaf to introduce the oral method to all of the schools for the deaf in Japan, while, in Nagoya, the Ministry of Education began a series of annual discussions on oralism. These meetings would surely convince the schools for the deaf in Japan to adopt the oral method.

It thus seems that JSL had already been introduced to the Taiwanese schools before oralism prevailed in Japan, and I think that we have figured out why the manual communication system was still in use after 1880 in both Japan and Taiwan.

SIGN LANGUAGE IN TAIWAN

According to Smith (1987b, 1989), the number of TSL signers on the island of twenty-two million is estimated to be 30,000 deaf people. In Taiwan, TSL is often called "natural sign language" and is the form of manual communication used in daily life by deaf people. It is distinct from a manually coded system called "grammatical sign language," which is actually Signed Mandarin used in the Taiwanese schools for the deaf.

Smith (1987a, 1987b, 1989) further explains that the vocabulary of TSL is derived from three major sources. The first is "the form of the language that was used in Taiwan before 1895" (Smith 1987b, 113–14), when Japan began its fifty-year colonial occupation of Taiwan. The second is JSL, which was brought into Taiwan between 1895 and 1945. Teachers were sent from the schools for the deaf in Japan and apparently contributed to introducing JSL to the deaf community in Taiwan. The third source is Chinese Sign Language (CSL) of mainland China, which was first brought to Taiwan in 1949, when the Chinese Communist

Party, headed by Mao Tse-tung, took over the administration of mainland China and the Nationalist Party, headed by Chiang Kai-shek, fled to Taiwan, along with approximately two million refugees, including many deaf Chinese and former teachers at schools for the deaf. In addition to these major sources, Smith (1987a) claims that Taiwanese deaf people have been adding new signs to the TSL vocabulary by coining and borrowing signs from other sign languages, such as American Sign Language (ASL).[11]

Smith (1987b, 1989) states that TSL has two major dialects, the Taipei and the Tainan. This dialectal difference seems to be related to the fact that, as mentioned earlier, teachers were sent from Japan during the colonial occupation of Taiwan. According to Smith, teachers at the Tokyo School for the Blind and the Mute were sent to the school in Taipei, whereas teachers from the Osaka Prefectural School for the Deaf were sent to the school in Tainan. In addition, the fact that Lin Wen-sheng, who was educated at the Tokyo School for the Blind and the Mute (1904–1917), was the first and only deaf principal at the Taipei school (1946–1951) may reinforce a possible link between the Tokyo dialect of JSL and the sign system used in northern Taiwan.[12]

Several syntactic characteristics of TSL should be briefly mentioned here. According to Smith (1987b, 1989), TSL has the basic word order of Subject-Verb-Object (SVO). Because some sign languages use the word order of the surrounding spoken languages (e.g., the basic word order of ASL is SVO, following spoken English, whereas in JSL it is Subject-Object-Verb (SOV), following spoken Japanese), it could be argued that the word order of Chinese is reflected in that of TSL. Other interesting syntactic features are that TSL has three different types of auxiliary verbs (AUX1, AUX2, AUX11)[13] and that, unlike JSL, TSL does not have any form of fingerspelling (Smith 1987b).[14]

Smith and Ting (1979) and Smith (1987b, 1989, 1990) claim that JSL, TSL, and KSL belong to a single language family (i.e., the Japanese sign language family). However, that designation should be carefully reexamined. Campbell (1998, 165) defines a language family as "a group of *genetically related* languages, that is, languages which share a linguistic kinship by virtue of having developed from a common ancestor" (emphasis mine). As reviewed earlier, Smith (1987a, 1987b, 1989) explains that TSL is derived from three different sources. In addition, JSL does not share the first and third sources with TSL (i.e., what existed in Taiwan before 1895 and the sign language of mainland China, respectively). Given Campbell's definition of "language family," the hypothesis of a Japanese Sign Language family that includes TSL is questionable. Other factors such as grammar should also be taken into account. Considering the fact that the basic word order of TSL is different from that of JSL and the fact that AUX2 and AUX11 do not appear in JSL, it seems that the notion of a "Japanese sign language family" is problematic and should be readdressed.

PREVIOUS STUDIES

This section includes information about previous studies that compare lexical items among various sign languages. Specifically, methods that have been used to collect and analyze the data are highlighted here. This summary provides a context from which to consider the collection and analysis performed in the present study.

In a series of works, Woodward (e.g., 1978, 2000, among others) has compared many pairs of sign languages and/or dialects of a sign language. Based on the original 200-word list developed by Swadesh (1952), Woodward developed a 100-word list modified for sign language research. Since the original 200-word Swadesh list includes many items such as body parts and pronouns that are frequently represented indexically or by pointing in many sign languages, Woodward excluded those items to avoid the problems of overestimation. Using a very similar format across his studies, Woodward has compared "possible cognates" based on the theory developed in glottochronology and lexicostatistics, but his studies are problematic in several respects. First, he provides no definition of "possible cognates." Second, his studies do not include phonological explanations of the compared signs. And third, no coding method whatsoever is specified.

Woll first compared twelve sign languages (including ten used in Europe) and then five (1984, 1987). In each study, she mentioned Swadesh's 100- and 200-word lists, as well as one prepared by Stokoe and Kuschel (1979), but she claimed that "[N]one of these three lists is, however, wholly useful for a study of urban deaf populations, as all three have been designed for anthropological research amongst 'third-world' groups" (Woll 1987, 13; emphasis in the original). Since she argued against the use of the lists prepared by Swadesh (1952) and Stokoe and Kuschel (1979), she proposed her own list of 257 items, many of which, though, seemed to be from the very lists she had criticized.[15] Using her own list, Woll coded signs based on features such as "orientation of fingers and palm, point of contact between hand and the location of the sign, and fine handshape details" (1984, 85).

In her dissertation (1999) and a later article (Guerra Currie, Meier, and Walters 2002), Guerra Currie made a lexical comparison of four sign languages: Mexican Sign Language (Lengua de Señas Mexicana: LSM), French Sign Language (Langue des Signes Française: LSF), Spanish Sign Language (Lengua de Signos Española: LSE), and JSL. She used two commercially available sets of flash cards and elicited 190 signs. The data were analyzed using the following metric: *Similarly articulated signs* are signs that share "at least two of the three main parameters of handshape, movement, and place of articulation, as well as the same approximate meaning" (Guerra Currie 1999, 51), and "a subset of similarly-articulated signs includes those signs that are articulated similarly or identically on all three major parameters" (Guerra Currie, Meier, and Walters 2002, 227).

Mckee and Kennedy (2000) compared lexical items of Australian Sign Language (Auslan), British Sign Language (BSL), New Zealand Sign Language (NZSL), and ASL. They used both the modified 100-word list developed by Woodward and a new list of 200 signs that were randomly selected from an NZSL dictionary for comparison. Signs were classified as follows: identical, completely different, related but different, and not found, and the authors adopted four major parameters: handshape, location, movement, and palm orientation.

The coding methods of these studies are summarized in Table 1.

THE STUDY

In order to form an idea of the extent to which JSL has influenced the TSL vocabulary, I compared lexical items of JSL and TSL to determine the degree of lexical similarity.

METHODOLOGY

I used dictionaries of JSL and TSL as sources of data. For JSL signs, I used *Nihongo-syuwa ziten* (Japanese-Japanese Sign Language Dictionary), edited by the Japan Institute for Sign Language Studies of

TABLE 1. Summary of Coding Methods

Sign Parameters	Woodward	Woll	Guerra Currie	McKee and Kennedy
Handshape	("possible cognates";	yes	yes	yes
Orientation	the term, however,	yes	NA	yes
Location	is undefined)	yes	yes	yes
Movement		NA[a]	yes	yes

NA = not available

a. The movement of the hands (Woll 1987, 20) was also used as an additional parameter to diachronically compare lexical items of BSL in the second half of Woll (ibid.), although it was adopted neither in the synchronic comparison of lexical items in Woll (1984) nor in the first part of Woll (1987).

the Japanese Federation of the Deaf (hereinafter JISLS-JFD) (1997). As the title indicates, this is a dictionary of Japanese words with corresponding Japanese signs. For TSL signs, I used Smith and Ting (1979) and Ting and Smith (1984), namely, volumes 1 and 2 of *Shou neng sheng qiao* (Your hands can become a bridge). They are predominantly written in Chinese, but an equivalent English gloss is given to each sign entry. At the end of the dictionary, each volume has an English index of the TSL signs.

I used three different sets of lexical items (word lists) for the comparison between JSL and TSL signs: the 100-word modified Swadesh list developed by Woodward (2000), the 199-word list developed by McKee and Kennedy (2000),[16] and a third list that included all of the 752 sign entries in Smith and Ting (1979). To distinguish the phonological identicalness, distinctness, and similarity of the signs in question, I used four phonological parameters: handshape, palm orientation, movement, and location, following McKee and Kennedy (2000). In addition, I used the number of hands involved in the production of a sign in question (i.e., one-handed versus two-handed or the loss or addition of a hand) as a fifth parameter to distinguish among signs. Any additional feature that distinguishes a pair of signs is noted and considered in the analysis.

Based on the similarity or difference of values within these parameters, signs were classified into three categories: phonologically identically articulated signs, phonologically distinctly articulated signs, and phonologically similarly articulated signs. In phonologically identically articulated signs, all of the parameters mentioned earlier must be identical between the JSL and TSL sign forms; at the same time, they must share the same meaning. Signs are identified as phonologically similarly articulated if they share the same meaning and only a single difference is observed in any one of the five parameters.[17] All of the other signs are regarded as phonologically distinctly articulated.

In addition, two more categories were considered. The first is "semantic mismatches." Semantically mismatched signs are identical in form but different in semantics.[18] They were excluded from the comparison because they cannot be easily compared. The second additional category is "missing data," which includes signs that were not found in either or both of the dictionaries; they were also excluded from the comparison.

RESULTS

The results of the three analyses (one for each word list) are summarized in Table 2.[19] First I present an explanation of how the categories of "semantic mismatches" and "missing data" were treated. The percentages of these items were calculated based on the total number of items in each analysis. For example, in the third analysis, 752 items were included in Smith and Ting (1979) and were used for comparison; thus 752 was the total number that was used to calculate the percentages of "semantic mismatches" and "missing data." In Analysis 3, 135 items or dictionary entries in Smith and Ting (ibid. (18.0 percent) were not found in JISLS-JFD (1997). Naturally enough, 16 Chinese family names and 6 Taiwanese place names listed in the TSL dictionary were not included in the JSL dictionary. In addition, 10 items (1.3 percent) showed semantic mismatches between the two sign languages. For example, the TSL sign WHICH, in which the 1 handshape on the dominant hand, with the palm outward, repeats a short, back-and-forth movement from left to right in the neutral space, is phonologically identical to the JSL sign WHAT; the JSL sign WHICH is a two-handed sign in which the 1 handshape on both hands moves up and down alternatingly. In Analysis 3, for example, since the total of 145 signs cannot easily be compared between the two languages, they were excluded from the further comparison, and the remaining 607 items were compared to calculate the percentages of "phonologically identically articulated signs," "phonologically similarly articulated signs," and "phonologically distinctly articulated signs."

Of 607 items, 231 (38.1 percent) were phonologically identically articulated; 105 (17.3 percent) were regarded as phonologically similarly

TABLE 2. Summary of the Three Analyses

	Identically Articulated	Similarly Articulated	Distinctly Articulated	Semantic Mismatches	Missing Data
Analysis 1 (100 signs)	33 (42.3%)	16 (20.5%)	29 (37.2%)	7 (7%)	15 (15%)
	49 (62.8%) out of 78 signs				
Analysis 2 (199 signs)	37 (38.5%)	20 (20.8%)	39 (40.6%)	5 (2.5%)	98 (49.2%)
	57 (59.4%) out of 96 signs				
Analysis 3 (752 signs)	231 (38.1%)	105 (17.3%)	271 (44.6%)	10 (1.3%)	135 (18.0%)
	336 (55.4%) out of 607 signs				

articulated; and 271 (44.6 percent) were considered phonologically distinctly articulated. The total of phonologically identically articulated and phonologically similarly articulated signs was 336 items (55.4 percent).

DISCUSSION

The phonological comparison of JSL and TSL lexical items helps us to consider how signs in these two languages may have been articulated years ago — before they were recorded on paper or video. Unlike spoken languages with written forms, it was rather difficult to record sign languages in linguistic detail until we had notation systems (cf. Stokoe 1960; Stokoe, Casterline, and Croneberg 1965; Prillwitz et al. 1989, to name a few) and video recording devices. As far as I know, there are no film recordings or illustrations of JSL and TSL signs from the early 20th century, unlike ASL (Frishberg 1975, 1979; Supalla 1998, 2004) and BSL (Woll 1987), and it is a challenge to reconstruct forms from these sign languages from more than 60 years ago. Since we have no historical data about how signs were articulated, it is also difficult to determine whether a certain sign in JSL is historically related to a corresponding TSL sign. However, by comparing various contemporary signs that are similarly articulated between the two languages, we can perhaps form a picture of what the older signs were like in the two languages.

I suggest that phonologically similarly articulated signs may be more useful for an initial JSL-TSL lexical comparison than phonologically identically and distinctly articulated signs. The latter may or may not be related historically, but because of differences in more than one parameter, the analyses of such signs require more in-depth investigation. Similarly, phonologically identically articulated signs pose challenges for the researcher because their identity may be coincidental or based on shared symbolism (e.g., iconicity), as Greenberg (1953, 1957) suggests, although such similarity could also be due to genetic relationship or borrowing. As a result, this work takes a careful look at phonologically similarly articulated signs and does not address comparisons of phonologically identically and distinctly articulated signs. Such comparisons are left for future work on this topic.

One hundred and five signs coded as phonologically similarly articulated can be classified into the following seven types according to parametric differences and other factors:

Difference in handshape	30 signs
Difference in palm orientation	14 signs
Difference in movement	37 signs
Difference in location	8 signs
One-handedness vs. two-handedness	13 signs
Compound signs	2 signs[20]
Relation of hands	1 sign[21]
Total	105 signs

Overall, movement was the most prominent parameter in the present research,[22] and handshape showed the next highest number of observed differences. Compared with the results of previous studies, in particular of Woll (1987) and McKee and Kennedy (2000), I found an unusually high rate of difference in the movement parameter.[23]

My primary purpose is not to compare the lexicons of JSL and TSL and to show to what extent they may have been shared, but rather to look closely at how the resemblance of phonologically similarly articulated signs can be explained according to parametric differences. In this section, I focus on phonologically similarly articulated signs in which the only observed difference occurs in the handshape.

Difference in Handshape

Of 105 phonologically similarly articulated signs in JSL and TSL, 30 showed differences only in handshape. These 30 signs were subcategorized into five subtypes.

FIGURE 1. *Handshape for* AIRPLANE *(TSL)*

The first subtype includes one-handed signs (i.e., signs that involve the use of only one hand [typically the dominant hand] for articulation), in which the only difference appears in the handshape and all the other parameters are coded as identical between the two sign languages. Six signs (AIRPLANE, DIRTY, HAT, SKY, SLEEP, and STRANGE) fall into this category. For example, for AIRPLANE, the dominant hand moves in a straight path from ipsilateral space to contralateral space. The JSL sign uses a handshape in which the thumb, little finger, and index finger are extended, and the other fingers are closed. In the TSL sign (see Figure 1), however, the thumb, little finger, and middle finger (instead of the index finger) are extended. If you try to articulate these handshapes by yourself, you will realize that the handshape for the JSL sign is easier to articulate than its TSL counterpart.[24] For SKY, a B handshape,[25] a flat handshape in which all of the fingers are extended and together, is used in the JSL sign, whereas a handshape that is identical to THREE in ASL or SEVEN in JSL and TSL (a so-called 3 handshape, where the thumb, index, and middle fingers are extended and separated and the other fingers are closed) is used in TSL.

The second subtype shows the difference in the handshape of the dominant hand in two-handed signs (i.e., signs in which two hands are involved). In these, the nondominant hand often functions as a base

FIGURE 2. SUBORDINATE *(TSL)*

hand, and different handshapes may be used across the two hands. Six signs are classified into this subtype: CALENDAR, CHINESE-CHARACTER, MEDICINE, STAND, SUBORDINATE, and YARD. For SUBORDINATE, for example, while the JSL sign uses a so-called A-dot handshape[26] (where only the thumb is extended and the other fingers are closed) in both hands, the corresponding TSL sign (see Figure 2) uses two different handshapes: an A-dot handshape in the nondominant hand and a bent A-dot handshape (the extended thumb is bent at the first joint) in the dominant hand.

In addition, for YARD, the JSL sign is symmetrical: Both hands use a B handshape. The corresponding TSL sign is asymmetrical: The nondominant hand uses a B handshape, as in the JSL counterpart, but the dominant hand uses a 1 handshape[27] (only the index finger is extended; the other fingers are closed). MEDICINE may be another interesting example. For the TSL version, the middle finger is bent at the base joint while the other fingers are extended, and the tip of the middle finger makes contact with the palm of the nondominant hand. In JSL, however, the ring finger is bent at the base joint while the other fingers are extended, and contact is made between the tip of the ring finger and the palm (see Figure 3). I presume that this is related to the fact that, in Japanese, the ring finger is called *kusuri yubi*, which literally means "medicine finger," and I hy-

FIGURE 3. MEDICINE *(JSL)*

pothesize that, to grasp the meaning of this name, a seemingly hard-to-articulate handshape is instead selected in the JSL sign.

The third subtype is the opposite of the second; in this category a difference occurs in the handshape of the nondominant hand in two-handed signs. This category contains five signs: BANANA, CAMERA, LAST-YEAR, MIDDLE, and TRY. In JSL, BANANA uses an S handshape (a closed fist with the thumb enclosing the index and middle fingers) in its nondominant hand, presumably showing the holding of a banana. In TSL, the nondominant hand extends only the middle finger, and the other fingers are closed.[28] For LAST-YEAR, an S handshape is used in the nondominant hand of the JSL sign, whereas a closed, flat, so-called Baby O handshape (where the thumb and index finger are extended to form a flat circle and the other fingers are closed) is used in the TSL sign (see Figure 4). In these pairs of signs, the S handshape is much easier to articulate than the others. In fact, according to Battison (1978), the handshape is one of the seven unmarked handshapes.[29] For CAMERA, on the other hand, the JSL sign is symmetrical: Both dominant and nondominant hands use a Baby C handshape (the thumb and the index finger are extended and curved, and the other fingers are closed). The TSL sign is asymmetrical: The nondominant hand uses a regular C handshape (all of the fingers are extended and curved), and the dominant hand uses a Baby C handshape.

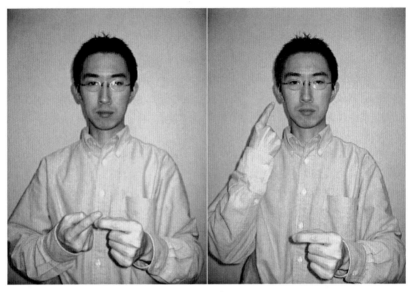

FIGURE 4. LAST-YEAR *(TSL)*

The fourth subtype consists of two-handed symmetrical signs that show handshape differences in both hands; seven signs (COW, EVEN-MORE, ORDINARY, PANTS, PUT-ON-CLOTHES, SHELL, and SIGN-LANGUAGE) compose this category. In JSL, SIGN-LANGUAGE uses a 1 handshape in both hands, whereas in TSL, SIGN-LANGUAGE uses a B handshape in both hands. For COW, a Baby C handshape is used in JSL; in TSL, a Y handshape (the thumb and little finger are extended, and the other fingers are closed) is used.

Signs in the fifth subtype exhibit handshape variations (i.e., hand-internal changes from one handshape to another), and I suggest that they be treated differently from signs that involve changes in path movement.[30] Six signs (BASE, CHOOSE, FEW, NOT-GOOD, TEN-THOUSAND, and YOUNG) are included in this subtype. For BASE, an S handshape, articulated beneath the elbow of the nondominant hand, opens to a 5 handshape (all of the fingers are extended and separate) in the JSL sign; the TSL counterpart makes a completely opposite movement: A 5 handshape closes to become an S handshape. For NOT-GOOD, the JSL sign uses a 1 handshape throughout the articulation without involving a hand-internal change, whereas in the TSL sign an S handshape changes to a 5 handshape during articulation.[31] This is true of YOUNG: The JSL sign uses a B handshape throughout and involves no hand-internal changes, whereas

FIGURE 5. YOUNG *(TSL)*

in TSL (see Figure 5), a B handshape changes to a 5 handshape in the course of articulation.

A HISTORICAL PERSPECTIVE ON CHANGES IN SIGNS

On the basis of the data analyzed here and other data discussed in Sasaki (2003), I assume that certain features that could be regarded as complex in the present-day TSL signs were also observed in the JSL signs that existed when they were introduced to the Deaf community in Taiwan. In other words, the present-day TSL signs may retain some older features (archaisms) of JSL signs that existed more than 60 years ago, and we may thus be able to reconstruct older forms, or protoforms, of JSL signs by looking at the present forms of both JSL and TSL signs. According to Baugh and Cable (2002, 360–61), "[A]ccordingly it has often been maintained that transplanting a language results in a sort of arrested development. . . . In language this slower development is often regarded as a form of conservatism, and it is assumed as a general principle that the language of a new country is more conservative than the same language when it remains in the old habit. . . . And, it is a well-recognized fact in cultural history that isolated communities tend to preserve old customs and beliefs." Baugh and Cable (ibid., 360) explain that several archaic features are found in American English when we compare it with British English. For example, the preservation of the postvocalic *r* sound in American English is characteristic of English speech in the seventeenth and eighteenth centuries. In this section, I discuss two characteristics observed through the comparison of phonologically similarly articulated signs.

The first characteristic that I have observed concerns the concept of symmetry. In the present study, it seems that two-handed asymmetrical signs in TSL are realized as symmetrical signs in JSL. For example, TSL YARD is asymmetrical: The nondominant hand with a B handshape does not involve any movement, whereas the dominant hand with a 1 hand-shape draws an arc on the horizontal plane in neutral space. For the JSL counterpart, on the contrary, the dominant hand makes a B handshape, which is now identical to the handshape of the nondominant hand. Other examples include CAMERA and SUBORDINATE. For TSL CAMERA, different handshapes are used, with a C handshape in the nondominant hand and a Baby C handshape in the dominant hand. CAMERA in JSL is a symmetrical sign, in which a Baby C handshape is used in both hands. Comparing two-handed symmetrical signs with asymmetrical signs, we could postulate that asymmetrical signs are more difficult to articulate than their symmetrical counterparts, presumably because two different handshapes have to be processed simultaneously. If we posit a protosign for JSL and TSL before and during World War II and assume that, due to conservatism, it did not change its form in TSL, whereas it did change in JSL due to the economy of language, we may assume that the present-day TSL signs show what JSL signs once looked like.

The second characteristic observed in this research is simplification; that is, hand-internal movements that are observed in some TSL signs are no longer involved in the corresponding JSL signs. Signs such as CHOOSE, NOT-GOOD, and YOUNG involve hand-internal movements in TSL, but no such movement occurs in the JSL counterparts. In addition, some JSL signs use purportedly easier handshapes than TSL signs do. The TSL sign SKY uses a 3 handshape, but the JSL counterpart uses a B handshape. As Battison (1978) explains, the B handshape is among the unmarked hand-shapes and may be easier to articulate than the 3 handshape. On the other hand, as reviewed in the previous section, the thumb, little finger, and middle finger are extended in the TSL sign AIRPLANE, whereas the thumb, little finger, and index finger are extended in the JSL counterpart. In addition, the nondominant hand of BANANA in JSL is an S handshape, whereas the corresponding TSL sign uses a handshape in which only the middle finger is extended and the other fingers are closed.

Based on the anatomical and physiological constraints on bones and muscles in the hand, Ann (1993) proposes an "ease score" for hand-shapes to enable us to calculate their complexity.[32] According to Ann, the ease score for the handshape of TSL AIRPLANE is 2 and that for the handshape of JSL AIRPLANE is 1.[33] For BANANA, the S handshape of the JSL sign has an ease score of 0, whereas that of the TSL sign has a score of 2.[34] With respect to where to make the dividing lines between "easy," "hard," and "impossible," Ann simply lets the physiology determine them: According to her criteria, for handshapes in which some of the fingers are selected (for extension, curving, or bending) and the rest are closed, a handshape with an ease score of 1, 2, or 3 would be considered hard (but not impossible), but one with an ease score of 4 or more is regarded as physically impossible. If her argument is valid, the JSL handshapes for AIRPLANE and BANANA are easier to articulate than the corresponding TSL signs, and we can assume first that signs in JSL have changed over time according to the economy of language and also that, because of archaism or conservatism, those in TSL did not change.

CONCLUSION

In comparing the lexicons of JSL and TSL, I have focused on the handshape parameter of phonologically similarly articulated signs. Of 105 phonologically similarly articulated signs, 30 showed differences in handshape, and these were further classified into five subtypes: one-handed signs, two-handed signs in which a difference occurs in the dominant hand, two-handed signs in which a difference is observed in the nondominant hand, two-handed signs in which both hands exhibit a difference, and signs that involve hand-internal changes. The data here suggest diachronic changes: two-handed asymmetrical signs have become symmetrical in terms of handshape, and handshape has been simplified. This historical change may well be due to archaism or conservatism in TSL.

However, the present study also raises several additional issues. First, I have defined "phonologically similarly articulated signs" as those that share the same meaning and differ in just one parameter, following Guerra Currie (1999) and Guerra Currie, Meier, and Walters (2002). This strict definition permits as much researcher bias to be avoided as possible. At the same time, however, the strictness of the definition may have eliminated probable pairs of phonologically similarly articulated signs, as reported in Sasaki (2003). Future studies should consider whether this definition is appropriate for "phonologically similarly articulated signs" and how much of researchers' and/or native signers' intuition should be included or excluded for comparisons.

Second, I have shown that there is a definite limit to the comparison of signs using sign language dictionaries. Sign languages are visual-gestural languages, and the two-dimensional illustrations in a paper dictionary lack significant information with respect to three-dimensional space (specifically, location and movement). The most effective way to obtain more precise data is to interview native signers. Future studies on comparisons of this nature must include such data.

Third, data of this nature should be collected from native signers not only of JSL and TSL but also of KSL. Just as the comparison of signs in JSL and TSL is important, so are those between JSL and KSL and between TSL and KSL. In addition, we should bear in mind that marginal areas in Japan might retain older forms of JSL signs, as is implied by Kunio Yanagida's (1930) theory that archaic words remain in marginal areas, which may apply to sign language as well. Such comparisons may well bring to light important and interesting insights into the developmental processes of signs in each area.

Finally, a clear relationship among Asian sign languages has not yet been revealed. As mentioned earlier, TSL may exhibit some influence from CSL of mainland China (Smith 1987a, 1987b). Also, Fischer (2001) claims that Hong Kong Sign Language (HKSL) seems to be related to the southern dialect of CSL.[35] In addition, considering the fact that the written languages of many Asian countries use Chinese characters to an extent and share some degree of cultural characteristics through the use of these characters, it would be reasonable to hypothesize that some measure of cultural commonality may affect the formation of each sign language. This would appear to occur particularly at the lexical level in view of the fact that many borrowed signs display the shape of Chinese characters. In future studies, other Asian sign languages (as well as JSL, TSL, and KSL) should be compared both lexically and grammatically.

NOTES

1. Ichida (pers. comm.) later recalls that the impression reported in his article (2002) might be a bit exaggerated. According to him, KSL signs for formulaic expressions (THANK-YOU, I-AM-SORRY), basic verbs (older forms of EXIST and BE), basic words regarding human relationships (MAN, WOMAN, FATHER, MOTHER, SIBLING, MARRY, FRIEND), basic adjectives and adverbs (TRUE, GOOD,

BAD, YOUNG, VERY, OKAY, ALSO, ALWAYS), *wh*-words (WHERE, WHO, WHEN), and conjunctions (IF) are similar to corresponding JSL signs.

2.   This fairly high mutual intelligibility can be realized only when signers employ signed languages as natural languages that are used among deaf people and whose structure is completely different from that of the spoken languages surrounding them. Ichida (2002) also reports on his experience with the hearing principal of the National Seoul School for the Deaf. In their meeting, the principal fluently used "hearing sign language" (or manually coded Korean or simultaneous communication), but Ichida and his Deaf colleagues had to rely on their interpreters to understand what the principal tried to say by his "signing."

3.   Smith (1976, 1990) makes a similar observation.

4.   In 1946, the school changed its name to the Taiwan Provincial Tainan School for the Blind and the Mute. In 1962, it became the Taiwan Provincial Tainan School for the Blind and the Deaf. Then in 1968, when the division of deaf education was separated from the division of blind education, the Taiwan Provincial Tainan School for the Deaf was established. It is now referred to as the National Tainan School for the Deaf.

5.   Its present name is the National Taichung School for the Deaf.

6.   A total of eight resolutions were passed at the conference. Here are the first two (Gallaudet 1881, 5–6; quoted in Jankowski 1997, 51–52):

> 1. The Convention, considering the incontestable superiority of speech over signs, (1) for restoring deaf-mutes to social life, (2) for giving them greater facility of language, declares that the method of articulation should have preference over that of signs in the instruction and education of the deaf and dumb.
> 2. Considering that the simultaneous use of signs and speech has the disadvantage of injuring speech and lipreading and precision of ideas, the Convention declares that the pure oral method ought to be preferred.

7.   The school's original name in 1880 was the Rakuzen-kai Training Institute for the Blind. The name was changed to the Rakuzen-kai Training Institute for the Blind and the Mute in 1884 and to the Tokyo School for the Blind and the Mute in 1887.

8.   However, the present school, the University of Tsukuba School for the Deaf, regards its founding year as 1875, when the Rakuzen-kai group was formed to establish a school for the blind and the deaf (Saito 2005).

9.   They are the parents of Edwin Oldfather Reischauer (1910–1990), former U.S. ambassador to Japan (1961–1966) and professor at Harvard University.

10.   Kawamoto later headed the Tokyo School for the Deaf and, after World War II, became a professor at the Tokyo University of Education.

11.   Chao and Chu (1981/1988) and Chao (1999) state that the Private Chi-Ying School for the Deaf started out as the Private Chinese School for the Deaf

in Keelung, a northern seaport near Taipei. It was founded by Lu Junou and Jiang Sinong, both of whom were teachers at the Nantong School for the Deaf in Zhejiang Province in mainland China. Most of the teachers at the Keelung school had graduated from the National Nanjing School for the Deaf and were all signers of Nanjing Sign Language. Therefore, Nanjing Sign Language may be a fourth influence on TSL.

12. However, MCCE (1999), seemingly a group of researchers who have collaborated to publish sign language books, casts some doubt on this widely believed explanation. The group maintains that the Tainan school also had teachers from Tokyo and that teachers were sent to the Taipei school from Osaka and Nagoya; thus some uncertainty remains regarding the reasons for the dominance of the Tokyo dialect of JSL in Taipei and of the Osaka dialect in Tainan.

13. In Smith (1989, 1990), these auxiliary verbs, all of which show the direction of some action from the agent to the theme or from the source to the goal, are named after the handshape that is used in each auxiliary verb. For example, a handshape meaning "one" (only the index finger is extended, and the other fingers are closed) is used for AUX1.

14. I use English glosses to represent both JSL and TSL signs, following a general convention in the literature of sign linguistics. With regard to readability, however, I avoid using Japanese and Chinese glosses to represent JSL and TSL signs, respectively. Whenever I need to specify whether a sign is from TSL or JSL, I indicate the language name for such a sign (e.g., TSL AIRPLANE).

15. Woll (1984, 81) says, "The full list appears in the Appendix with the Swadesh and Stokoe and Kuschel lists," but the full list as well as other lists are not actually included anywhere. Thus we have no way of finding out what items she included.

16. The list prepared by McKee and Kennedy (2000) is actually composed of 199 items since it includes two occurrences of NERVOUS.

17. In Guerra Currie, Meier, and Walters (2002, 227), the authors identify "similarly articulated signs" as those that have "approximately the same meaning and the same values on any two of the three major parameters of handshape, movement, and place of articulation." They further explain that "[A] subset of similarly articulated signs includes those signs that are articulated *similarly or identically* on all three major parameters" (emphasis mine), and they call these "equivalent variants." In this regard, their "similarly articulated signs" are slightly different from mine in that the latter do not include "phonologically identically articulated signs."

18. Quinto-Pozos (2002, 61) calls these "similarly articulated but semantically unrelated (SASU) signs."

19. The results shown here are slightly different from those reported in Sasaki (2003) after reanalyzing the data.

20. Two monomorphemic signs in JSL were realized as compound signs in TSL. OLDER-BROTHER and YOUNGER-BROTHER are monomorphemic in JSL (the extended middle finger with the other fingers closed is moved upward for OLDER-BROTHER and downward for YOUNGER-BROTHER); in the corresponding TSL signs, a bound morpheme that shows blood relationship is added at the outset of the signs, resulting in compound signs. This bound morpheme is also found in FATHER, MOTHER, GRANDFATHER, and GRANDMOTHER in both JSL and TSL.

21. In one sign, the relation of hands is a mirror image across JSL and TSL. In LITTLE, the Chinese character for "small" is represented by the two hands, one with a 1 handshape, which functions as the middle vertical stroke, and the other with a V handshape, which represents the two dots on both sides of the middle stroke. In JSL, the 1 handshape is articulated by the nondominant hand (i.e., the left hand for right-handed signers), and the V handshape is represented by the dominant hand (i.e., the right hand for right-handed signers). In TSL, however, this relationship is the opposite: The V handshape is represented by the non-dominant hand, whereas the 1 handshape is articulated by the dominant hand.

22. See Sasaki (2005) for a lexical comparison of JSL and TSL with respect to the differences in the movement parameter.

23. In the second half of her study, Woll diachronically compared lexical items of BSL with regard to parameters such as "location of the sign, handshapes of the left and right hands, orientation of the fingers, and movement of the hands" (1987, 20) and found that handshape showed the greatest number of differences (43 percent); the parameter with the next highest number was location (24 percent); and the third was movement. In McKee and Kennedy (2000), hand-shape also had the greatest number of parametric differences in all three comparisons between NZSL and ASL (13 out of 32 related signs), between NZSL and Auslan (15 out of 41), and between NZSL and BSL (23 out of 47); move-ment ranked second in all three comparisons (NZSL and ASL: 5 out of 32 related signs; NZSL and Auslan: 10 out of 41; and NZSL and BSL: 10 out of 47).

24. However, I have observed that some native signers of JSL use the hand-shape of TSL AIRPLANE, and I suspect that there may be idiosyncratic variations between two handshapes with regard to ease of articulation.

25. "B handshape" refers to the handshape of the fingerspelled letter *B* in ASL. This type of notation also applies to other fingerspelled letters and num-bers, such as "S handshape," "V handshape," "1 handshape," and so on.

26. The name "A-dot" is attributed to Stokoe (1960) and Stokoe, Casterline, and Croneberg (1965), who used a diacritic dot to transcribe a sign with the extended thumb.

27. In the literature of ASL, this handshape has traditionally been called the G handshape, following the fingerspelled letter *G*, although both the thumb and the index finger are extended in the actual fingerspelled letter *G*. For a clearer

distinction, I use "1 handshape" for a handshape in which only the index finger is extended and the other fingers are closed.

28. This handshape is often offensive to people in the Western culture, but it *is* used in signs in JSL and TSL, such as ELDER-BROTHER and YOUNGER-BROTHER (in both JSL and TSL).

29. The seven unmarked handshapes that Battison (1978) has proposed are the A handshape (all of the fingers except the thumb are closed, and the thumb is beside the closed index finger), the S handshape, the B handshape, the 5 handshape, the 1 handshape ("G handshape" in Battison's terminology), the C handshape, and the O handshape (all of the fingers are curved and together, and they form the shape of the letter O).

30. In the field of sign phonology (cf. Brentari 2001), hand-internal changes are sometimes treated in the movement parameter. However, in the present analysis, these changes are considered to be those in handshape since they are independent of path movements and therefore can co-occur with path movements, as in ASL THROW, which uses a handshape in which the thumb, the index finger, and the middle finger are curved so that they first form a circle (while the ring finger and the little finger are closed), then the curved fingers open and are extended in the course of articulation (hand-internal movement), while the arm makes a throwing motion (path movement).

31. Ichida (pers. comm.) points out that the TSL version of NOT-GOOD could be a compound sign in which GOOD is followed by a marker for negation.

32. The algorithm for the calculation of the ease score is as follows:

$$(\text{IE/SS} + \text{P/JT}) \times \text{MOC}_{\text{of selected fingers}}$$

where IE/SS = Independent Extensor/Sufficient Support; P/JT = Profundus/Juncturae Tendinum; and MOC = Muscle Opposition in Configuration (Ann 1993, 163).

Each criterion is calculated as follows. The IE/SS is related to whether each finger in this group has either an independent extensor or sufficient support to extend, and the P/JT has to do with whether the middle, ring, and pinky fingers are all included or all excluded from the group. If the answer is "yes," a plus value, which is equal to "0," is assigned; if the answer is "no," a minus value, which is equal to "1," is given. These values are added, and the sum is multiplied by the value for the selected fingers as follows:

closed = 0
bent = 1
extended = 2
curved = 3

33. The values for the IE/SS and P/JT criteria in TSL AIRPLANE are both 1; those in JSL AIRPLANE_are 0 and 1, respectively. For both TSL and JSL AIRPLANE, the selected fingers are considered to be bent, not extended, according to Ann (1993). For TSL AIRPLANE, $(1 + 1) \times 1 = 2$; for JSL AIRPLANE, $(1 + 0) \times 1 = 1$.

34. The ease score for the S handshape in JSL BANANA is automatically 0 since the ease score for all "one-group" handshapes (i.e., handshapes in which all of the fingers act together — they are all either extended or closed) is 0. The values for the IE/SS and P/JT criteria in the nondominant handshape of TSL BANANA are both 1. For this handshape, the selected fingers are again considered to be bent, not extended. For TSL BANANA, $(1 + 1) \times 1 = 2$.

35. Woodward (1993) also supports Fischer's claim.

REFERENCES

Ann, J. 1993. A linguistic investigation of the relationship between physiology and handshape. PhD diss., University of Arizona.

Battison, R. M. 1978. *Lexical borrowing in American Sign Language.* Silver Spring, Md.: Linstok.

Baugh, A. C., and T. Cable. 2002. *A history of the English language*, 5th ed. London: Routledge.

Brentari, D. 1998. *A prosodic model of sign language phonology.* Cambridge, Mass.: MIT Press.

Campbell, L. 1998. *Historical linguistics: An introduction.* Edinburgh: Edinburgh University Press. Reprint, Cambridge, Mass.: MIT Press, 1999.

Chao, (J.) C.-M. 1999. *Ziran shouyu jiaoxue diyice* [Natural sign language teaching, vol. 1]. Taipei: Zhonghua minguo qiting xiehui [Chinese Deaf Association, Republic of China].

———, and H.-H. Chu, eds. 1981/1988. *Taiwan ziran shouyu* [Taiwan Natural Sign Language]. Taipei: Shouyu zhi jia [House of Sign Language].

Fischer, S. D. 2001. The importance of studying Asian sign languages. Paper presented at the Conference on Sign Linguistics, Deaf Education, and Deaf Culture, Chinese University of Hong Kong, Hong Kong, December 17–19.

Frishberg, N. 1975. Arbitrariness and iconicity: Historical change in American Sign Language. *Language* 51: 696–719.

———. 1979. Historical change: From iconic to arbitrary. In *The signs of language*, ed. E. S. Klima and U. Bellugi, 67–83. Cambridge, Mass.: Harvard University Press.

Gallaudet, E. M. 1881. The Milan Convention. *American Annals of the Deaf and Dumb* 26: 1–16.

Greenberg, J. H. 1953. Historical linguistics and unwritten languages. In *Anthropology today: An encyclopedic inventory*, ed. A. L. Kroeber, 265–86. Chicago: University of Chicago Press.

———. 1957. *Essays in linguistics.* Viking Fund Publications in Anthropology 24. New York: Wenner-Gren Foundation for Anthropological Research. Reprint, Chicago: University of Chicago Press, 1963.

Guerra Currie, A.-M. P. 1999. A Mexican Sign Language lexicon: Internal and cross-linguistic similarities and variations. PhD diss., the University of Texas at Austin.

———, R. P. Meier, and K. Walters. 2002. A cross-linguistic examination of four signed languages. In *Modality and structure in signed and spoken languages*, ed. R. P. Meier, K. Cormier, and D. Quinto-Pozos, 224–36. Cambridge: Cambridge University Press.

Ichida, Y. 2000. *Syuwa bunpoo kenkyuusitu: Syuwa ni tuite siritai* [Japanese Sign Language Grammar Research Laboratory: Want to know sign language]. http://jsl.gn.to/former/whatjsl.htm (no longer available).

———. 2002. Kankoku o hoomon site [Visiting Korea]. *Nihon syuwa gakkai nyuusuretaa* [Japan Association of Sign Linguistics Newsletter] 125 (April; online).

Jankowski, K. A. 1997. *Deaf empowerment emergence, struggle, and rhetoric.* Washington, D.C.: Gallaudet University Press.

Japan Institute for Sign Language Studies of the Japanese Federation of the Deaf (JISLS-JFD: Zen-nihon rooa renmee nihon syuwa kenkyuu-dyo), ed. 1997. *Nihongo-syuwa ziten* [Japanese-Japanese Sign Language dictionary]. Tokyo: Zen-nihon rooa renmee [Japanese Federation of the Deaf].

McKee, D., and G. Kennedy. 2000. Lexical comparisons of signs from American, Australian, British, and New Zealand sign languages. In *The signs of language revisited: An anthology to honor Ursula Bellugi and Edward Klima*, ed. K. Emmorey and H. Lane, 49–76. Mahwah, N.J.: Erlbaum.

Modern Classics Cultural Enterprises, Ltd., Division of Sign Language Books, Research and Compilation Committee (MCCE: Xiandai jingdian wenhua shiye youxian gongsi shouyu shuxi yanjiu bianji weiyuanhui). 1999. *Shouyu dashi IV: Taiwan shouyu wanquan xuexi shoucezhi zhuanyepian* [Sign language master IV: Taiwan Sign Language perfect study for the professional]. Taipei: Xiandai jingdian wenhua shiye youxian gongsi [Modern Classics Cultural Enterprises Ltd.].

Nakamura, K. 2002. *About Japanese Sign Language.* http://www.deaflibrary.org/jsl.html.

Osugi, Y. 1995. Kaigai dyoohoo: Rotyesutaa dayori [Overseas information: Letter from Rochester], Part 5. *Nihon syuwa gakkai kaihoo* [Japanese Association of Sign Linguistics Bulletin] 54: 7–9.

Prillwitz, S., R. Leven, H. Zienert, T. Hanke, J. Henning, et al. 1989. *HamNoSys, Version 2.0. Hamburg Notation System for Sign Languages: An introductory guide.* International Studies on Sign Language and Communication of the Deaf, vol. 5. Hamburg: Signum.

Quinto-Pozos, D. G. 2002. Contact between Mexican Sign Language and American Sign Language in two Texas border areas. PhD diss., The University of Texas at Austin.

Saito, S. 2005. *Sooritu 130-syuunen kinen sikiten: Gakkootyoo sikidi* [The celebration of the 130th anniversary of the foundation: School principal's address]. http://www.deaf-s.tsukuba.ac.jp/ce130/sikiji.htm.

Sasaki, D. 2003. Comparing the lexicon of sign languages in East Asia: A preliminary study focusing on the influence of Japanese Sign Language on Taiwan Sign Language. Qualifying paper, Department of Linguistics, the University of Texas at Austin.

———. 2005. Comparing the lexicon of Japanese Sign Language and Taiwan Sign Language: A preliminary study focusing on the difference in the movement parameter. *Proceedings of the Sophia University Linguistic Society* 19: 21–39.

Seino, S. 1997. Syoowa syoki syuwa-koowa ronsoo ni kansuru kenkyuu [A study on the dispute between sign language and pure speech method in the early Showa era]. *Siritu nayoro tanki daigaku kiyoo* [Bulletin of Nayoro City College] 29: 57–80.

Smith, W. H. 1976. History and development of deaf education and sign language in Taiwan. Unpublished manuscript.

———. 1987a. China, Republic of. In *Gallaudet encyclopedia of Deaf people and deafness,* vol. 1, A–G, ed. J. V. Van Cleve, 184–87. New York: McGraw-Hill.

———. 1987b. Taiwanese (s.v. Sign Languages). In *Gallaudet encyclopedia of Deaf people and deafness,* vol. 3, S–Z, Index, ed. J. V. Van Cleve, 113–16. New York: McGraw-Hill.

———. 1989. The morphological characteristics of verbs in Taiwan Sign Language. PhD diss., Indiana University.

———. 1990. Evidence for auxiliaries in Taiwan Sign Language. In *Theoretical issues in sign language research,* vol. 1, *Linguistics,* ed. S. D. Fischer and P. Siple, 211–28. Chicago: University of Chicago Press.

——— (Shi, W.-h.), and L.-f. Ting, eds. 1979. *Shou neng sheng qiao* [Your hands can become a bridge], vol. 1. Taipei: Zhonghua minguo longren shouyu yanjiuhui [Deaf Sign Language Research Association of the Republic of China].

Stokoe, W. C., Jr. 1960. Sign language structure: An outline of the visual communication systems of the American Deaf. *Studies in linguistics: Occasional papers* 8. Buffalo: Department of Anthropology and Linguistics, University of Buffalo, State University of New York. Reprint, Silver Spring, Md.: Linstok, 1978. Revised reprint, Burtonsville, Md.: Linstok, 1993.

———, D. C. Casterline, and C. G. Croneberg. 1965. *A dictionary of American Sign Language on linguistic principles.* Silver Spring, Md.: Linstok. Revised reprint, Silver Spring, Md.: Linstok, 1978.

———, and R. Kuschel. 1979. *A field guide for sign language research.* Silver Spring, Md.: Linstok.

Supalla, T. 1998. Reconstructing early ASL. Paper presented at the Sixth International Symposium on Theoretical Issues in Sign Language Research, Gallaudet University, Washington, D.C., November 12–15.

———. 2004. The validity of the Gallaudet lecture films. *Sign Language Studies* 4: 261–92.

Swadesh, M. 1952. Lexico-statistic dating of prehistoric ethnic contacts: With special reference to North American Indians and Eskimos. *Proceedings of the American Philosophical Society* 96: 452–63.

Ting, L.-f., and W. H. Smith (Shi, W.-h.), eds. 1984. *Shou neng sheng qiao* [Your hands can become a bridge], vol. 2. Taipei: Zhonghua minguo longren shouyu yanjiuhui [Deaf Sign Language Research Association of the Republic of China].

Woll, B. 1984. The comparative study of different sign languages: Preliminary analyses. In *Recent research on European sign languages*, ed. F. Loncke, P. Boyes Braem, and Y. Lebrun, 79–92. Lisse, the Netherlands: Swets and Zeitlinger.

———. 1987. Historical and comparative aspects of British Sign Language. In *Sign and school: Using signs in deaf children's development*, ed. J. Kyle, 12–34. Multilingual Matters, vol. 33. Philadelphia: Multilingual Matters.

Woodward, J. 1978. Historical bases of American Sign Language. In *Understanding language through sign language research*, ed. P. Siple, 333–48. New York: Academic Press.

———. 1993. Lexical evidence for the existence of South Asian and East Asian sign language families. *Journal of Asian Pacific Communication* 4: 91–106.

———. 2000. Sign languages and sign language families in Thailand and Viet Nam. In *The signs of language revisited: An anthology to honor Ursula Bellugi and Edward Klima*, ed. K. Emmorey and H. Lane, 23–47. Mahwah, N.J.: Erlbaum.

Yanagida, K. 1930. *Kagyuu koo* [Thoughts on cochlea]. Tokyo: Toko shoin.

Part 3　Language Attrition

Evidence for First-Language Attrition

of Russian Sign Language among

Immigrants to Israel

Judith Yoel

You can not keep language safe and deep within you; it must get exercise. You must use it, or else it gets rusty, atrophies, and dies.
Triolet (French/Russian bilingual)

People who immigrate to another country where the citizens speak a different language stand a good chance of losing some of their first-language skills. Often perceived as simply forgetting or regression, such loss is known as *natural language attrition.*[1] Linguistic research has proven beyond a doubt that signed languages are natural modes of communication that possess linguistic properties. This chapter discusses the ways in which Deaf people who immigrate from one country to another lose their native language skills over time when contact occurs between signed languages.

ATTRITION OF SPOKEN AND SIGNED LANGUAGES

General Points

Attrition is defined as a gradual but progressive eroding of language skills (Grosjean 1982). In 1980, at the inaugural conference on language attrition in Pennsylvania, Bert Weltens stated that "broadly defined, language attrition may refer to the loss of any language or portion of the language by an individual or community. It may refer to the declining use of the mother tongue skills by those in a bilingual situation or among

The epigraph to this chapter is drawn from Obler and Mahecha (1991, 53).

ethnic minorities in [some] language contact situations where one language for political or social reasons comes to replace another" (1989, 51).² Seliger's comment that language attrition is the "loss of first language by predominant use of the second language" is also particularly relevant to this study (1991, 5–6). Attrition implies the degradation of one's linguistic ability in comparison to that of a fluent speaker of the same language. The degree of loss differs from person to person, ranging from minimal (in which an individual still feels comfortable with the mother tongue but experiences some difficulty retrieving specific lexical items) to more serious loss (in which interactive communication is hindered or the individual claims no recollection of the native language).

Two well-attested theories about the rate of first-language attrition posit that (1) the attrition of any language, at any age, and under the right conditions sets in quickly (Kennedy 1932; Godsall-Myers 1981; Weltens 1989) and that (2) it occurs after an initial, undefined period of no or little loss (called "stable competence"). According to the second theory, a transitional period ensues, in which the individual who has acquired a new language can move back and forth between languages. When language loss sets in, it is characterized by "a decrease in one's speech repertoire" (Sharwood-Smith 1983, 51). No single, current model of first-language attrition can account precisely for the amount of language loss or its effects on linguistic skills, which are affected differently. Research suggests that phonology suffers minimally, whereas syntax is more vulnerable. Violations of syntactic constraints appear in simple utterances and commonly show the imposition of second-language syntax upon that of the native language. A host of additional factors such as age, language typology, language prestige, and the language learner's personality may also contribute to first-language attrition.

Natural attrition (in contrast to pathological attrition, which is language loss resulting from brain damage that occurs as the result of a stroke, an accident, or senility) can be categorized as follows: (1) first-language loss in a first-language environment (e.g., as it occurs with the onset of old age); (2) first-language loss in a second-language environment (e.g., as it occurs among immigrant populations); (3) second-language loss in a first-language environment (e.g., an English-speaking person who learns French but lives in an environment that offers no opportunity to use it will eventually lose some French language skills); (4) second-language loss in a second-language environment (e.g., as seen among immigrants who learn a second language but revert to their first language in old age) (Gonzo and Saltarelli 1983).

The most common type is attrition of the first language in a second-language environment, which is the focus of this chapter. I have adopted Schoenmakers–Klein Gunnewiek's (1983) definition of attrition because it cites language contact within a community as a key cause of first-language attrition, "a form of language change caused by a break with the L1 [first-language] community, having as effects, a restricted use of the L1 [caused by] intensive contact with the L2 [second language]" (cited in Waas 1996, 36). Major notes that "an American who learns three words of Japanese is unlikely to suffer any loss of English, while one who has spent the last twenty years in Japan probably will" (1993, 463). Language conflict and contact are essential factors in most cases of attrition. Pavlenko (2002) states that, in most cases, L1 attrition does not lead to a total loss of the L1 but rather to a convergence of the L1 with the L2.

The area most commonly affected by attrition is the lexicon (Cohen 1989; Olshtain and Blum-Kulka 1989; Altenberg 1991). Lexical knowledge is a complex process that encompasses more than merely recalling and producing a word. It includes the meanings of words, connotations, and an awareness of the appropriate linguistic and social circumstances in which certain words, synonyms, and idioms appear (Weltens and Grendal 1993). Not all lexical items are equally vulnerable to attrition.[3] Linguistic frequency plays a significant role in the susceptibility of lexical items to loss. Both infrequent and frequent items are at risk of loss. On the one hand, since infrequently used words are difficult to access, the second language may replace the first. On the other hand, frequently used and readily accessible words in the second language may replace first-language items. Generally, high-frequency items in the first language appear to show more stability. Kaufman and Aronoff (1991) cite the early loss of frequently used lexical items as one of the most puzzling features of attrition. Various compensation strategies (e.g., paraphrasing and the use of fillers) often accompany attempts to recall lexical items.

ATTRITION IN SIGNED LANGUAGE

Signed language is perhaps the only focus of study left relatively untouched by cross-linguistic theories of attrition. Although Battison and

Jordan noted as early as 1976 that "when a signer of one country moves to a country where there is a different sign . . . they forget their own sign as rapidly as they acquire the signs of the new country," anecdotal accounts of a similar process come from Deaf people who have relocated from one country to another, where a different signed language is used (Battison and Jordan 1976, 63; Grosjean 1982). Gerner de García (1995) follows the immigration of a nine-year-old deaf child from Mexico to the United States. She presents an account of the girl's attempt to cope with two new languages (English and ASL), two new cultures (both American and American Deaf culture), and her (and her family's) language conflict within a multilingual context. Grenoble (1992) set out to study Russian Sign Language through Deaf ex-Russians living in the United States but was forced to abandon the work when it became clear that "the informants exhibited significant interference from ASL in their RSL" (1992, 337).

The Current Study and Frameworks for Analyses

This chapter investigates the first-language attrition of Russian Sign Language among Deaf immigrants to Israel. It is an examination of first-language loss in the retrieval and production of lexical items, not of attrition as it may be evident in data from natural discourse. The mass immigration of Jews from the former Soviet Union (FSU) to Israel enabled this research.[4] Among nearly one million immigrants who have left the FSU since 1988 are an estimated one thousand Deaf immigrants. This preliminary examination of attrition in a signed language focuses on the lexicon and tests the widely held assumption that frequently used lexical items are vulnerable to attrition. Evidence for language loss is investigated through two theories: (1) the model of ethnolinguistic vitality (Giles, Bourhis, and Taylor 1977; Allard and Landry 1992) and (2) the theory of interference (Freed 1982; Lambert and Freed 1982; Seliger 1991). Evidence of attrition is provided as a result of L2 interference in the L1 and also by the existence of lexical gaps.

The model of language vitality first introduced by Giles, Bourhis, and Taylor (1977) places social and psychological processes in sociocultural contexts and relates them to interethnic linguistic behavior. "[The researchers] developed a taxonomy of support variables believed to affect a group's Ethnolinguistic Vitality (EV)," defining EV as "that which makes a group likely to behave as a distinctive and active collective entity in inter-group situations" (Allard and Landry 1992, 176). The model of language vitality has been supported by Giles, Bourhis, and Taylor (1977), Bourhis, Giles, and Rosenthal (1981), Giles and Byrne (1982), Bourhis and Sachdev (1984), and Hamers and Blanc (2000), all of whom have noted a correlation between social and psychological variables and linguistic behavior (Allard and Landry 1986).

The model adapted by Allard and Landry (1986, 1992) outlines specific variables that contribute to the loss or maintenance of language, culture, and identity when two or more groups come into contact. During language contact, users of one language interact with users of another language or language variety. In situations of prolonged contact one language usually exerts some influence on the other. The more support there is for a demographic, sociopsychological, or psychological variable, the more likely it is that a group will remain an entity with its language, culture, and identity intact. A lack of support, however, means that aspects of language, culture, or identity may disappear. "Additive bilingualism occurs when conditions favor the development and maintenance of the maternal language, while permitting the learning and use of a second language. Subtractive bilingualism [and attrition] occurs when conditions favor the development of a second language to the detriment of the maternal language" (Allard and Landry 1992, 173). The three levels of the model of ethnolinguistic vitality include (1) the social level (demographic, political, economic, and cultural capital), (2) the sociopsychological level (interpersonal contacts, the media, and educational support), and (3) the psychological level (language aptitude and vitality beliefs), and they are outlined later with regard to Deaf immigrants from the FSU to Israel. The application of the EV model shows the linguistic outcome for Deaf people.

The theory of interference is one of the most widely accepted explanations of language loss (Freed 1982; Lambert and Freed 1982). The basic premise is not that the first language is erased from memory but that contact with an additional language causes difficulty in recalling the other language. It assumes that language contact causes a situation of language conflict, which results in linguistic conflict for the individual; in turn some reduction in the linguistic system will occur. The theory posits interplay between dynamic language processes. It predicts that the existing patterns of the first language will be modified and reorganized in favor of the second or additional languages. Interference may be sporadic and idiosyncratic (Grosjean 1989). Lexical items in the L1 may eventually be lost or replaced by items in the L2.

Hypothesis

This study hypothesizes that with limited opportunity to use and maintain Russian Sign Language (RSL), immigrants are forced to master the new signed language, Israeli Sign Language (ISL), and that the latter will eventually encroach upon the former. The outcome is attrition of the first-language (RSL) lexicon.

Subjects

Twenty-two deaf Russian immigrants (eight males and fourteen females) were located through my connections in the Israeli Deaf community. Subjects were videotaped following a Hebrew language class for new immigrants in Rishon L'Zion (near Tel Aviv) and at weekly Deaf club gatherings in Jerusalem, Tel Aviv, and Haifa.[5] Seven of the subjects have been deaf since birth; twelve became deaf before the age of three, and three became deaf between the ages of five and ten. Fifteen people claimed hearing parents, seven have immediate family members who are deaf (e.g., parents or siblings), and two people have extended family members who are deaf (e.g., a grandfather and cousins). The subjects also include two married couples and a father-and-daughter pair.

The majority of subjects learned RSL at school between ages four and six. Four subjects said they had learned RSL before attending school. Three subjects learned RSL postlingually. The latter became deaf at ages five, seven, and ten and learned sign language at ages seven, ten, and thirteen, respectively, when they enrolled in residential schools for Deaf students. Educational policy in the former Soviet Union, until quite recently, mandated residential schools for everyone. Therefore, all of the subjects received a similar education. In the residential schools for Deaf students in the FSU, RSL is restricted to mainly to out-of-class activity. Its use in the classroom is discouraged and still results in occasional punishment even today. Outside of a formal class setting, RSL is the main means of communication between Deaf students.

In order to determine whether one's L1 communicative performance has suffered attrition, evidence of a certain level of L1 competence must first exist. No testing was conducted to affirm this. However, since all of the subjects attended residential school (where RSL served as the primary means of communication), identified themselves as members of a larger Deaf community in the FSU, and stated that RSL was their native language, it was assumed that all of them were competent users of RSL.

Factors such as the onset of postlingual deafness or immigration at a young age may account for varying degrees of RSL proficiency. In no way is it implied that these subjects form a homogenous linguistic or cultural group.

The subjects came from various regions of the former Soviet Union (e.g., Saint Petersburg, Moscow, the Ukraine, Belarus, Georgia, Moldova, Kazakhstan, and Cryazovets). Michael Pursglove, cofounder of the Bilingual School for the Deaf in Moscow, notes, "the influence of region is unclear. Just how many different signed languages are currently in the FSU is an open question. Different reference works present different signs for the same items, but whether these are dialectal variation, idiolectal or generational boundaries is unknown." (Pursglove 1995, personal communication). Some evidence of regional lexical variation exists. A different manual alphabet for the Baltic republics of Estonia, Latvia, and Lithuania suggests that perhaps a different signed language is in use there (Grenoble 1992). However, RSL researcher Galina Zaitseva (1996) asserts that, due to centralized schooling and national sociocultural organizations, even in the various republics (e.g., Kazakhstan, Uzbekistan, the Ukraine), where different spoken languages exist, a single signed language is found throughout the FSU. Moreover, RSL researcher Anna Komorova (1994) suggests that a "standard" variety of RSL is understood by all users, as are regional varieties. For political reasons and so that individuals may assert their identity and diversity, she urges users to employ terms such as "Uzbek Sign Language" and "Georgian Sign Language," but they seem to prefer the term "Russian Sign Language."

Over such a large geographical area, some degree of dialectal variation seems inevitable, and this may have some effect on the subjects' performance. In order to deal with regional variation, three different interpreters from three different regions (i.e., the Ukraine, Saint Petersburg, Uzbekistan) viewed the data independently of one another. In analyzing the data, for instance, one subject's articulation of a single-handed sign was deemed unacceptable by interpreters from Saint Petersburg and the Ukraine, but the interpreter from Uzbekistan declared the same sign an "acceptable variation." Although the interpreters were able to shed some light on the effects of regional variation, questions remained. (Questions also remained because six of the twenty-two subjects did not complete the questionnaire as to where they were originally from in the FSU).

The subjects, who had immigrated to Israel between the ages of eleven and sixty-six, ranged from sixteen to seventy. Four of them had studied in an Israeli high school, in classes for Deaf and hard of hearing pupils. Two of the subjects are still in school; two completed their formal education in grade nine, two in grade ten, three in grade eleven, and ten after twelve years of formal education. Three of the subjects (a social worker, a theater director, and a physical education teacher and sports coach) hold university (or equivalent) degrees. Others include a welder, two seamstresses, and a draftsman. At the time the study was conducted, their period of residence in Israel ranged from one to twelve years. The limited number of subjects in this study posed limitations for a statistical analysis. As a result, this chapter focuses on providing ethnographic analyses, and showing (via raw numbers and percentages) how Deaf participants fare on tasks of lexical retrieval, describing in general presumed cases of language loss.

Methods

Each subject completed a questionnaire in written Russian since, for each of them, Russian had been the language of instruction at school. A native Russian speaker and an RSL interpreter aided those who required help; she explained the questions and sometimes wrote the subjects' answers. The questionnaire was divided into three sections: (1) general background (e.g., age, level of schooling, type of education, profession, year of immigration), (2) linguistic background (e.g., mother tongue, age at which the subject became deaf, the age of first exposure to signed language), and (3) present linguistic circumstances (e.g., involvement in the Deaf community in the FSU and Israel, extent of interaction with other users of RSL and ISL, language use in specific domains). The questionnaire allowed the subjects to express themselves in ways not possible in the study's two experimental language situations.

The subjects performed two language tasks. Before each one they were given instructions in written Russian, and a native signer of RSL confirmed their comprehension. Each individual was videotaped consecutively performing the two tasks in a familiar and comfortable setting (the subjects' classroom or Deaf club). Each person signed to a native RSL signer. A camera operator was also present. No help or feedback was given.

The first task, adapted from the Language Skills Attrition Project (LSAP) (Lambert and Moore 1986), was used in the first testing of frequently named items in attrition studies. The process assumes that (1) a connection exists between conceptual recognition and the two signed languages; (2) the second language may interfere with the production of the first language; and (3) frequency is particularly vulnerable in the lexicon of the attriter (i.e., the individual who is losing first-language skills). It entails recognition, visual processing, retrieval from the mental lexicon, and production. This analysis considers only the surface production: picture naming. Presented with twenty-two large (32 cm × 24 cm), colorful illustrated prototypes of everyday items on laminated cards (e.g., an airplane, a bed, an umbrella, a tea cup), subjects were instructed to sign what they saw. When an item was signed, the next card was shown. There was no measured time-reaction analysis. When the subjects failed to name an item, the next card was presented; all previously unnamed items reappeared once at the end. The pictures represented items familiar in both cultures and consisted of nouns only, as concrete items are the most unambiguous. Also included were a limited number of distracters — identical signs in RSL and ISL (e.g., an airplane, a fish).

The second lexical task was adapted to examine first-language attrition by Waas (1996), who administered it to native German speakers in Australia. This study replicates Waas's experimental situation, and the only difference is language modality. The task involved RSL facility, recall, and production of lexical items. Such tests are common in attrition studies because of the insight they offer into lexical organization (Cohen 1989). This task focuses on the items produced. The subjects had a sixty-second time limit, within which they were asked to list as many different animals as possible. The precise instructions were "I would like to see how many different animals you can name in sixty seconds. Any animal will do." Subjects who stopped signing before the time limit was up were encouraged to continue and were recorded for a full sixty seconds.

Three experienced RSL interpreters and I analyzed the data. All three interpreters are children of Deaf adults (CODAs), and RSL is their first language. All continue to use RSL in a personal and professional capacity. In addition to testing the subjects, I conducted two face-to-face interviews with two individuals actively involved with Deaf immigrants from the FSU to Israel.[6]

ANALYSIS

Ethnolinguistic vitality examines the potential long-term consequences of a language for a speech community. No single factor indicates a language's future; rather, it is the combination of sociological, sociopsychological, and psychological factors that indicates whether a language will be maintained.

Ethnolinguistic Vitality: The Sociological Level

In order for a language to survive, a critical mass of language users who possess a certain degree of power is required. The sociological level of EV posits a correlation between the sociological strength of a language community, its demographics (numbers), the group's political representation and strength, and its economics (monetary resources) and cultural capital. Specifically, the more active a group is, the more likely it is to survive.

DEMOGRAPHIC CAPITAL

In the FSU, residential schools not only provided a shared experience for Deaf people but also physically united people in central locations that served as the base for an informal Deaf collective, which often included adult residential villages, social clubs, and sports clubs.[7] However, upon immigration to Israel, their demographic status weakened significantly. A government-imposed policy of absorption resulted in the dispersion of Deaf people across the country, often to peripheral areas, where few other Deaf people were living.[8] With Deaf initiatives located in central, urban locations, they are inaccessible to many Deaf immigrants. With insufficient finances to relocate or travel to cities, many Deaf newcomers rarely experience social and linguistic interaction with other Russian Deaf people. Thus, their demographic capital in Israel is weak.

POLITICAL CAPITAL

Politically, Deaf people had weak status in the FSU. The national organization for Deaf people, VOG (All-Russian Federation of the Deaf), is administered mainly by hearing and hard of hearing individuals. In his assessment of obstacles that Deaf people encounter (Pursglove and Komorova 1991), Igor Abramov (1993), chair of the Moscow branch of VOG, states that, until 1991, Russian legislation categorized Deaf and blind people, as well as those with physical disabilities, together under the single heading of what translates into English literally as "invalidity" (Pursglove 1995, 58). Of the twenty-six laws, drafts, ministerial orders, and presidential decrees in the FSU that relate to Deaf people (e.g., regarding studying, traveling, owning a car, buying medicine), few were enforced (Pursglove 1995).

The FSU has a chronic shortage of interpreters for Deaf people, but when they are available, their services are free of charge. A 2006 update ensures that each individual is entitled to thirty hours of interpretation a year; beyond that, each person must pay the equivalent of ten U.S. dollars for such services. In contrast to Western countries, Deaf people in the FSU have few Deaf role models. In Israel, Deaf immigrants also have little power. They fall under the auspices of national social services, disability, National Insurance, the Ministry of Absorption, and other institutions; but little consideration is given to this group's special needs. A government budget allotted specifically for Deaf immigrants lasted a single year (1998–1999) before it was discontinued. A branch of the National Association for the Deaf in Israel, specifically for Deaf immigrants, exists mostly in name. Its chair, Emmanuel Slutzsky, sends an annual report to the Israeli Minister of Absorption and summarizes progress in three areas: absorption, education, and culture. Activities, funded in part by the Ministry of Absorption, have been restricted to two social gatherings (1999 and 2000). Slutzsky states that, "[d]espite the rich experience and high level of Deaf Russians in Israel, they have contributed little [in Israel]" (Slutzsky, 2000, personal communication). Having gone from a weak status to a still weaker one, it will be difficult for this group to secure the political capital necessary for recognition and representation.

ECONOMIC CAPITAL

Prior to the dissolution of the Soviet Union, the government disability payment for Deaf people afforded them relative stability. Currently, the only state pension for Deaf people is insufficient for a person to live on. Once every five years, the government of the FSU reimburses Deaf people for the purchases of necessary technological devices (e.g., fax machines, modems, pagers, flashing indicators, and teletext cellular phones). While economic capital for Deaf people in the FSU is currently meager, they have at least some opportunities to progress beyond a secondary school education (e.g., a hair-dressing school, a school for drama and mime, and a pharmaceutical college for Deaf people [Ignatova 1996]).

In addition, a number of institutions have separate tracks for Deaf people within a hearing environment. These include a technical school (with Deaf faculty) and a teacher-training college that trains graduates of the Moscow Bilingual School for the Deaf to be teachers of Deaf children. Moreover, special agreements exist, such as that with the Moscow city authorities, whereby a certain number of Deaf individuals are provided with training and employment (ibid.). Moreover, VOG operates sixty-three factories employing Deaf people in the production of a variety of goods. In 1991 legislation was changed so that no Deaf VOG employee could be fired (Komorova 1994), and in 1993 an independent organization was established to defend the economic and social interests of Deaf people (Ignatova 1996).

Upon immigration to Israel, Deaf Russians take a cut in their disability payments. Immigrants struggle to find suitable employment and often have to adjust occupations downward. Some fail to find any employment at all. Emmanuel Slutzsky, a former VOG administrator in the FSU, presently works with Deaf immigrants; he cites employment as the biggest obstacle that Deaf immigrants must overcome. "It is impossible," he says, "for most [Deaf immigrants] to find work" (Slutzsky, 2000, personal communication). And there are fewer educational opportunities for Deaf people beyond a secondary level. Education is often limited to a five-month intensive Hebrew/ISL course. Deaf immigrants in Israel do not yet fare well along the lines of economic capital.

CULTURAL CAPITAL

Deaf cultural activities in the FSU, although not always formally defined, supported, or recognized as such, were abundant. In 1995, 155,590 deaf individuals (more than half of the estimated 300,000 deaf people in the entire FSU) were officially registered with the seventy-one regional branches of VOG. The Moscow branch of VOG alone had 12,000 members (Pursglove 1995, 50). In the 1990s the FSU had more than five hundred Deaf clubs, excluding Deaf athletic clubs, which are numerous and play an important role in Deaf cultural life. Church services (e.g., Russian Orthodox and Evangelical) are available in RSL. Deaf people in the FSU have their own organization of painters *(kolorit)*, writers and poets *(kamerto)*, and a theater *(Teatr Mimiki i Zhesta)*. They also boast the purported oldest Deaf theater in the world, which was established in 1962 and is considered prestigious by Deaf and hearing people alike (Pursglove 1995). Despite the existence of what appears to be a community, Russia has no linguistic concepts to portray this. Galina Zaitseva (1996), Russia's foremost researcher of RSL, employed the term *mikrosotism* [microsocietal unit] in an article to refer to the Deaf community in the FSU.

In Israel, the notion of a "community" for immigrants is weak. Opportunities for immigrants to become culturally involved with other

Russian Deaf people are limited. Of the fourteen Deaf clubs, only three (Tel Aviv, Bat Yam, and Ashdod) have gatherings specifically for immigrants. The largest club in Tel Aviv holds a weekly gathering in RSL for people from all over the country. In other words, their interaction with other Deaf people who use RSL (outside of the immediate family) is determined by external and practical factors such as physical proximity and accessibility (e.g., means and cost of transportation). At the remaining eleven clubs, Deaf Russians and Israelis socialize together using ISL. Immigrants attend functions, lectures, courses, sports events, trips, and holiday celebrations with Israeli Deaf people. At the only sports club in Tel Aviv these two groups also mix. However, participation in these activities is restricted by both individual and institutional financial hardship. For example, the Deaf club in Haifa has cut back all activities — for Russians and Israelis alike — to a single day a week. Immigrants who require basic services are affected by fiscal restraints. For instance, the only RSL interpreter in the northern region explained in an interview with me that, at least temporarily, her services have been officially suspended. Deaf individuals must do without Hebrew/ RSL translation services unless they are able pay privately (Haimov, 2000, personal communication). Cultural opportunities have declined upon immigration.

ANALYSIS

Ethnolinguistic Vitality: The Sociopsychological Level

Whereas the sociological level of EV is concerned with the group as a whole, the sociopsychological level is concerned with individuals, specifically with the extent to which they are exposed to their native language and culture. If the exposure is substantial and positive, language maintenance is the expected outcome; if it is limited and negative, language loss is anticipated. Exposure occurs mainly through one's network of interpersonal contacts (family and friends), exposure to the media, and education. These experiences are an essential step in the eventual formation of culture-related attitudes and values.

INTERPERSONAL CONTACTS

Ethnic groups find vitality at not only a sociological but also a sociopsychological level. In doing so, they must have access to people like themselves, with whom they can establish relationships. Deaf people in the FSU have strong ties to one another. There is a high rate of endogamous marriage, and they share numerous social and life-experience commonalities that extend beyond their hearing loss and common language. Deaf people identify with other Deaf people. They interact on formal levels (e.g., schools, church), as well as informal levels (e.g., social activities, long-lasting school ties). In the last decade, technology (e.g., the Internet) has brought increased opportunities for interaction between Deaf and hearing people. Public awareness of Deafness and RSL among hearing people has increased.

Deaf immigrants to Israel share commonalities, but they lack opportunities to interact with others like themselves. Situations of immediate family support often remain intact because Deaf people from the FSU tend to immigrate with extended family members, but gone is much of their familiar social network (e.g., acquaintances, friends, colleagues). Although they have a desire to connect with people from the home country, logistically this is difficult to accomplish. For Deaf immigrants, the degree of contact with other Deaf people from the FSU is not only reduced but also lacking.

THE MEDIA

In an examination of American Sign Language, Baker suggests that "the absence or presence of a minority language in the mass media (e.g., television, radio, newspapers, magazines, tapes and computer software) affects the status of a language" (1996, 55). "The attitude toward Russian Sign Language prior to *glasnost* and *perestroika* that ranged from downright hostile to lukewarm has improved, although some prejudice against signed language remains" (Pursglove and Komorova 1991, 5).[9] Some elevation in the status of Deaf people has occurred, which, in turn, has sparked new professional activity. For example, in 1996, a Moscow conference on sign language and Deafness drew 150 delegates from the FSU and other countries (Zaitseva, Pursglove, and Gregory 1999, 13), and an RSL dictionary is available on the Internet (Kautz 2004).

Because of limited media exposure to RSL, Deaf immigrants in Israel experience further isolation. Videotapes, as well as cable and satellite television channels, are available in Russian but without subtitles or captioning. For those immigrants who can afford the costly cable television, a single brief report is broadcast daily in Signed Russian, not RSL. There is a Russian press in Israel, but for some Deaf people, written language is difficult. The reading level of Deaf people is documented as frequently lagging behind that of their hearing peers (Zaitseva 1996; Baker 1999). Deaf immigrants must rely mainly on the Hebrew and ISL media (e.g., captioned television broadcasts and Internet sites) for news and important information. Even with these opportunities, Deaf immigrants from the FSU have limited exposure to media in ISL — and even less to RSL.

EDUCATIONAL SUPPORT

Before 1990, all Deaf children in the FSU attended residential schools. As is common in Eastern Europe, residential villages formed the continuation of the residential school experience. Until recently, there was no mainstreaming or inclusion in the FSU (Pursglove 1995). Educational methods for Deaf pupils were based on oralism, which is regarded there as successful. Oral methods are praised, while views to the contrary are rarely expressed in the news media. When they are, they are accompanied by hostile editorial comments, state Pursglove and Komorova (1991), educators of Deaf people in the FSU. Signed Russian, also referred to as "calqued speech," is the dominant language used in the media, although Deaf people have protested that these broadcasts are sometimes difficult to understand.[10] Signed Russian has the syntax and lexicon of spoken Russian and is not a natural sign language. Until recently, "[the] Signed Russian [seen mainly in the media] was clearly the high style at which speakers aimed, believing it to be more prestigious than RSL" (Grenoble 1992, 323). However, RSL remains the main means of communication among Deaf people.

In 1992, the Moscow Bilingual School for the Deaf was established. Pursglove, one of its founders, reported to me that this is the only school in the FSU that teaches both in and about RSL. Its teachers travel to other schools to disseminate a bilingual/bicultural ideology; although people have expressed interest and support, no other schools for Deaf children have developed a similar ideological approach. Graduates of the Moscow Bilingual School have continued their education by attending the Center for Deaf Studies (established in 1993), Moscow City Pedagogical University, and Teacher Training College Number Four to become teachers of Deaf children. Educational support for RSL is thereby slowly increasing.

For the Deaf child who is a part of a linguistic minority, uses a majority language in the classroom, and lives in a place where both the educational and societal aim is assimilation, the outcome is acculturation (Baker 1996). In Israel, Deaf immigrants who are too old to attend school study in an *ulpan* (immigrant language class) provided by the Ministry of Absorption. No separate or specific instruction is offered in ISL; rather, a Deaf Israeli teacher teaches Hebrew to newcomers via ISL. The immigrant, therefore, learns two new languages, Hebrew and Israeli Sign Language, simultaneously.

Battison and Jordan (1976) present evidence that Deaf people understand a foreign signed language with more ease than a hearing person would understand a foreign spoken language, thus making the aforementioned situation possible but by no means easy. Although the visual manual modality is familiar, Russian Sign Language and Israeli Sign Language are mutually unintelligible. Furthermore, classes are not restricted to immigrants from the FSU. "The individual is often so overwhelmed at attempting to master a new sign language at the same time as a new oral language that they cannot hear, written in a different alphabet, that even socializing opportunities are limited," says one new immigrant who experienced this system.

For young Deaf immigrants, school could provide a setting in which to use RSL. At home, opportunity to use RSL is limited because only about 10 percent of Deaf children have Deaf parents. Moreover, educational policy in Israel does not recognize or foster the maintenance of RSL. Deaf immigrants from the FSU have failed to have any impact on the Israeli educational system for Deaf people. Deaf youngsters must therefore adapt to what exists, and that means learning ISL as soon as possible, with social acceptability a significant added incentive. The current educational setting and policy fail to provide circumstances that encourage the retention of the native culture or mother tongue.

Ethnolinguistic Vitality: The Psychological Level

The final stage of EV relates to the individuals and specifically to their language skills. This stage is characterized by two main factors: (1) the language aptitude and competence of the individuals and (2) their cognitive-affective disposition, their beliefs about learning an additional language, and their use of that language. At this stage, the individuals ask themselves questions such as, is my language inferior, is my cultural or linguistic group stable or unstable, and to which group do I currently belong? The answers contribute to their linguistic disposition and ultimately have an impact on their identity and language use. Language choice can serve as a marker of identity. In turn, people's outlook regarding their language use and affiliation with a speech community has an impact on the viability of that language.

L A N G U A G E   A P T I T U D E   A N D   V I T A L I T Y
B E L I E F S
Although RSL is the dominant language of Deaf people in the FSU, an air of inferiority has surrounded it until fairly recently. A host of factors (e.g., an oral method of education and a preference for Signed Russian) contributed to this perception. It was not until 1990 that RSL was officially recognized, and even then it was considered only an "auxiliary language" (Pursglove 1995, 56). As cross-cultural contact between Deaf people increased, the term "Russian Sign Language" gained currency only in 1991 by analogy with British Sign Language and American Sign Language. The phrase did not appear in print until February 1995, when a footnote drew attention to the new terminology (Zaitseva and Gregory 1995). The term "RSL" is still often misunderstood, and many people assume that Signed Russian and Russian Sign Language are one and the same. At a conference on Deaf education in Moscow (1999), upon hearing the term "Deaf pride," which is commonly used within European and North American Deaf populations, one hearing participant objected with "What rubbish! What is there to be proud about in that?" (Pursglove, 2002, personal communication). In the FSU, a low group image is reinforced by the dominant hearing society.

Deaf immigrants are forced to decide which linguistic and cultural group they belong to and which group they want to identify with. This is only partially determined by language competence, for linguistic behavior is also formulated in terms of language attitude. They must also begin to establish personal goals in the new surroundings, and their degree of success in fulfilling them will have some effect on language maintenance or loss (Allard and Landry 1992, 175).

Deaf immigrants are further challenged by the necessity of mastering not one but two new languages (one signed and one written) and two new cultures (one Deaf and one hearing). This task is intensified by the weakening of the aforementioned sociological and psychosociological factors that afforded them some stability in the past. The weak status of RSL brought from the FSU, as it was reinforced by a dominant hearing society, in combination with the new and difficult circumstances and the daily challenges that accompany immigration, may result in an unstable linguistic situation.

CONCLUSION

The Model of Ethnolinguistic Vitality and Deaf Immigrants

An analysis of the ethnolinguistic vitality of Deaf Russian immigrants to Israel reveals that their demographic status is weak, their economic resources are meager, and their prospects for employment are few. They lack opportunities to interact with other Deaf Russian immigrants, and the occasions for social interaction they once had have been substantially diminished. They have limited exposure to the media. Furthermore, immigrants of school-attending age are encouraged to assimilate. They are faced with major decisions to make about their identity with regard to culture, subculture, and language. These conclusions are confirmed by the information in the questionnaires the subjects completed and the ethnographic interviews I conducted.

The result for both the individual and the language group is that the new culture does not perceive their language, RSL, as "significant." As RSL becomes increasingly difficult to access, the predicted outcome for RSL users in Israel is eventual subtractive bilingualism. The strong need to master additional languages and participate in local culture comes at a cost. In order for Deaf immigrants to become independent and successful members of Israeli society they must, at least to some degree, assimilate culturally and linguistically.

ANALYSIS

The Questionnaire

The results of the questionnaire administered to the subjects reveal a situation of language conflict that arose as the result of RSL users coming into regular contact with ISL and ISL users, as well as spoken and written Hebrew. Although the questionnaires admittedly had some drawbacks (e.g., introspective and subjective reporting; fewer than 100 percent of the questionnaires were completed), the answers provide an overall picture of the situation. Details such as the extent of interaction with other RSL and ISL users varied from person to person, depending on whether the subject had immediate family members who were Deaf and the subject's physical location and proximity to Deaf clubs. Three main trends appeared. The first was a positive attitude toward the L2 in that the subjects expressed a willingness to learn ISL. Their statements included the following: "I would like to know ISL and Israeli culture," "ISL and Hebrew are important because I live in Israel," "ISL is getting increasingly easier for me to learn," and "ISL is easy." The subjects' growing comfort with ISL hints at the more prominent role ISL may play in their future.

The second trend was an indication of disruption in RSL fluency. Although some subjects were reluctant to directly acknowledge any disturbance, others specifically mentioned accounts of unintentionally mixing up the two languages, signing the "wrong language" to someone, and unconsciously alternating between RSL and ISL (also known as code switching, which occurs when a person uses one language in combination with another). Code switching can occur at the level of a sign or phrase or as the result of a pragmatic situation. It may be the outcome of an attempt to retain continuity and nativelike fluency in spite of changes induced by language contact. (Code switching as it is used in this study refers only to the use of different signed languages, not to a convergence of spoken and signed language systems. Code mixing, a similar term, is often used in signed languages to indicate language use that incorporates elements of spoken language into signed language use [Davis 1989].) Quinto-Pozos (2002) discusses code switching as a natural consequence of language contact, not as a strategy specifically related to language attrition. In an interim form of language, the L1 may fill in when the L2 is not known (Romaine 1989), and the L2, it seems, may fill in when the L1 is temporarily inaccessible. Subjects admitted experiencing difficulty in the momentary retrieval of RSL lexical items.

A third trend — the replacement of the L1 by the L2 — was also evident. This was not investigated further due to the lack of more detailed questions pertaining to domain-specific language use. Fishman defines a domain as a "sociocultural construct abstracted from topics of communication, relationships between communicators, and locales of communication, in accord with the institutions of society and the spheres of a speech community" (1972, 442). The subjects generally indicated that RSL dominates mainly in a household domain, while ISL is becoming increasingly common as the dominant language in the areas of employment and social interaction.

The Theory of Interference

The articulations of signs contrary to the citation form or of those deemed unacceptable by native users were assumed to be evidence of cross-linguistic lexical interference, that is, the L2 (ISL) in the L1 (RSL). The term "miscues" (Goodman 1986) is adopted in order to avoid value implications (e.g., guessing what the signer meant or speculating about how the error may be connected to the subject's background). Although the term can include idiosyncrasies and other temporary production mistakes (e.g., slips of the hands; Klima and Bellugi 1979), it generally refers to "errors." Miscues include forms articulated in ISL instead of RSL either partially or in their entirety. They also include forms with one or more parameters (e.g., handshape, movement, orientation, location) that are different from the stipulated form, as well as anomalous forms, such as a combination of the L1 and L2 or the L2 form followed by an L1 self-correction.

The first experimental task, picture naming, required the retrieval and production of frequently used lexical items, including many common items such as household objects (e.g., bed, key), easily recognized animals (e.g., hen, polar bear), and vehicles (e.g., bus, truck). This task served as the main source of evidence of language interference. The lowest rate of accuracy for any of the subjects was 50.0 percent, and the highest was 91.2 percent. The average rate of error was 25.0 percent. On average, subjects correctly named 16.5 out of the 22 items.

The most obvious example of second-language intrusion was the unconscious presentation of an ISL sign when only RSL was requested. For example, in RSL, BED is formed by bending the extended middle two fingers on each hand and bringing the fingertips into contact. A slight hand-internal movement (e.g., bouncing) may occur, but no movement occurs beyond this. The index finger and pinky remain extended upward, forming an iconic representation of a bed. In its place, one subject used the dissimilar ISL sign (see Figure 1), parting the flat hands with extended digits outward, followed by contact between the back of the hand and the cheek, as if mimicking the resting of the head on the hands or a pillow. The individual continued without any obvious realization that what was produced was not RSL. The very different RSL sign is illustrated in Figure 2.

Two subjects correctly signed RSL BED but followed it with the second movement from the ISL sign. This can also be interpreted as *con-*

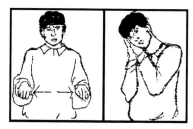

FIGURE 1. BED *(ISL)*

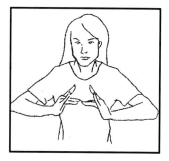

FIGURE 2. BED *(RSL)*

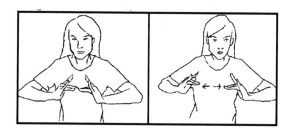

FIGURE 3. BED *A miscue
combination of RSL
and ISL*

structed action (Metzger 1995), a combination of characterization and classifiers to convey characteristics or events. The sign commonly used, the citation form, although requested, was not produced. Another person signed the correct form in RSL but also articulated the second movement of the ISL sign (i.e., bringing one hand up to his cheek). This hand used the hand configuration seen in the RSL sign instead of the ISL hand configuration — with all fingers extended. In yet another incident, illustrated in Figure 3, a subject combined the two different articulations, retaining the hand configuration of RSL but adding the path of movement to each hand seen in ISL. The subject did not appear to be aware of any error.

Signs composed of both RSL and ISL seem to be the result of language contact. Tarone's (1980) study of the attrition of Russian in an English-speaking environment documented similar lexical innovations. Signers struggled with some signs. For example, the RSL citation form of RAIN-BOW (see Figure 4) is articulated with a single hand forming an arc-shaped path from one side to the other slightly above the signer's forehead. (Whether the sign moves from left to right or right to left depends on the signer's hand preference). In ISL, also illustrated in Figure 4, two hands in a position of initial contact just above the forehead move downward from the central location in opposite directions, forming an arc.

FIGURE 4. RAINBOW: *RSL*   RAINBOW: *(ISL)*   RAINBOW: *Miscue*

Other phonological parameters (e.g., a C hand configuration and palm orientation) are identical. Miscues also included signing an otherwise correct RSL sign at an incorrect location (e.g., at chest height instead of over the forehead) and an ISL sign at the same location, when RSL was requested (the latter is illustrated in Figure 4).

Other subjects used incorrect hand configurations in otherwise correct signs (e.g., an incorrect G and an incorrect U handshape instead of an open handshape with all fingers extended and bent, a C handshape). These types of miscues have plausible explanations (e.g., a miscue in the location parameter may be a phonological reduction); monolingual native language users and stable bilinguals also show evidence of miscues. This study examines the hypothesis that miscues may result from language contact and the notion that their relation to attrition is worth exploring. In combination with additional factors (e.g., a rate of error of 25 percent), such a relation may exist.

When spoken languages come into contact with one another, speakers commonly paraphrase in order to overcome the resulting confusion (Andersen 1982; Cohen 1989). When one subject looked at the illustration of the rainbow and signed AFTER RAIN [pause] RAINBOW, self-explanation seemed to aid recall ability in that the target sign appeared after a related sign and a long pause. Semantically related items or one that is used when another is present may direct the signer toward the target item. There was also evidence of the subjects' failing to produce the target item and instead providing a semantically related item such as RAIN-SHOWER instead of UMBRELLA; FOOD and EAT instead of SAND-WICH; and KETTLE and DRINK instead of TEACUP. Also present was the classifier for "vehicle," which was used in place of a specifically requested and clearly illustrated taxi, bus, and car.

When subjects realized interference had occurred, RSL self-repairs sometimes followed. When a speaker's fluency has decreased due to language attrition, it is common for the number of self-repairs to increase (Hansen 1999). When signs were identical in RSL and ISL, a rate of error of 10 percent still occurred, explained perhaps by the too-good-to-be-true phenomenon. That is to say, momentarily confused by the existence of a single sign common to both languages, subjects produced an anomalous form. Feeling a need to clarify their utterances, they added information even when it was not specifically requested. For example, after signing "toothbrush," two subjects added "toothpaste." In an attempt to move between languages, the subjects also produced incorrect word-for-word renditions. For example, in RSL, "polar bear" is BEAR-WHITE, whereas in ISL it is BEAR-NORTH. One person signed BEAR-NORTH in RSL. Although this is comprehensible, it is nevertheless a miscue.

It has been observed that bilinguals who experience L1 interference in the L2 have a greater tendency to make literal translations from the L1 to the L2, particularly if the L2 is weaker (Dornic 1978). In this case, it was the L2 that interfered with the L1. Similarly, Waas (1996, 43) observed literal cross-linguistic translations among German speakers in Australia, who, for example, labeled an octopus an "ink fish," a German concept imposed upon English.

Interestingly, two unanticipated features also showed evidence of interference: mouth patterns and fingerspelling. Mouth borrowings involve the articulation of words, partial words, and lip movements that are derived from contact between signed and spoken languages. "It is clear that mouthings arise in a situation . . . of strong language contact" (Sutton-Spence and Boyes Braem 1998, 4).[11] However, mouthings can also be an indication of contact between two signed languages. In some signs, it is obligatory to move the mouth, without voice cocurrently with its production, as an integral part of the sign (Siple 1973; Boyes Braem and Sutton-Spence 2001). This is particularly common in European signed languages, including RSL and ISL. (This type of mouth movement is unrelated to those that co-occur with signs related to emotion and to mouth gestures, which have no connection to spoken language.)

In RSL signs requiring mouthing, three different subjects signed RSL but simultaneously mouthed Hebrew words. For example, while signing "bed" in RSL, the subjects either said or formed the word "divan," which is "bed" in Russian (with no voice); but one subject signed the RSL sign while simultaneously orally producing "mita," the word for "bed" in spoken Hebrew. Another subject, upon viewing the illustration of a "sandwich," signed "food" in RSL and orally produced "Burger Ranch," a popular Israeli hamburger chain. Attrition may be one factor that lies behind such behavior, but there also may be others. Quinto-Pozos (2002) discusses mouthings as they occur in a situation of language contact, with no relation to attrition. Mouthings from different spoken languages are also common in the signing of Deaf users in nonattrition situations (e.g., Deaf users of Langue des Signes Québécoise [LSQ], American Sign Language [ASL], and French and English in Quebec, Canada).

In fingerspelling, handshapes represent the letters used in the orthography of the spoken language. Russian Sign Language and Israeli Sign Language have different manual alphabets. RSL fingerspelling substituted for signs with an existing citation form. One subject confidently declared, "There is no sign in RSL [for rainbow]," and proceeded to spell R-A-I-N-B-O-W in the Russian manual alphabet. Three RSL interpreters and seventeen other signers (including the subject's daughter) confirmed the existence of an RSL sign for "rainbow." In this particular incident, it may be that fingerspelling substituted for a temporarily inaccessible sign. However, in some signed languages, even in monolingual sign use, a sign exists for a concept (e.g., CAR), yet the signer sometimes chooses to fingerspell. In this study, when subjects fingerspelled, there were no instances of the ISL manual alphabet used in place of the RSL manual alphabet, of letters from one system inserted into the other, or of vowels systematically omitted in RSL fingerspelling, as is common in ISL/Hebrew fingerspelling.

The final example of interference involves abandoned attempts. On items they failed to name, 5.3 percent of subjects indicated a desire to pass. I assume that interference of the L2 in the L1 (and perhaps frequency, too) is partly, if not largely, responsible for the momentary inaccessibility of a commonly used L1 item.

EXPERIMENTAL TASK #2

In Experimental Task #2, the animal recall task, 97 out of a total of 237 (40.9 percent) signs were miscues of some form. In this same task conducted in spoken language, Waas (1996) noticed that her subjects were unsure whether the names they offered were in the L1. Seven subjects signed the names of animals in ISL instead of RSL. These included CAT and MOUSE, forms with a relatively high degree of frequency in the L2, thus presumably explained by rapid and initial L2 access. Other ISL signs implied that the subjects' immediate environment influenced their choice of items. Species typical of the L2 locale (e.g., SNAKE, SCORPION, and CRAB) were signed in ISL, but none of these appeared in RSL, where these animals are less common.

Waas's (1996) research revealed that her subjects avoided typically Australian animals (e.g., koalas, emus, kangaroos) in German. They named an average of 10.5 animals within the sixty-second time limit. Six subjects opted out of the task before a full minute had passed. One subject stands out, for he named only four animals, all with L2 interference, and refused to complete the task. An explanation for this may lie in the subject's profile. Lavi (a pseudonym) is sixteen years old and immigrated to Israel with his parents when he was twelve. In the FSU, he attended a residential school for Deaf children for six years. He now attends an Israeli high school and is in a class for Deaf students. In class, he uses mainly Signed Hebrew, and with his classmates, he uses ISL. He lives at home with his Deaf parents, who use RSL. He said he communicates with them in a mixture of RSL and ISL. He was unable to fill out the questionnaire alone since he is no longer able to read and write Russian sufficiently. He stated that he remembered very little RSL. In his questionnaire, he said that he felt a part of Israeli culture but not of Russian culture (only one other subject indicated this). He was not even willing to reveal what his name had been in the FSU before it was changed to the name he uses in Israel, saying it was "no longer important."[12]

As lexical items, signs for animals can be difficult to analyze for interference because constructed action is often employed. In other words, the signer changes perspective and "becomes" the object signed, acting out animal movement or portrays a salient feature of that animal (e.g., ears, paws). Initially referred to as "puppeting" (Mandel 1977) because the movement is usually restricted to the hands (Coulter 1979, 2), this is more commonly referred to as constructed action (Metzger 1995; Aarons and Morgan 2003; Quinto-Pozos 2006) — the signer's construction of another's actions (Aarons and Morgan 2003). Constructed action is not limited to animate objects. In Figure 5, RSL AIRPLANE is illustrated. Also illustrated in Figure 5 is the way in which one subject employed constructed action to indicate the wings of an airplane (and the RSL sign WINGS).

The utilization of constructed action can provide additional information such as mood or emotion or give human characteristics to an inanimate object (Quintos-Pozos 2006). Its usage was perceived to stray from

FIGURE 5. AIRPLANE: *RSL* WINGS: *RSL: Miscue*

the citation form requested and thus deemed a miscue. Constructed action may be an alternative strategy utilized by signers to fill in for a momentarily inaccessible form. It enables them to demonstrate their "intention" based on the characteristics of an animal or the salient features of an object.

RESULTS

Lexical Gaps

EXPERIMENTAL TASK #1

In spite of the simple name-this-item procedure in the first task, lexical gaps were evident. Miscues included signing COMB in neutral space in front of the body at chin height rather than in its correct location close to the signer's head or hair. (In ISL, COMB is also articulated on the signer's head). Incomplete signs also appeared. One was both incomplete and ambiguous. In RSL, TRUCK comprises two parts: (1) a two-handed A handshape articulated close to the chest (as if grasping a steering wheel) and (2) the outline (made by the thumbs and index fingers) of a rectangular shape over one's shoulder. With only the initial part evident and the second half omitted entirely, the subject's sign was also CAR in RSL and ISL. This can be interpreted as a *coordinate term*. Olshtain and Barzilay's (1991) study of attrition among native Hebrew speakers in an English-speaking environment revealed the use of coordinate terms, which are linked grammatical elements of equal status. For example, "rabbit" was uttered when the person really wanted to say "gopher." Table 1 compares the use of coordinate terms that were observed in this study of RSL.

The significance of visual perception in signed languages came to light with the subjects' failure to retrieve the target sign. In its place they produced anomalous variations, constructed action, miscues, or other RSL

TABLE 1. Use of Coordinate Terms in RSL

Picture Represented in the RSL Picture-Naming Task (Experimental Task #1)	Coordinate Terms (Miscues) Produced by Subjects in RSL
ARMCHAIR	BENCH
BUS	CAR[a]
	TAXI
TEACUP (with saucer)	DRINKING GLASS[b]
	HOT TEA
FEET (from the ankles down)	LEGS
	LEGS
	LEGS
	LEGS
	LEGS[c]
ROOSTER	HEN[d]
SANDWICH	HAMBURGER
BICYCLE	MOTORCYCLE
TRUCK	CAR

Each of the forms in the left-hand column exists as a commonly known sign in RSL.
a. The use of CAR instead of BUS and TRUCK can also be attributed to the use of constructed action in place of a specific sign.
b. Miscues such as this one could indicate cultural issues at work. Russians often drink hot tea from what is considered a drinking glass (for cold drinks) in Israel, while Israelis would be more likely to drink hot tea from a teacup with a saucer (as illustrated).
c. This was used by five different subjects and may be evidence of language contact from Hebrew. In spoken Hebrew, the same word can refer to both "legs" and "feet." It may also be due to the fact that, despite the existence of citation forms, it is not uncommon for signers to point downward to indicate "feet."
d. The picture clearly identifies a rooster with a large, red crown on its head, but for some individuals, language use as it relates to real-life experience would not prompt them to differentiate between a rooster and a hen.

signs that shared the same general shape as the target item. In some cases overlapping phonological parameters cropped up as well. AIRPLANE, for example, was produced both as the constructed action seen in Figure 5 and as a variation of this (also a constructed action), with both arms outstretched straight from the shoulder, extending beyond the conventional signing space. While acknowledging the role of visual representation in this modality and the fact that constructed action is commonly used in signed languages, the evidence also suggests that visual representation may play some part in the miscues. Additional examples, some with overlapping phonological parameters, included MUSHROOM for UMBRELLA and BRIDGE for RAINBOW.[13]

Since there is no semantic relation between an umbrella and a mushroom in one case and a rainbow and a bridge in another, one may assume the commonality is the visual representation and perception of shape. In RSL, UMBRELLA is a one-handed representation of a person holding an umbrella (as an instrumental classifier would normally be used) (Supalla 1986), as illustrated in Figure 6.[14] A satisfactory and equally accepted variation is a two-handed representation of an umbrella pole being held over one shoulder. Miscues of UMBRELLA included a 1 HC with a bent B handshape formed over the index finger to represent the shape of an umbrella (which may also be interpreted as a classifier) and the same sign again but with a thumb in place of the index finger (which the interpreters judged unacceptable). See Figure 6. Another miscue was the formation of RSL MUSHROOM, where a bent 5 handshape appeared under the bent B (Figure 6). (Regional variation did not appear to account for any of the miscues.) The observations are summarized in Table 2.

Variations of RSL RAINBOW included signs that were initiated with contact at the nondominant hand and signs that were not. This was determined irrelevant, as both are acceptable. Miscues included incorrect handshape (e.g., a G and U handshape instead of a C handshape), incorrect location (e.g., at chest height),[15] an incorrect path of movement (e.g., an ISL, not an RSL, path of movement), and an incorrect articulation of RSL BRIDGE rather than RAINBOW.[16] Figure 7 and Table 3 summarize these observations.

EXPERIMENTAL TASK #2

In Waas's (1996) use of the animal recall task, her results in spoken language ranged from "a great deal of attrition" to "little, if any at all," depending on the individual. However, she concluded that most of her subjects had "extensive difficulties in retrieving animal names in the L1" (ibid., 142). This task provided the majority of evidence for the lexical

FIGURE 6. UMBRELLA: *RSL* UMBRELLA: *Miscue* MUSHROOM: *RSL: Miscue*

TABLE 2. Articulations of RSL UMBRELLA, MUSHROOM, and RAIN-SHOWER

Sign	Handshape	Number of Hands	Location	Palm Orientation	Movement
UMBRELLA variation #1	closed A	one	over shoulder	toward the body	None
UMBRELLA variation #2	closed A	two	over shoulder	toward the body	None
UMBRELLA[a] variation #3 (classifier)	bent B over 1 handshape, contact at palm	two	over shoulder	facing down	None
umbrella	**bent B over extended thumb, contact at palm**	two	in front of signer	facing down	None
mushroom	bent B over closed 5 handshape, contact at palm	two	in front of signer	facing down	None
rain-shower	bent B	one	**next to ear**	**facing down**	**yes (fingers wiggling)**

Miscues are indicated by bold text.

a. This sign is acceptable if it is interpreted as a classifier for some type of umbrella (e.g., beach umbrella, sun umbrella).

The phonological parameter of nonmanual signals (e.g., facial expression) was not considered.

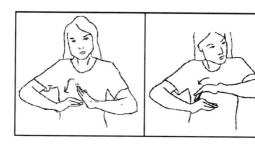

FIGURE 7. RAINBOW: *RSL: Miscue* BRIDGE: *RSL: Miscue*

TABLE 3. Articulations of RAINBOW and BRIDGE in RSL

Sign	Handshape	Location	No. of Hands	Initial Contact	Path of Movement	Orientation
RAINBOW	C handshape	forehead	one	yes (3) no (14)	left to right[a]	palm outward
RAINBOW	U handshape	forehead	one	no	left to right	palm outward
RAINBOW	G handshape	forehead	one	no	left to right	palm outward
RAINBOW	C handshape	**chest**	**two**	no	**outward from center**	palm outward
BRIDGE	**bent B handshape**	**chest**	one	yes	**right to left[a]**	**palm down**

Miscues are indicated by bold text.
a. Whether a sign moves from right to left or left to right may be influenced by the signer's preference of a dominant hand.

One subject did not sign the requested form. He declared that there was no RSL sign for "rainbow" and then fingerspelled the word.

The phonological parameter of nonmanual signals (e.g., facial expression) was not considered.

gaps in RSL. Despite the task's relatively short time limit (sixty seconds), subjects repeated animals (e.g., HORSE was mentioned twice nonconsecutively in RSL). Subjects repeated animals in both languages (e.g., MOUSE first appeared in ISL, then in RSL).

The research of Turian and Altenberg (1991) presents various methods of compensation employed by children undergoing L1 attrition. The compensation methods, as exemplified, are used by adults as well. One strategy consisted of grouping animal types together to ease the demand on the recall process. Strings included domestic animals (e.g., COW, GOAT, SHEEP, HORSE, DONKEY) and African animals (e.g., ELEPHANT, GIRAFFE, MONKEY, HIPPO, ZEBRA). One individual, after confirming comprehension of the instructions, set the list within a context and signed WHEN BOY POSS. I HAVE CHICKEN, COW, HORSE, DOG, CAT.

One subject's idiosyncratic addition of adjectives to the animals did not increase the number of items; however, it may have provided the individual with the impression that he was buying time until he could recall another item (e.g., ELEPHANT BIG, SNAKE LONG, FISH LOTS). The naming of one animal often seemed to trigger the next (e.g., JACKAL, WOLF, F-O-X, ROOSTER, CHICKEN, LION, TIGER, CAT).

Fingerspelling was more prevalent in the second task. The patterns in which it appeared suggest that fingerspelling is a strategy employed by some of the subjects to name a lexical item when the RSL sign does not readily come to mind. When subjects are pressured by a time limit, fingerspelling presumably substitutes for signs and fill lexical gaps. Subjects fingerspelled animals that others signed and vice versa. Examples included C-H-I-C-K-E-N, F-O-X, L-I-O-N, H-O-R-S-E, C-O-W, and Z-E-B-R-A. Those who fingerspelled an animal later signed the same animal; other subjects began to fingerspell but did not continue because they recalled the sign and produced it. A total of thirteen animals were fingerspelled in the RSL manual alphabet, all of which have corresponding signs. Although this could be indicative of idiosyncratic style, the evidence seems to suggest that those who fingerspelled more often may have done so because they were unable to recall the target lexical item within the time allotted.

Accompanying this task was an enhanced degree of physical unease not observed in the previous task, no doubt the result of a combination of having to retrieve L1 items that had not been accessed for some time and thus were not readily accessible, the pressure of a time limit, and the presence of a video camera directed at the signer. Some examples include holding both arms outstretched, palms up and shrugging (a familiar I-don't-know gesture common in spoken languages), as well as tapping the forehead with an index finger (which can be interpreted as attempts to trigger the memory). These may also be evidence of idiosyncratic habits. One subject apologized for his inadequate RSL skills. Additional remarks concerned memory (e.g., "I don't remember," "I forget," "I must remember"), requests for a break (e.g., "Just a minute"), and an inability or a desire not to carry out the task (e.g., "I can't do this," "That's all," "Enough!"). Furthermore, four subjects requested help from the nonparticipating addressee, the native RSL signer to whom they were signing. Waas's (1996) study of attrition revealed similar remarks, such as "Is a minute up yet?" and "I'm finished" (41).

CONCLUSION

The results of this study suggest that a signed language user who moves from one place to another, where people use a different signed language, exhibits certain reoccurring linguistic behaviors. In terms of Russian Deaf immigrants who have immigrated to Israel, if one considers ethnographic vitality, the individual experiences significant changes with regard to social, sociopsychological, and psychological factors; Deaf people who immigrate to Israel encounter numerous challenges and find their status there generally weakened. One of the most significant challenges is establishing a new identity in a new culture and community through language use.

With regard to the two data-elicitation language tasks, the Deaf immigrant signers also illustrated reoccurring behaviors, mainly in the form of miscues and temporary production errors. These appear to be connected to language contact between the different spoken and signed languages. Some evidence exists for the influence of one signed language on another. Quinto-Pozos (2002) has established that, when Mexican Sign Language and ASL came into contact with one another (in Texas), interference from one language appeared in certain domains of the other (e.g., phonology and the use of nonmanual signals). The nature of the data from this current work suggests that, when RSL and ISL come into contact, the subjects' use of RSL is affected by exposure to ISL. The data also demonstrate that it is possible to look at how first-language attrition may function in a signed language. Conclusive evidence, however, would require the systematic examination of additional variables. This preliminary examination of RSL and ISL in contact with one another demonstrates the complexity involved in examining language loss. It also adds perspective to the ways in which languages in contact are affected and how they function. Furthermore, it has implications for further research about how attrition can apply to language of a visual-gestural modality, which in turn has implications for the human capacity for language.

NOTES

1. Early work on "language decay," as it was once called, was mainly of a pathological nature (e.g., senility, aphasia, brain damage resulting from stroke or accident).

2. Workshops on first-language attrition have since been held at the Second-Language Research Forum (Madison, Wisconsin, 2000) and the Third International Symposium on Bilingualism (Bristol, United Kingdom, 2001).

3. Lexical items thought to be relatively immune to attrition include "well-learned items . . . tied to a redundant cognitive structure" (Power 1993, 230),

items learned as part of an original or unique learning experience, routinelike processes (e.g., counting, days of the week, prayers; Berko Gleason 1993), and emotion-laden words (e.g., curses, body parts, body functions; Weltens 1989).

4. The term "Former Soviet Union" refers to what was once the USSR. The more common "CIS" (Commonwealth of Independent States) does not include the three Baltic states and Georgia. Since the subjects in this study stemmed from one of those areas, CIS was not adopted.

5. This setting required that subjects switch from language to language. To reduce language interference, the questionnaire was administered between the language class and the videotaping of data, ensuring that the subjects had to move only from written Russian to RSL, without adding Hebrew and ISL.

6. The first interview was conducted with E. Slutsky, a sixty-year-old Deaf sports instructor originally from Moscow. At the time of the interview, he had lived in Israel for seven years with his Deaf daughter. Formerly employed in the FSU as a sports instructor and the administrator of a sports club, he manages Israel's only sports club for Deaf people (for both new immigrants and Israelis), which meets at the Helen Keller Center in Tel Aviv. The second interview was conducted with E. Haimov, a forty-two-year-old hearing daughter of Deaf parents, who has lived in Israel since 1988. She worked as a sign language interpreter in the FSU and is currently employed as a nurse and an RSL interpreter in Israel. Information from these interviews was transcribed and confirmed when necessary. Additional information was obtained by correspondence with M. Pursglove, cofounder of the Moscow Bilingual School for the Deaf.

7. The characteristics of an informal Deaf collective suggest that Deaf people in the FSU may form a "community." Although a lack of reference to the term "community" has been noted (Pursglove and Komorova 2002), the notion of a Deaf community in the FSU has not formally been studied.

8. Government policy in Israel, until mass immigration from the FSU, consisted of gathering new immigrants in an absorption center to ease their transition into society. Once the number of immigrants increased significantly, a policy of "direct absorption" was adopted, whereby new immigrants were placed directly into the communities in which they would live. These areas consisted mainly of development towns and outlying areas.

9. *Glasnost* was a policy introduced by Gorbachev in 1985 to encourage openness in the USSR. *Perestroika* was a system of economic and bureaucratic reforms for restructuring the USSR introduced by Gorbachev in 1987.

10. The term "calqued speech," as it is used in Russian, is not related to the linguistic process of borrowing and literally translating semantic items and word combinations from one language to another.

11. Mouthing is not connected to vocalization, which is idiosyncratic and can be related to personal style, educational background, or pragmatic

circumstances. Mouth patterns observed among the subjects can also be related to a number of sociolinguistic variables, such as culture, age, and dialect.

12. It is common practice in Israel for immigrants, especially children, to change their original Russian first names to Hebrew names.

13. The five major phonological parameters of signed languages are location, movement, handshape, orientation, and nonmanual markers (e.g., facial expressions, mouth movements). Despite the vast number of possible combinations, only those that conform to phonological constraints are permitted.

14. The use of an instrumental classifier in place of a sign was observed in this study elsewhere in the picture-naming task, specifically in TOOTHBRUSH, where, in three instances, the sign was not made with a 1 handshape but instead with a closed fist that represented holding a toothbrush.

15. As previously mentioned, although the chest may be interpreted as a reduction in location, in light of the evidence it is considered a miscue. The signer was a high school student with a higher than average rate of error. Moreover, the sign was articulated in combination with an incorrect path of movement (e.g., from a central location instead of from one side to the other) and with two hands instead of one.

16. I was unable to explain why "rainbow" might be confused with "bridge."

REFERENCES

Aarons, D., and R. Morgan. 2003. Classifier predicates and the creation of multiple perspectives in South African Sign Language. *Sign Language Studies* 3(2) (Winter): 125–56.

Abramov, I. 1993. History of the Deaf in Russia: Myths and realities. In *Looking back: A reader on the history of Deaf communities and their sign language*, vol. 20 of *International Studies on Sign Language Communication*, ed. R. Fischer and H. Lane, 199–206. Hamburg: Signum.

Allard, R., and R. Landry. 1986. Subjective ethnographic vitality viewed as a belief system. *Journal of Multilingual and Multicultural Development* 7(1): 1–12.

———. 1992. Ethnolinguistic vitality beliefs. In *Maintenance and loss of minority languages*, ed. W. Fase, 171–95. Amsterdam: John Benjamins.

Altenberg, E. 1991. Assessing first-language vulnerability to attrition. In *First-language attrition*, ed. H. Seliger and R. Vago, 189–206. New York: Cambridge University Press.

Andersen, R. 1982. Determining the linguistic attributes of language attrition. In *The loss of language skills,* ed. R. Lambert and B. Freed, 83–118. Rowley, Mass.: Newbury House.

Baker, C. 1996. *Foundations of bilingual education and bilingualism.* Philadelphia: Multilingual Matters.

———. 1999. Sign language and the Deaf community. In *Handbook of language and ethnic identity*, ed. J. A. Fishman, 122–39. New York: Oxford University Press.

Battison, R. M., and I. K. Jordan. 1976. Communication with foreign signers: Fact or fancy. *Sign Language Studies* 15: 53–68.

Bell, A. 1984. Language style as audience death. *Language in Society* 13: 145–204.

Berko Gleason, J. 1993. Neurolinguistic aspects of first-language acquisition and loss. In *Progression and regression in language: Sociocultural, neuropsychological, and linguistic perspectives*, ed. K. Hylenstam and A. Viberg, 147–77. New York: Cambridge University Press.

Bourhis, R., H. Giles, and D. Rosenthal. 1981. Notes on the construction of a subjective vitality questionnaire for ethnolinguistic groups. *Journal of Multilingual and Multicultural Development* 2(2): 145–55.

Bourhis, R., and I. Sachdev. 1984. Vitality perceptions and language attitudes: Some Canadian data. *Journal of Language and Social Psychology* 3: 97–126.

Boyes Braem, P., and R. Sutton-Spence, eds. 2001. *The hands are the head of the mouth: The mouth as articulator in sign languages.* Hamburg: Signum.

Burling, R. 1981. Social constraints on adult language learning. In *Native language and foreign language acquisition*, ed. H. Wintz, 279–90. New York: Academy of Science.

Cohen, A. 1989. Attrition in the productive lexicon of two Portuguese third-language learners. In *Language attrition in progress*, ed. K. de Bot and T. van Els, 135–50. Dordrecht, the Netherlands: Foris.

Coulter, G. 1979. American Sign Language typology. PhD diss., University of California–San Diego. Ann Arbor: UMI Dissertation Service.

Davis, J. 1989. Distinguishing language contact phenomena in ASL interpretation. In *The sociolinguistics of the Deaf community*, ed. C. Lucas, 85–102. San Diego: Academic Press.

de Bot, K., P. Gommans, and C. Rossing. 1991. First-language loss in a second language environment: Dutch immigrants in France. In *First-language attrition*, ed. H. Seliger and R. Vago, 87–98. New York: Cambridge University Press.

Dornic, S. 1978. The bilingual's performance: Language dominance, stress, and individual difference. In *Language, interpretation, and communication*, ed. D. Gerver and H. Sinaiko, 259–71. New York: Plenum.

Fishman, J. 1972. Domains and the relationship between micro- and macro-sociolinguistics. In *Directions in sociolinguistics: The ethnography of communication*, ed. J. Gumperz and D. Hymes, 435–53. New York: Holt, Rinehart, and Winston.

Freed, B. 1982. Language loss. In *The loss of language skills*, ed. R. Lambert and B. Freed, 177–86. Philadelphia: University of Pennsylvania Press.

Gal, S. 1979. *Language shift: Social detriment of linguistic change in bilingual attrition*. New York: Academic Press.

Gerner de García, B. 1995. Communication and language use in Spanish-speaking families with deaf children. In *The sociolinguistics of the Deaf community*, ed. C. Lucas, 221–52. Washington, D.C.: Gallaudet University Press.

Giles, H., R. Y. Bourhis, and D. M. Taylor, eds. 1977. *Language, ethnicity, and intergroup relations*. New York: Academic Press.

Giles, H., and J. L. Byrne. 1982. An intergroup approach to second language acquisition. *Journal of Multilingual and Multicultural Development* 3(1): 17–40.

Godsall-Myers, J. E. 1981. The attrition of language skills in German classroom linguals: A case study. Abstract in *Dissertation Abstracts International*.

Gonzo, S., and M. Saltarelli. 1983. Pidginization and linguistic change in emigrant languages. In *Pidginization and creolization as language acquisition*, ed. R. Andersen, 181–97. Rowley, Mass.: Newbury House.

Goodglass, H., and E. Kaplan. 1983. *The assessment of aphasia and other neurological disorders*. Baltimore: Williams and Wilkins.

Goodman, K. 1986. *What's whole in whole language?* Portsmouth, N.H.: Heinemann.

Grenoble, L. 1992. An overview of Russian Sign Language. *Sign Language Studies* 7 (Winter): 321–38.

Grosjean, F. 1982. *Life with two languages*. Cambridge, Mass.: Harvard University Press.

———. 1989. Neurolinguists beware! The bilingual is not two monolinguals in one person. *Brain and Language* 36: 3–15.

Hamers, J. F., and M. H. A. Blanc. 2000. *Bilinguality and bilingualism*, 2d ed. New York: Cambridge University Press.

Hansen, L. 1999. Not a total loss: The attrition of Japanese negation over three decades. In *Second-language attrition in Japanese contexts*, ed. L. Hansen, 142–53. New York: Oxford University Press.

Hutz, M. 2004. Is there a natural process of decay? A longitudinal study of language attrition. In *First-language attrition: Interdisciplinary perspectives on methodological issues*, ed. M. Schmidt, B. Kopke, M. Keijzer, and L. Weilmar, 189–207. Philadelphia: John Benjamins.

Ignatova, I. 1996. Sign language as an additional means of education in a traditional school for the deaf. In *Deaf children and bilingual education*, ed. G. Zaitseva, 75–79. Moscow: Zagrey.

Kaufman, D., and M. Aronoff. 1991. Morphological Disintegration and Reconstruction, In *First language attrition,* ed. H. Seliger and R. Vago, 175–188, Cambridge: Cambridge University Press.

Kautz, J. 2004. *The RSL dictionary: The Russian Sign Language project.* Stanford University, Stanford Digital Language Laboratory, Stanford, California, January 21, 2006. http://www.stanford.edu/group/ll/data2/rsl.

Kennedy, L. 1932. The retention of certain Latin syntactical principles by first- and second-year students after various time intervals. *Journal of Educational Psychology* 23: 132–46.

Klima, E., and U. Bellugi. 1979. *The signs of language.* Cambridge, Mass.: Harvard University Press.

Komorova, A. 1994. Bilingual school for the deaf. *World Federation of the Deaf News* 7(1): 1–24.

Lambert, R., and B. Freed, eds. 1982. *The loss of language skills.* Philadelphia: University of Pennsylvania Press.

Lambert, R., and S. Moore. 1986. Problem areas in the study of attrition. In *Language attrition in progress,* ed. B. Weltens, K. de Bot, and T. van Els, 177–86. Dordrecht, the Netherlands: Foris.

Major, R. C. 1993. Sociolinguistic factors in language and acquisition of phonology. In *Progression and regression in language,* ed. K. Hyltenstam and A. Viberg, 463–78. New York: Cambridge University Press.

Mandel, M. 1977. Iconic devices in American Sign Language. In *On the other hand: New perspectives in American Sign Language,* ed. L. Friedman, 57–107. New York: Academic Press.

Metzger, M. 1995. Constructed dialogue and constructed action in American Sign Language. In *The sociolinguistics of the Deaf community,* ed. C. Lucas, 255–71. Washington, D.C.: Gallaudet University Press.

Milroy, L. 1987. *Observing and analyzing natural language.* New York: Blackwell.

Obler, L., and N. Mehecha. 1991. First-language loss in bilingual polygot aphasics. In *First-language attrition,* ed. H. Seliger and R. Vago, 53–67. New York: Cambridge University Press.

Olshtain, E. 1989. Is second-language attrition the reversal of second-language acquisition? *Studies in Second-Language Acquisition* 11: 151–65.

———, and M. Barzilay. 1991. Lexical retrieval difficulties in adult language attrition. In *First-language attrition,* ed. H. Seliger and R. Vago, 139–50. New York: Cambridge University Press.

Olshtain, E., and S. Blum-Kulka. 1989. Happy Hebrish: Mixing and switching in American-Israeli family interactions. In *Variation in second language acquisition,* vol. 1: *Discourse and pragmatics,* ed. S. Gass, C. Madden, D. Preston, and L. Selinker, 1–30. Philadelphia: Multilingual Matters.

Pavlenko, A. 2002. Poststructuralist approaches to the study of social factors in L2. In *Portraits of the L2 user,* ed. V. Cook, 331–54. Philadelphia: Multilingual Matters.

Polinsky, M. 1995. American Russian: An endangered language. University of California at San Diego, Jan. 21, 2006. http://ling.ucsd.edu/polinsky/pubs/american-russian.

Power, Des, 1993. Very long term retention of first language without rehearsal: A case study, In *Applied Cognitive Psychology,* vol. 7, 229–237.

Pursglove, M. 1995. The silent majority: Deaf people in Russia since 1991. In *The new Russia,* ed. M. Pursglove, 49–59. London: Intellect Books.

———, and A. Komorova. 1991. The Deaf in Russia: Some current issues. *Rusistika* 4(12): 5–9.

———. 1996. *The changing world of Russia's Deaf communities.* Washington, D.C.: Gallaudet University Press.

———. 2002. The changing world of the Russian Deaf community. In *Many ways to be deaf,* ed. L. Monaghan, K. Nakamura, C. Schmaling, and G. Turner, 249–60. Washington, D.C.: Gallaudet University Press.

Quinto-Pozos, D. 2002. Contact between Mexican Sign Language and American Sign Language in two Texas border areas. University of Texas–Austin. Ann Arbor: UMI Dissertation Services.

———. 2007. Can constructed action be considered obligatory? *Lingua* 117(7): 1285–314.

Romaine, S.1989. *Bilingualism.* New York: Blackwell.

Schoenmakers–Klein Gunnewiek, M. 1983. The use of person deixis by Portuguese migrants. In *Proceedings of the International Conference on Language Attrition.* University of Amsterdam, August 17–20.

Seliger, H. W. 1991. Language attrition: Reduced redundancy and creativity. In *First-language attrition,* ed. H. W. Seliger and R. M. Vago, Introduction. New York: Cambridge University Press.

Selinker, L. 1972. Interlanguage. *International Review of Applied Linguistics* 10: 209–31.

Sharwood-Smith, M. 1983. On explaining language loss. In *Language development at the crossroads,* ed. S. Felix and H. Wode, 45–59. Tübingen, Germany: Narr.

Siple, P. 1973. *Constraints for a sign language from visual perception data.* La Jolla, Calif.: Salk Institute.

Supalla, T. 1986. The classifier system in American Sign Language. In *Noun classes and categorization,* ed. C. Craig, 181–214. Amsterdam: John Benjamins.

Sutton-Spence, R., and P. Boyes Braem. 1998. *The hands are the head of the mouth: Workshop on mouthings and mouth gestures.* Leiden, Germany. http://www.sign-langua.uni-hamburg.de/intersign/Workshop2/Braem_Spence.html.

Tarone, E. 1980. Communication strategies: Foreign talk and repair in interlanguage. *Language Learning* 30: 417–31.

Turian, D., and E. Altenberg. 1991. Compensatory strategies of child first-language attrition. In *First-language attrition*, ed. H. Seliger and R. Vago, 207–26. New York: Cambridge University Press.

van Uden, A. 1970. *A world of language for deaf children*. Rotterdam: Rotterdam University Press.

Waas, M. 1996. *Language attrition downunder: German speakers in Australia*. New York: Lang.

Weltens, B. 1989. *The attrition of French as a foreign language*. Dordrecht, the Netherlands: Foris.

———, and Grendal, M. 1993. Attrition of vocabulary knowledge. In *The bilingual lexicon*, ed. R. Schreuder and B. Weltens, 135–56. Amsterdam: John Benjamins.

Yukawa, E. 1996. L1 Japanese attrition: Three case studies of early bilingual children. Paper presented at the symposium on language attrition in cross-linguistic perspective at the Eleventh World Congress of Applied Linguistics, University of Jyväskylä, Jyväskylä, Finland, August 4–9.

Zaitseva, G. and S. Gregory. 1995, Developing collaborative research projects in bilingual education: Russia and the UK, In *Proceedings of the 18th International Congress in the Education of the Deaf*, 22–26. Tel Aviv: Ramot.

Zaitseva, G. 1996. The use of different language means in the bilingual approach. In *Deaf children and bilingual education: Proceeding of the International Conference on Bilingual Education of Deaf Children*, 162–68. Moscow: Zagrey.

———, M. Pursglove, and S. Gregory. 1999. Vygotsky, sign language, and the education of deaf pupils. *Journal of Deaf Studies and Deaf Education* 4(1) (Winter): 9–15.

Part 4 Foreign Assistance and Language Contact

Albanian Sign Language: Language Contact,

International Sign, and Gesture

Karin Hoyer

After World War II, Albania was the most inaccessible country in Europe. The Communist regime under the longtime party leadership of Enver Hoxha was characterized by isolation from the rest of the world, propaganda, and political persecution. When people adjusted their TV antennas to illegally receive broadcasts from Yugoslavia and Italy, deaf people were sometimes able to get a glimpse of Italian signed news programs. Manipulation of one's TV antenna was, however, a very dangerous act because one never knew who in the neighborhood was spying for the regime. A suspicious-looking antenna was enough of a crime to result in imprisonment.

Living in Communist Albania was a challenge for everyone. Moreover, the lives of deaf people were, to a great extent, determined by the rules set by hearing people, who regarded visual communication in public as shameful. Many deaf people were thus socially isolated within their hearing family. An important consequence of this was that no Deaf community emerged despite the fact that a school for deaf children was founded in the 1960s. According to Andoni, Shabani, and Baçi (2003), the collapse of Communism and the opening up of the country in the 1990s enabled linguistic minorities to come out of the woodwork and become visible in Albanian society. The end of the isolation meant freedom to move about the country and to think freely. For deaf people, this new era signaled the genesis of a community and the rapid development of a language that has come to be known as Albanian Sign Language (AlbSL).

In this chapter, I discuss the post-Communist situation in Albania with regard to deaf people and Albanian Sign Language, including the recent development of AlbSL as a result of its contact with International Sign. I also discuss the relationship between conventional, emblematic gestures in use among Albanian hearing people and their apparent influence on the signs of AlbSL.

In this section, I provide a short overview of the recent history of Albania, the situation of deaf people there during the Communist regime, and the recent and current state of deaf education. I also discuss the establishment of a Deaf organization after the opening up of the country and its activities during the first five years of the new millennium.

A Balkan country, Albania is situated north of Greece, east of Italy (on the other side of the Adriatic Sea), south of Serbia and Montenegro, and west of the former Yugoslavian Republic of Macedonia (FYR Macedonia). Modern Albania, which has a long and belligerent history, was first inhabited in the centuries before Christ. After enduring several invasions and the rule of various conquerors, the people of the region in 1912 proclaimed their independence (Prifti 2002). During World War II, the country was occupied by Italy, and after the war, the Communist Party in Albania seized power.

In the 1990s, the opening up of the country was characterized by political and economic instability. The Democratic Party, the first non-Communist party in the postwar era, was founded in 1990. In 1997, collapsing pyramid schemes caused rioting all around Albania. In 1999, in response to the Serbs' attack on ethnic Albanians in Kosovo, NATO started an air war in neighboring former Yugoslavia. Hundreds of thousands of Kosovar refugees crossed the border into Albania and were welcomed into the homes of Albanians as a token of the strong tradition of hospitality of these long-suffering people. Today, Albania is taking its first tentative steps toward real democracy — hoping for future membership in the European Union.

The population of Albania is about 3.2 million.[1] According to SIL Ethnologue, the majority of the population claims Standard Albanian (Tosk) as their mother tongue. Spoken minority languages are Gheg (an Albanian variety spoken in the northern part of the country), Greek, Macedonian, Romani, Romanian, and Serbian. The Albanian National Association of the Deaf (ANAD) estimates the deaf population to be about three thousand, but no reliable numbers are available.

During the Communist regime, deaf education was rooted in oralism. An elementary school for deaf children was established in the capital of Tirana in 1963. However, many deaf children from poor families in mountain villages have never had a chance to attend this boarding school. They still live isolated from other deaf people, hidden by parents who consider their deafness a shameful punishment from higher forces.[2]

In addition to spoken Albanian, teachers, at least in part, also used fingerspelling in the classroom. According to the executive director of ANAD, Eduard Ajazi, a former student of the school in Tirana, the school's teachers visited the Soviet Union in the 1960s to obtain training in deaf education within an oralist philosophy. Pursglove and Komarova (2003, 257) maintain that, in the Soviet Union, "the oral tradition predominated, especially after Stalin appeared to advocate for it in 1950." In the Soviet era, sign language was not allowed in the classroom, although fingerspelling was used. In the 1970s (before Albania's alliance with China collapsed in 1978), the school collaborated with China. The school in Tirana is still the only educational institution for deaf people in Albania.

After finishing their schooling, the majority of the pupils usually returned to their homes in the countryside and no longer socialized with other deaf people. This was especially true for the deaf women, who were guarded in their homes by their fathers and brothers and later by their husbands or sons. However, deaf men living in the same cities or villages would meet with each other (Eduard Ajazi, pers. comm., March 10, 2005). Before Communism collapsed in 1990 and ANAD became an active organization at the beginning of the new millennium, the deaf people of Albania did not gather in an organized way on a regular basis.

The isolation and lack of interaction were the result of several factors. During the Communist era, no one was encouraged to think or act freely; on the contrary, such independence was actively prohibited. Moreover, attitudes toward people with disabilities were negative. Andoni, Shabani, and Baçi (2003) show that even a declaration of belonging to a certain linguistic minority group (e.g., Romas, Egyptians, Bosnians, Serb-Montenegrins) was too daring and could entail negative social and political consequences. In addition, the Communist regime did not allow the population to move around freely within the country.

In 1993, ANAD was established, and in 1996, it became a member of the World Federation of the Deaf. But it was not until deaf Albanians contacted the Finnish Association of the Deaf (FAD), which resulted in a cooperative agreement between FAD and ANAD, that ANAD became an active organization. In 2000, an Organizational Support Project, funded by the Finnish Ministry for Foreign Affairs, was launched within ANAD.[3] In 2000, a group of five deaf Albanians visited Finland and

FAD for two weeks. Eduard Ajazi, who was one of the members of the group (pers. comm., March 10, 2005), commented about the eye-opening experience of coming from formerly isolated Albania and encountering many new concepts through his interaction with an almost one-hundred-year-old Deaf organization. Unknown to many deaf Albanians was a whole new world of ways to run an organization democratically (e.g., the process of decision making, financial management, and activities such as advocacy work). Also, seeing the equipment (e.g., visual or vibrating alarms) used by deaf people in some countries was another novel experience. These new domains of knowledge led to a need for linguistic signs that did not yet exist in their vocabulary. This need became even more urgent when ANAD began implementing the organizational training provided by the advisors from abroad.

I have been working as a sign linguist for FAD since October 2002 and am responsible for advising and training deaf (and hearing) Albanians in planning, organizing, and implementing sign language work within ANAD.[4] The long-term goal of this work is to improve the status of AlbSL so that it will be recognized as the first language (i.e., primary language or mother tongue) of deaf people. One of the objectives of the project was to document sign language use on video and to publish a description of part of the lexicon. A videocassette and a booklet dictionary titled *Gjuha e Shenjave Shqipe* 1 [Albanian Sign Language 1], containing about 250 sign entries and signed example sentences, were released in 2005. For the documentation of the language and the publication, I worked with two deaf Albanian research assistants, Brunilda Karaj and Florjan Rojba, as well as a group of fifteen deaf persons from different parts of Albania.

At present, AlbSL is not acknowledged at any official level, and it does not receive any institutional support whatsoever. Because it is not used in any official domains, its use is not tied to any political or economic power. There are no professional sign language interpreters in Albania, and within ANAD only two hearing persons have received some basic interpreter training through the Organizational Support Project.* No hearing adult children of deaf adults who sign have been found; if there are any, presumably they could function in some capacity as interpreters. Albanian Sign Language is used only within the emerging Deaf community.

*However, after a lot of lobbying, funding was arranged for a two-year interpreter training project, which started in Spring 2007.

THE TRANSITION FROM TRADITIONAL VISUAL-GESTURAL MEANS OF A COMMUNICATION BASED ON FINGERSPELLING TO A MORE EXTENSIVE USE OF ALBANIAN SIGN LANGUAGE

In this section, I discuss observations made during sign language work of the traditional visual-gestural means of communication based on fingerspelling, as well as the expansion of the sign vocabulary and language use of deaf people in Albania today. I suggest that the absence of a Deaf community during the Communist regime impeded the development of a full-fledged sign language. In addition, I discuss possible consequences of external language-planning activities when not enough indigenous language users are involved. The section ends with a brief discussion about the name of Albanian Sign Language in Albanian.

When I arrived in Albania for the first time at the end of 2002, I was told that those who had attended the school for deaf students used to communicate with each other by fingerspelling Albanian words with a one-handed alphabet and interspersing a few signs. I call these *indigenous signs*, in contrast to the new signs that have appeared through language contact situations after the collapse of Communism.[5] Hearing teachers in the school for deaf children reported the nonexistence of any sign language in Albania; they told me that only *daktilim* ("fingerspelling") was used.

My first impression concurred with this because the deaf people who were neither frequent participants in ANAD activities nor in contact with people from the organization relied heavily on fingerspelling and mouthing of Albanian words. However, those who had been actively involved in the organizational work and received training from (or been in contact with) foreign advisors during the last three years used considerably more signs. They were mainly present and former members of the board and staff of ANAD (most of them from the capital of Tirana). Despite their more frequent use of signs, their language still lacked signs for certain semantic fields such as color and kinship terminology.

This observation of a more frequent use of signs among deaf people in Tirana is also in accord with the findings of a data collection survey that was carried out in 2003 and 2004 with 136 informants. Florjan Rojba, one of the Albanian deaf research assistants who conducted the interviews, reported that the 41 deaf interviewees from Tirana relied more on signs in their communication than did those from the provinces, who relied more on fingerspelling. When interviewing deaf people in the provinces, Rojba had to use more fingerspelling in order to be understood (pers. comm., March 30 and April 13, 2006).

Once I began my work, I found, however, that the traditional visual-gestural communication method based mainly on borrowing from Albanian (fingerspelling) had linguistic features. Evidence for this was present at all linguistic levels. At the beginning of the sign language project, we made a preliminary inventory of the handshapes in use in Albania, and here we reached full consensus among the working group members.[6] There was much discussion about indigenous Albanian signs compared to Italian or international ones, revealing a considerable degree of linguistic awareness of the signs of their own language. With regard to nonmanual signals, facial expressions were used for grammatical functions such as negation and question formation.

The members of the working group also mostly agreed on the semantics of the signs used. For instance, when we were discussing different signs for "brother," it turned out that the meaning of each sign varied. In Figure 1, VËLLAI 1 means "brother," "sister," "same," and "equal" (the difference in meaning is expressed by the mouthing derived from spoken Albanian accompanying the sign).[7] In Figure 2 VËLLAI 2 means "brother," "sister," "friend," "cousin," and "same," and in Figure 3 VËLLAI 3 (an initialized sign[8]) means only "brother."

The sign language I observed deaf Albanians using can be characterized in various ways. Full fingerspelling was not always required (sometimes only part of an Albanian word or sentence was fingerspelled). The use of fingerspelling seemed to be systematized in some way; for example, there were many lexicalized fingerspellings that were loans from Albanian (i.e., originally fingerspelled words that had gone through a lexicalization process and resulted in a sign with a reduced but fixed form). By changing the orientation of the palm (toward or away from the signer) and the direction of the hand movement (a motion from one location in signing space to another), one could modify lexicalized fingerspellings according to the subject and the object.[9] My task was to give training in lexicography, mainly on the practical methods of documenting and publishing part of a dictionary lexicon. Within the scope of our assignment, we did not have sufficient resources to perform comprehensive studies of various linguistic aspects of the language (e.g., phonology, morphology, syntax).

There is no documentation of the communication based on fingerspelling used by deaf people during the Communist regime and therefore

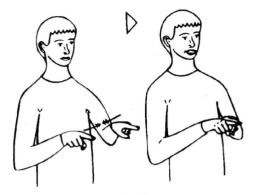

FIGURE 1. VËLLAI 1: *"brother," "sister," "same" and "equal."*

FIGURE 2. VËLLAI 2: *"brother," "sister," "friend," "cousin" and "same"*

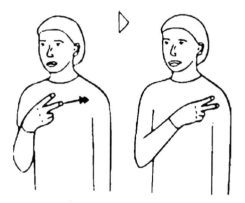

FIGURE 3. VËLLAI 3: *"brother"*

no evaluation of the linguistic status of this manner of communicating. In comparison with other signed languages, the biggest difference in this case seems to be the lack of an extensive use of signs; instead, the vocabulary is based on fingerspelling. However, AlbSL users are now developing an extended sign vocabulary. Despite the efficiency of communication between Albanian deaf people and the observed linguistic patterns, AlbSL, as used in the Albanian Deaf community in 2005, is still a developing language.[10] At all levels, idiolectal variation in AlbSL is more the rule than the exception. This became quite obvious during our sign language work. One of the aims of the dictionary publication (Hoyer and Çabej 2005) was to demonstrate examples of this variation, which was evident when we were videotaping signed example sentences for the dictionary. The signers generally did not agree on how to sign a specific sentence; they all had their own expression, and the other members of the group typically accepted their preference. The language has not yet reached a level of standardization in which all of the users can recognize a specific utterance as AlbSL and nothing else and in which everyone agrees on the lexicon and grammar.

Consequently, deaf people today use two varieties of communication; AlbSL, which makes more frequent use of signs, has greater prestige. Presently deaf people in Albania generally prefer to abandon finger-spelling. Many whom I have met expressed the joy they experienced upon learning new signs. The deaf research assistants were told the same thing when they traveled around the provinces in 2005 while delivering the dictionary to the Deaf community. They also reported that deaf people who traveled abroad for work or studies after the collapse of Communism have changed the way they communicate and that the frequency of fingerspelling has decreased. Florjan Rojba has told me that, when these people return to Albania on vacation, they use many signs that have originated in the country to which they have moved (e.g., Greece, Italy, Germany, the United States).

Why is the Deaf community so eager to abandon the fingerspelling tradition? Why does a method of communication based on signs have greater prestige? There are no known studies that might illuminate the reasons for this change; therefore, I can only refer to discussions with Albanian deaf people and make general assumptions. Signing is said to be easier and quicker than fingerspelling, and the message may be more clearly transmitted through signs than fingerspelling. At the same time, I also believe that the pride reflected by the new Deaf identity is the main reason for abandoning fingerspelling. A comment made by Florjan Rojba illustrates a commonly held belief: "We want to use signs like the Deaf in all other countries." It means that the extensive use of signs, as in other signed languages deaf Albanians have come in contact with, is a mark of membership in a transnational Deaf community. It symbolizes the abandonment of the isolating Communist era and its oppression of Albanian deaf people.

The active development and use of AlbSL can be tied to the association of ANAD in the capital city of Tirana. The most typical user of Albanian Sign Language today is a deaf male, aged twenty to forty, living in Tirana, and frequently taking part in ANAD activities. The younger generation of deaf people in Tirana is also starting to use AlbSL when communicating with their hearing children, leading to a new generation of CODAs.

The most common profile of the deaf user of the traditional finger-spelling is a middle-aged deaf woman with little or no contact with ANAD and living isolated in a village in the Albanian countryside. During the first-ever conference for deaf women in Albania, which took place in October 2004, I noticed that not all of the deaf women in the audience understood the presentations given in AlbSL. To accommodate them, summaries of the talks were given in fingerspelling. In addition, the need for interpreters who use only fingerspelling during the national conferences arranged by ANAD has been discussed. Albanian deaf people themselves are very aware of the divided communication situation. Thus, during the last few years, deaf people have been coming together more frequently, and the use of AlbSL has started to spread from Tirana to the countryside.

During the past few years, the expansion of the vocabulary of AlbSL has likely taken place because, although the traditional communication based on fingerspelling was not just a manual code of spoken Albanian, it was not a full-fledged language either. As I see it, the Communist era reflects two important factors that affect the development of the language. The restricted method of communication reflected the absence of a community in which a signed language could flourish; at the same time, the limited language use and the restricted world of concepts were also the result of the harsh political and social climate in this extremely isolated country.

Since the opening up of Albania, the language use of deaf people has also become freer. The new era has created opportunities for deaf people to interact more extensively. Washabaugh (1986) discusses the social circumstances that affect language acquisition and development. Through studies of Providence Island Sign Language (PSL), he suggests that a complete and mature sign language will not necessarily develop even if deaf people interact with one another and children have access to sign language input and are not prohibited from signing by their hearing parents. Washabaugh claims that PSL has a more context-dependent lexicon and syntax than full-fledged sign languages. He argues that something in the social relationship between deaf and hearing persons impedes language acquisition and inhibits the development of a mature sign language.

Deaf people experience paternalism and victimization at the hands of the hearing community and are socially isolated within their hearing families. This results in an unbalanced power relationship and an attitude in which deaf people prefer interaction with hearing people to contact with other deaf people. On Providence Island, many deaf people are forced to interact mostly with hearing people also for geographical reasons. Interactions among deaf people are often characterized by miscommunications. They do not form their own communities either within or between villages. Deaf children are not raised to become culturally Deaf; instead, they grow up to identify with hearing people and aspire to become like them. Washabaugh maintains that appropriate social circumstances are a prerequisite for full language acquisition and development. This will not happen if the language users do not have an identity as members of a community that defines itself as a group with a language of its own.

The plight of deaf Albanians during the Communist era is somewhat similar to the situation Washabaugh describes. The strong family ties during the hardships of that period led deaf people in Albania to rely on interactions with their hearing families. However, with regard to education and communication, the Albanian case is different from that of Providence Island. In Albania, a school for deaf children has been in operation since 1963; consequently, deaf children have lived together in an organized way, and some of them have kept in touch after leaving school.

The fingerspelling used by the teachers was the model for communication among the deaf pupils. This was not the case on Providence Island, where no school for deaf children existed. Instead, hearing people used signs in communications with deaf people, therefore making some communication possible. In Albania, hearing people did not sign, but the use of gestures in Albanian culture (discussed later) ensured at least some communication between hearing and deaf people. Since deaf people are usually in the minority in any community, they are surrounded by a hearing majority using spoken language. However, hearing people often use gestures associated with their spoken utterances, and this fact likely influences the form of an emerging sign language. Still, in the case of both Providence Island and Albania, the common denominator that impedes the development of a full-fledged sign language appears to be the lack of a community. In Albania, the absence of a community can be ascribed to the strict rules that limited interactions during the Communist regime. The political change in Albania and the international contacts that have arisen since the end of the 1990s have greatly contributed to the emergence of a Deaf community. The latter have also influenced the form of the language, especially the vocabulary, which has grown rapidly.

Nicaragua is another example. There, societal attitudes that led to the isolation of deaf individuals were one factor that impeded the formation of a Deaf community until the late 1970s (Senghas and Coppola 2001). The genesis and rapid development of Nicaraguan Sign Language is well documented and goes hand in hand with the development of the educational system for deaf children. Senghas and Coppola describe the significant role the child learners played in the creation and development of the spatial grammar of the language. Later cohorts of deaf children that were exposed to a partly developed language systematized it. Limitations on the input resulted in a new language developed by these later cohorts of the child learners.

One of the consequences of the ending of Albania's isolation was that the country received international aid in different forms. Some of the assistance was directed to the school for deaf children, and an attempt was made to introduce sign language into deaf education. The publication *Libër me shenja* [Book with Signs], containing 360 signs to be used at the school, was published in 1996 with Dutch support. *Libër me shenja*, however, was apparently not a success in the Albanian Deaf community. One problem may have been that practically no deaf people were involved in creating the book — a classic example of how language planning can go wrong. New words or signs can rarely be coined by outsiders; they should instead emerge into a language through its users.

The adult Deaf community firmly rejected *Libër me shenja*. In 2002, after the book was reviewed by three different groups of deaf people in Tirana (on the initiative of ANAD), it was found to contain numerous invented or foreign signs that had never been used in Albania. However, because some of the hearing teachers at the school were starting to use it, some of the signs (which had not previously been in use in Albania) have become a part of the AlbSL vocabulary of today's younger generation.

Before the sign language work started, even the name of Albanian Sign Language had no fixed form; it was alternatively referred to as "Gjuha shenjave e shqip" [literally, "language sign of Albania] or "Gjuha shqip e shenjave" ["language of Albanian sign"]. The two names were considered equally acceptable even if the latter gives the incorrect impression that it is a signed version of Albanian. Deaf people refer to the language simply as "signing." As a result of the increased linguistic knowledge made possible by the sign language work, the Albanian name in use today is Gjuha shenjave e shqip.

The name of a language is an important statement of language policy, as is evident in Berenz's (2003, 180) description of the beginning of the use of the term "língua de sinais" [sign language] for Brazilian Sign Language instead of "mímica" [mimicry], which the language was called up to that time. The choice of the name occurred at the same time a political decision highlighted the equal linguistic status of spoken and signed languages.

CONTACT WITH INTERNATIONAL SIGN

In his discussion of the sociocultural setting of language contact, Weinreich (1970) mentions language proficiency, specialization in the use of each language, the manner of learning each language, and attitudes toward the languages as factors at the individual level. At the community level, the crucial issues are the size of the bilingual group, demography, political and social relations, and prestige. In this section, I discuss language proficiency and attitudes toward languages among Albanian deaf individuals and the way in which issues such as prestige and social relations have affected the outcome of such contact in Albania. I also describe the circumstances and effects of contact with International Sign, including signs borrowed for new concepts and changes in indigenous signs. At the end of this section, I discuss a nonindigenous way of coining new signs and present the first impressions of two native Auslan users of the communication among deaf Albanians in relation to International Sign.

International Sign is used by deaf signers who do not share a common sign language. Socially, it functions somewhat as a pidgin language in that it fosters communication between people who use different sign languages. However, a study of the linguistic status of International Sign by Supalla and Webb (1995) revealed that it has complex structures that can be compared to those found in full-fledged sign languages. They found systematic patterns of word order, markers of negation, and verb agreement patterns that are more similar to those found in creoles and in full sign languages than in spoken language pidgins. Supalla and Webb contend that this complexity is due to a high degree of similarity between the sign languages in contact. According to the authors, International Sign's circumstances of usage resemble those of a pidgin but is more structurally complex than a typical pidgin. Rosenstock (2004) notes that International Sign can more appropriately be defined by its function than by its linguistic status since there are no native users of International Sign. It can be seen as a communication system with the purpose of conveying meaning, and it is used as a lingua franca in the international Deaf community. Rosenstock adds, however, that the label "lingua franca" depends greatly on its users' comprehension of the system. In the case of deaf Albanians, the almost complete absence of contact with International Sign before the 1990s prevented its use as a tool for mutual understanding between the deaf people of Albania and deaf people elsewhere.

Currently, AlbSL demonstrates elements of contact with International Sign, other sign languages, and Albanian. Due to their reliance on traditional fingerspelling, many Albanian deaf people know written Albanian to some extent. Knowledge of other signed languages and International Sign is still relatively limited since contacts abroad have been permitted for only the past fifteen years. Most of these have occurred within Albania when signing foreigners have visited the country or when deaf Albanians have returned to their homeland while on vacation after moving abroad. Exceptions to this rule are those deaf people who have been active in ANAD and have attended conferences or other events for deaf people abroad. It is still possible to see contact-induced change in AlbSL that can be traced to exposure to International Sign during the two-week trip to Finland in 2000. Four of the five deaf persons attending this trip later became members of either the ANAD staff or board and have therefore been key persons in the development of AlbSL. Additionally, television, videotapes, and the Internet enable deaf Albanians to become familiar with other signed languages.

Even though AlbSL still relies heavily on fingerspelling for signs that do not yet appear in the language, more and more signs have come into the lexicon because of the extension of the world of concepts, which creates a need for new linguistic symbols. New signs are coined through more frequent contact among the language users in the Albanian Deaf community, and the language is starting to be used in various linguistic domains. This is due to the natural evolution of a language, the need for new signs, and contact-induced change.

Much of the influence of International Sign has taken place through foreign signing advisors working within ANAD, although other sign languages also induce changes.[11] From 2000 to 2005, four different Australian advisors and I from time to time trained the staff and board of ANAD on organization management, the documenting of signed language, dictionary work, awareness of Deaf culture, and interpreter issues and skills. This means that Albanian deaf persons with close contacts to ANAD have been quite exposed to foreign influence and have therefore likely been the most active sources of language change. It is too early to estimate how established the neologisms have become in everyday language use in the provinces outside ANAD contexts. However, it seems that the tendency is for new signs to first spread throughout the capital city of Tirana and only after that through contacts between individuals or organizational events arranged by ANAD to the more distant deaf population.

According to Winford (2003), the initiators of contact-induced change may be fluent bilinguals who are highly proficient in both languages and engage in frequent code mixing. What has triggered the contact-induced change in AlbSL is, however, not a situation with widespread bilingualism among the language users. Rather, the borrowing of signs from International Sign by monolingual deaf people (with linguistic proficiency in only one *signed* language) has been motivated by a clear need. New areas of knowledge (e.g., organizational development) have led to a need for linguistic symbols for these novel concepts. Also, existing gaps in the lexicon have been filled through borrowing. This lexical modernization is similar to what Reagan (2001) maintains has been taking place in Russia. The social, economic, and political changes that occurred after the collapse of the former Soviet Union resulted in widespread lexical borrowings and innovations in Russian. In AlbSL, lexical borrowing is quite visible, whereas the problem of estimating the extent of structural borrowing has to do with the fact that the grammatical features of AlbSL have not been studied; to some extent, they may also be in a developmental stage.

Signs Borrowed for New Concepts

Since we know the sociolinguistic context and background of the language and its users, we are able to analyze the nature of the contact-induced change and examine its linguistic consequences. According to Winford (2003), borrowed items are manipulated so that they conform to the rules of the recipient language. New lexical entries may be created, and existing ones may be modified.

When starting the leadership training program of the Organizational Support Project in 2000, Colin Allen, a native deaf Auslan user, found that deaf Albanians were unable to understand him when he used International Sign. He was also not able to understand them when their communication was based on fingerspelling. To convey his message, he used a method that can be described as "acting out the message" — using pantomime and facial expressions. Many of the signs he used are commonly used in International Sign (Colin Allen, pers. comm., February 6, 2005; March 13, 2006).

In her study on International Sign, Rosenstock (2004) discusses the conventionalized International Sign vocabulary and suggests that the limited number of conventionalized signs is partly due to the fact that International Sign is used in only a few domains. Many of the signs are used in interpreted International Sign at conference settings and are within the field of deafness-related topics.

Signs have been borrowed into AlbSL from International Sign as a result of the leadership training and the visit to Finland in 2000. Many of the borrowed signs belong to a special-purpose vocabulary and are not part of the core lexicon. Examples are BORDIT ("board"), PRESIDENT ("president"), QEVERIA ("government"), BUXHET ("budget"), PROGRAM ("program"), AVOKAT ("lobby, advocate"), NDIHMON ("support, help"), VIT ("year"), MOSHË ("age"), PARLAMENT ("parliament"), VENDOS ("approve, decide"), PROBLEM ("problem"), and ANGLISHT ("English language").[12] The corresponding signs PRESIDENT, GOVERNMENT, BUDGET, PROGRAM, and PARLIAMENT in International Sign are shown in the appendix, signed by Liisa Kauppinen, president emerita of the World Federation of the Deaf.[13]

It is too early to describe the possible phonological adaptations of the signs because of both the recency of the borrowing and the dearth of phonological descriptions of AlbSL before contact. The citation forms of the signs mentioned are mainly the same as those of the corresponding ones in International Sign. The only exception is QEVERIA ("government"); the AlbSL sign is articulated with a short repeated movement toward the forehead instead of the simple straight movement away from the forehead (as in the same sign in International Sign).

When it comes to morphosyntax, however, there is an interesting example of modification with regard to numeral incorporation. In AlbSL the numbers one through five can be incorporated into VIT ("year"). Rosenstock (2004) found that numeral incorporation is almost absent in her data on International Sign. She claims that "numeral incorporation is largely based on economic considerations. Bound morphemes only develop over time and in situations where conventional symbols can replace iconic ones. Since IS is a system with no native users and lacks the historic context, it seems logical that no numeral incorporation exists" (ibid., 83).

The vocabulary of International Sign consists partly of loans from natural sign languages, and some of the signs are shared among many different sign languages (see Rosenstock 2004 for examples and a discussion of the origin of signs in International Sign). Of the thirteen signs in AlbSL borrowed from International Sign (mentioned earlier), three of them — BUXHET ("budget"), PROGRAM ("program"), and MOSHË ("age") — are also found in Finnish Sign Language. This adds further evidence to the claim that most of the signs' origins may be in International Sign since it was used during the trip to Finland in 2000, when the group of five deaf Albanians were exposed to International Sign for the first time.

Before that visit, there were no signs for these concepts; the only exception is the indigenous sign meaning "problem." The concepts were mainly expressed by fingerspelling the Albanian word or by a combination of a paraphrase (such as "director high/first" for "president") and fingerspelling. Some of the concepts, such as board, budget, and lobby/advocate, were not a part of the vocabulary of deaf people during the Communist regime. Florjan Rojba reports that many concepts still lack signs and are expressed by fingerspelling the corresponding Albanian word (e.g., "use," "need," "social," "service," "private," "original," "bank," and "guarantee"). Furthermore, AlbSL does not have signs for certain time units (e.g., days of the week or months). Instead, they are fingerspelled (sometimes only partly) and accompanied with mouth movements derived from the corresponding Albanian word.

Contact-Induced Changes in Indigenous Signs

Indigenous signs have either given way to foreign ones or undergone changes in their structure or meanings. The native sign MËSOJ ("to teach") is more frequently used with the Ô handshape (as in the corresponding sign in International Sign) than with the original ʒ handshape (Figure 4).

A homonym of RRI, which originally meant "to wait," has appeared in AlbSL due to contact with International Sign and happens to be identical in form to WORK in International Sign. Today it seems as though the sign is more frequently used to mean "to work." This type of meaning shift may be motivated by prestige since AlbSL already had a native counterpart for "to work" (see Figure 5).

Colin Allen suggests that foreign signs may have more prestige (leading to the abandonment of the native signs) because many of the latter

FIGURE 4. MËSOJ *"to teach"*

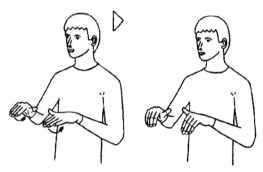

FIGURE 5. PUNOJ *"to work"*

are also used as gestures in the surrounding hearing community (e.g., "to work" in Figure 5; pers. comm., February 6, 2005; March 13, 2006). In beginning to identify themselves with the international Deaf community, Albanian deaf people might abandon a "hearing" gesture in favor of a Deaf sign. They might prefer to have signs in common with other sign languages instead of sharing their signs with the Albanian hearing community.

The signs for DEAF or DEAF PERSON also show the prestige factor associated with foreign influence. In Albanian, the words *shurdhër* ("deaf person") and *memec* ("mute," "deaf-mute") are both considered pejorative by deaf people; instead, the expression *nuk degjon* ("do not hear") is used.[14] The name of the Albanian National Association of the Deaf is Shoqata Kombëtare Shqiptare e Njerëzve që nuk Dëgjojnë (Association of National Albanian People Who Do Not Hear).

Albanian Sign Language has many variants of DEAF. The indigenous ones are the following:

1. The index finger moves into contact with the mouth/chin + JO ("no") (the sign is articulated with a mouth movement originating in *nuk flet* ["do not speak"]).
2. The index finger moves into contact with the ear/cheek + JO (with a mouth movement originating in *nuk degjon*).
3. The index finger moves from contact with ear/cheek to contact with mouth/chin + JO (with a mouth movement originating in *nuk flet* or *nuk degjon*).

The third variant of DEAF is favored in AlbSL within ANAD settings, although it seems as though this sign is becoming shorter in form, losing its second part (JO) and acquiring a mouth movement more like [df] originating in the English word "deaf." The result is a sign that resembles DEAF in both International Sign and FinSL (the index finger first touches the ear/cheek and then the mouth/chin). This is therefore a case in which the foreign influence is seen to favor a sign that resembles one from International Sign. In addition, the influence of English is evident in the mouth movement. In her study of International Sign, Rosenstock (2004) found that some very common signs were frequently accompanied by mouth movements derived from English. Interestingly, DEAF was one of these.

A Foreign Way of Coining New Signs

The sign language work has included training for deaf people in Deaf studies and raising awareness of one's language and culture. As a result, some deaf people have now begun to object to the tendency to copy foreign linguistic features when a domestic counterpart already exists. There have been extensive ideological discussions about linguistic issues such as the abandonment of indigenous signs in favor of international ones and how to respect the AlbSL manner of coining new signs. The shorter sign for DEAF or DEAF PERSON with the mouth movement [df] (mentioned in the third variant shown earlier) is one example of a sign that has been the target of such discussions within the Deaf community.

One of the most visible consequences of the 1996 book *Libër me shenja* is that deaf people began creating numerous initialized signs. Those that the book presented (e.g., kinship signs for "mother," "father," "sister," "brother," "grandmother," "grandfather," "nephew," "niece," "uncle" [mother's brother], "aunt" [mother's sister], "uncle" [father's brother], "aunt" [father's sister]) reflected a foreign manner of creating neologisms through initializing. Before the collapse of Communism in 1990 and the subsequent opening up of the country, there existed both indigenous initialized signs and lexicalized fingerspelled signs. Of 1,240 signs that have been taken from spontaneous video data during the sign language work that began in 2003, 13 have been noted as being indigenous initialized or lexicalized fingerspelled signs. In addition to these, Florjan Rojba mentioned at least 16 more signs of this kind in common use. The place of articulation for the 29 signs that include fingerspelling is restricted to the signing space in front of the signer, which is the general place of articulation for initialized or lexicalized fingerspelled signs in AlbSL.[15]

Incorporating the first letter of the corresponding Albanian word as the handshape of the sign and combining it with a specific place of articulation other than that in front of the signer is, however, nonindigenous and new to AlbSL. Of the twelve initialized one-handed kinship signs mentioned earlier from *Libër me shenja*, four are articulated on the face and eight on the body. Even if only a few new signs from the book become established in AlbSL (the first four of the twelve kinship signs mentioned are in use today), the book seems to have influenced a new nonindigenous method of coining signs.

The initialized signs for the names of Albanian cities illustrate this new process. According to Eduard Ajazi and Colin Allen, before the year 2000, Tirana and Korçë were the only cities that had a sign, both of which were created in an indigenous manner, with handshape and movement parameters combined in the neutral space in front of the signer. The city of Fier may have had a sign articulated on the top of the head with a 5 handshape, which was later changed to an F handshape. The signs for the cities of Elbasan and Gjirokastër are also the result of this nonindigenous manner of creating neologisms. Their signs are articulated on the top of the nondominant fist with the handshape of the Albanian letters *E* and *Gj* respectively. In addition, influence from a foreign hand-alphabet is evident in the sign for the city of Durrës, which is based on the letter *D* in the two-handed alphabet used in Auslan. All of these initialized signs were created before the linguistic awareness training took place. On the other hand, new signs for cities (e.g., Lezhë, which was created after the training started) do not include initialization. This awakening loyalty to AlbSL within the Albanian Deaf community may well encourage resistance to future influence from abroad with regard to the coining of new signs.

As mentioned earlier, Colin Allen has reported that, in the year 2000, he could not make himself understood while using International Sign with deaf Albanians. Susan Emerson's first impression of communication with deaf Albanians six years later was totally different. Like Allen, Emerson is a native Auslan user and has experience with International Sign through her work as an interpreter. She compared her first impression of two different Balkan sign languages: AlbSL and the sign language used in Kosovo, an area of former Yugoslavia. Emerson found that AlbSL was easier for her to comprehend than the sign language used in Kosovo. Her immediate impression of AlbSL was that it resembled International Sign (Susan Emerson, pers. comm., February 16, 2006). This observation reveals two important issues. First, her description of AlbSL differs substantially from that of Colin Allen six years earlier. These two Auslan users met with the same deaf individuals. This difference indicates that, in the six-year interim, the language of those who were actively participating in ANAD activities had apparently changed drastically.

The second issue has to do with a plausible reason that a signing foreigner with skills in International Sign finds AlbSL to be more intelligible than the sign language used in Kosovo. The latter is a close variant of the sign language used in other former Yugoslavian areas (e.g., Serbia, Montenegro, FYR Macedonia) and is presumably older than AlbSL. The oldest school for deaf students in the Balkans, Stefan Decanski School in Belgrade, was founded as a primary school in 1896, and the Association of the Deaf and Hard of Hearing of Serbia was established in 1944 (Allen and Walters 2005). Over time, a full-fledged natural sign language developed, much like the one used in Kosovo, which is more arbitrary in form and more abstract compared to a younger sign language. The structures of a full-fledged sign language are often more nontransparent than the corresponding ones in the much younger AlbSL, which demonstrates influence from International Sign. Rosenstock (2004) discusses the different levels of the iconic structures of International Sign. One of her hypotheses with regard to the comprehension of a foreign natural sign language compared with interpreted and noninterpreted International Sign is that "a fully developed natural SL like ASL has many structures that are arbitrary and highly abstract. These are presumably harder to understand than the more iconic structures in either form of IS" (247).

In AlbSL, borrowing from International Sign has only recently begun, and it is therefore difficult to know at this stage which signs will become an established part of the language (integrated borrowing) and which will remain temporary code switching or code mixing. Furthermore, in a contact situation, lexical borrowing may vary from casual to heavy and may sometimes result in bilingual mixed languages (see Thomason 1995). Today, AlbSL is borrowing extensively; as a result, its vocabulary is expanding suddenly and rapidly. Its deaf users see their sign language as a symbol of an awakening Deaf identity. Despite this, AlbSL is not a bilingual mixed language (which is created by bilinguals), because a widespread bilingualism (i.e., proficiency in two *signed* languages) cannot be said to be prevailing within the Albanian Deaf community.

CONTACT BETWEEN HEARING AND DEAF PEOPLE: GESTURES VERSUS SIGNS

In this section, I discuss gestural behavior with a focus on conventionalized gesture use in the Albanian hearing community. I present my initial study on Albanian emblematic gestures that have a sign counterpart in AlbSL. At the end of this section a discussion follows on the relationship between idioms in spoken Albanian and emblematic gestures and signs.

Gestures can be used differently in various countries and cultures. For example, in Western countries a headshake is interpreted as a "no," but Albanians traditionally shake their head for "yes." By comparing the gestures used by two groups of immigrants to the United States (Jews from Eastern Europe and Italians from the south of Italy) and the assimilated first-generation offspring of these immigrants, Efron (1972) showed that the usage is related to one's cultural tradition. Morris et al. (1979) conducted a field study in European countries to map the geographical distribution of gestural practice. They found that many gestures have several different meanings and that they were used across both national and linguistic boundaries. That study demonstrates that Europe has regions of culturally specific gestural usage.

Definitions of Gestural Behavior

The terminology for communicative gestural behavior is somewhat diverse. Attempts have been made to define and classify gestural behavior according to its meaning, form, or function.[16] Nevertheless, Kendon (2004) maintains that a consensus exists on a core of visible body expressions that are usually referred to as gestures. Gesture is visible action that can function either as part of an utterance or as an utterance in its entirety. As he suggests, "gestures produced in relation to speech are an integral component of the communicative act of the speaker. Regardless of whether and how they contribute to the interpretation of the communicative act by others, they must be seen as part of the speaker's final product, and not as symptoms of some struggle to attain verbal expression" (359).

The lexicographic approach of Johnston and Schembri (1999) defines gesture in contrast to sign language. They distinguish between nonlinguistic visual-gestural acts (e.g., gesticulation, gesture, and mime by nonsigners) and linguistic visual-gestural acts (e.g., signs). Sutton-Spence and Woll (1999) make a distinction between extralinguistic gestures and signs according to the following criteria: Signs are part of a sign language when they do not replace or add to any other sign. They are also part of a sign language when they obey morphological rules. Gestures can be borrowed into a sign language and become signs (i.e., part of the language). They cannot constitute grammatical sentences as signs do.

Conventional gestures or *emblems* (or *emblematic gestures*) differ from general gesticulation in many respects. McNeill (1992) describes emblems as wordlike gestures that are standardized in form and meaning, which they convey even when they are produced without speech. They are culture specific and have a historical tradition within the community. Emblems are not necessarily pantomimic or descriptive, and if there are iconic features, they are traces from the past and unimportant for the current function of the emblem. Goldin-Meadow (2003) gives as examples the gestures for "thumbs up," "okay," and "shush," which can be understood within a community without context or explanation. Emblematic gestures are not necessarily transparent to those outside the community. This means that, like signs, they do not seem to depend on iconicity. Goldin-Meadow contends that gestures (except emblematic ones) used in association with speech are heavily dependent on iconicity to convey meaning.

Other authors have also written about gesture use vis-à-vis signed language. Zeshan (2003) discusses the conventional gestures that hearing people use in relation to signed languages. She asserts that they often move into the lexicon of conventional sign languages. Moreover, Sutton-Spence and Woll (1999) recognize that some signs in British Sign

Language (BSL) were most likely emblematic gestures at one time. In addition, both BSL users and English speakers use emblematic gestures that are a part of the British culture of today.

Gesture Use in the Albanian Hearing Community

In Albania, as in southern Europe in general, hearing people use their body to communicate and interact with each other in a complex and sophisticated way. Compared to the extensive use of gestures in southern Europe, Nordic people do not use gestures that often.[17] In their comparison, Morris et al. (1979) found that in Denmark, Sweden, and Norway, only 60 to 80 percent of the twenty conventional gestures studied were used, compared to Italy and Greece, where all twenty were in use. Even though Finland and Albania were not included in the study, the results support the view of a difference between northern and southern Europe in the degree of gestural use.

My first contact with Albanian gestures occurred when I arrived at the airport at Tirana. As a foreigner, I was immediately spotted and surrounded by begging children who pulled at my coat sleeves. The children spoke to me in Albanian, a language that I did not know at that time, and they used gestures I also could not interpret. One of the children used a wiggling gesture with a flat hand moving repeatedly up and down in front of his face. Later I learned that this is a conventional Albanian gesture meaning "to eat" or "food." A sign identical to it also exists in AlbSL (see Figure 6).[18]

Some of the gestures I observed hearing Albanians using were similar to those used in the cultural contexts of northern Europe and Finland.

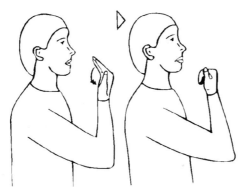

FIGURE 6. HA *"to eat," "food"*

They included gestures that depicted some of the content of what was said (e.g., specifying the size or the shape of an object or illustrating an action of some kind). Furthermore, the Albanians use pointing to visible or nonvisible referents and different kinds of gestures to structure their discourse (e.g., gestures linked to emphasis, which are often referred to as "beats/batons"; see McNeill 1992). My main interest, however, was the vocabulary of conventional gestures (i.e., emblems) used in the Albanian hearing society that were not transparent enough for me to guess the meaning from the context. This interest was due to the fact that I had started to learn AlbSL through interactions with deaf people, and I noticed that many of the conventional gestures used by hearing people were also signs in AlbSL. It seems that the AlbSL signs that resemble conventional gestures have their origins in the exposure deaf people have had to these gestures in the hearing community.

Albanian Conventional Gestures versus Signs in AlbSL: Preliminary Data

OBJECTIVES AND METHODS

As a consequence of my observations of the similarity between emblematic gestures used in the hearing community and signs in AlbSL, I elicited and analyzed some data in order to examine the possible relationship between certain gestures used by hearing Albanians and signs used by deaf Albanians. My objective was to investigate possible differences between these emblems in form, meaning, and use. I had made observations and kept notes about hearing people's use of emblematic gestures since my first arrival in Albania. By the end of 2005, I had visited the country nine times (in periods of four to eight weeks). The data are based on my observations and on several discussions about emblems with both deaf and hearing Albanians.

In addition, I collected data during interviews with two hearing informants who were unfamiliar with AlbSL. The informants were asked to list all of the gestures conveying meaning that they could think of in use among hearing people in Albania. In order to obtain complete information about emblematic gestures, I asked additional questions about gestures for a specific Albanian word. I also queried the informants about the use and the form of the gestures they produced. The form, meaning, and use of twenty emblematic gestures were compared to the corresponding sign and were discussed and analyzed together with the deaf research assistants involved in the sign language work.

ANALYSIS AND RESULTS

Some of the gestures in the interview data were also in use in the Nordic cultural context (e.g., the index finger to the lips for "be quiet" and the shrugging of one's shoulders for "I don't know").[19] However, the focus of the data analysis was culture-specific, nontransparent emblematic gestures, so all iconic gestures imitating an action were excluded. The emblematic gestures that were analyzed are presented in Table 1. Some of the observations and a few examples are presented here. The results seem to indicate that all of the emblematic gestures presented in Table 1 are in use by the Albanian hearing community and correspond to a sign with a similar form in AlbSL. Some of the gestures showed no difference from the corresponding sign (e.g., see Figure 7, MIRË ["good"], where the orientation of the palm can vary in both the gesture and the sign).

This does not necessarily mean that no difference whatsoever exists. Further studies are needed to analyze possible differences in meaning and

TABLE 1. Twenty emblematic gestures in Albania with a similar counterpart in AlbSL

Lexical Counterpart of the Gesture	English Translation
BUDALLA	"foolish," "crazy"
BUKUR	"beautiful"
BURG	"prison," "be imprisoned"
FALEMINDERIT	"thank you"
FËMIJË	"child"
HA	"to eat," "food"
NUK-FLET	"not on speaking terms"
KEQ	"bad"
KOKËBOSH	"empty headed," "incompetent"
KOKËFORTË	"hard headed," "obstinate"
MENDJEMADH	"arrogant," "conceited"
MËRZITUR	"worried"
MIRË	"good," "fine," "well"
POSHTËR	"vile," "base," "low," "indecent"
PUNOJ	"to work"
RRAH	"to beat"
SHKOJ	"to go"
TURP	"shame"
URI	"hunger," "to be hungry"
VONË	"to be late"

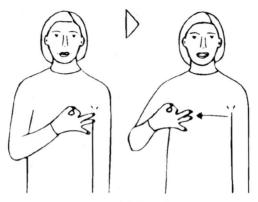

FIGURE 7. MIRË *"good," "nice"*

use. For example, FALEMINDERIT can mean "thank you," "please," and "excuse me"; this is not necessarily the case, however, for the corresponding gesture, where "thank you" seems to be the most common meaning. The gesture HA ("to eat," "food") in Figure 6 is articulated with a repeated movement, while observed patterns for this sign in AlbSL appear generally to indicate a reduction in the number of repetitions within a sentence. The sign BUKUR ("beautiful") can be applied to anything beautiful, whereas the most common use of the gesture is to refer to beautiful women.

It is too early to make blanket statements about the differences between the emblematic gestures and their corresponding signs. Since AlbSL is still under development, a wide range of variation is tolerated. The situation clearly needs to be examined again in the near future to determine how the process is unfolding. However, in some cases, differences are already clearly visible. Even if emblematic gestures are generally restricted in form, they become even more so when borrowed into a sign language and become units in a linguistic system. Zeshan (2003, 132–39) discusses the formational aspect in the lexicalization process. With increasing lexicalization, variation in the form is eliminated, and the form becomes more fixed. In the case of MENDJEMADH ("arrogant," "conceited"), the handshapes of the gesture may be a B handshape with thumb extended, a Y handshape, an L handshape, an X handshape, or a G handshape. In addition, the G handshape may be oriented either vertically or horizontally, while in the latter case, the orientation of the palm can be either upward or downward. For the corresponding sign (see

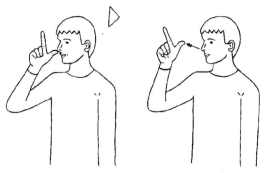

FIGURE 8. MENDJEMADH *"arrogant," "conceited"*

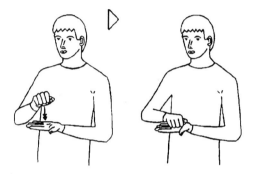

FIGURE 9. KOKËBOSH *"empty-headed,"*
"incompetent"

Figure 8), a smaller set of handshapes is accepted; only the L and Y hand-shapes are allowed.

Reduction in form also applies to KOKËBOSH ("empty headed," "in-competent"). The place of articulation is more flexible for the gesture than for the sign. According to the deaf informants, the most common place of articulation (among hearing people) for this gesture is on one's own head. If two speakers are both socially and physically close, the gesture may be jokingly articulated on the other person's head. The gesture can also be ar-ticulated toward a tabletop or against the palm of the nondominant hand. The deaf informants reported that, for this sign (see Figure 9), the younger deaf generation most commonly uses the palm of the nondominant hand as the place of articulation. This means that, in the borrowing process, more signlike features win, the result being a two-handed sign with the nondominant hand taking on the role of the tabletop.

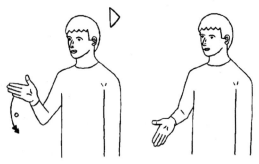

FIGURE 10. RRAH *"to beat"*

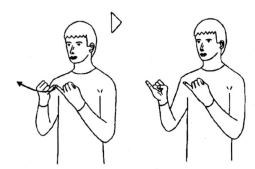

FIGURE 11. NUK-FLET *"not on speaking terms."* There exist also an alternative form that is one-handed and the starting point for the movement is at the mouth rather than the pinky of the nondominant hand.

In the case of RRAH ("to beat"), the transition from an emblematic gesture to a sign is most clearly seen in the morphosyntactic pattern. The gesture cannot be modified according to subject or object, but the verbal sign may be directionally inflected and is signed with a different orientation of the hand and with a movement toward the signer to mean "you beat me" (the citation form is shown in Figure 10).

NUK-FLET ("not on speaking terms") is an example of a difference in use between the gesture and the sign. They both have the same variation in form, but the gesture appears to be used primarily by children. The sign, however, is used by adults as well (see Figure 11).

Some of the processes (e.g., simplification, symmetricalization) are similar to ones that take place when complex visual depictions change into signs in a signed language.[20]

Due to the absence of a Deaf community during the Communist era in Albania, deaf people socialized with hearing people to a great extent, and communication was thus significantly influenced by the gestures they used. Deaf people who had attended the deaf school communicated mainly through fingerspelling and with the use of only a few signs. The claim that many of these signs seem to be those originating in the emblematic gestures used in the surrounding hearing community is supported by this initial study. Washabaugh (1986, 85–87) reports that the deaf residents of Providence Island also use emblems. Those used by hearing people were important for the deaf residents when they were trying to make sense of the spoken communication in the surrounding community. Washabaugh found that all of the emblems used by the hearing people had become signs used by deaf residents.

Researchers have recently been addressing the relationship between gestures and the structures used in sign languages. For example, Casey (2003) suggests that role shift and directionality in signed languages have a gestural origin. Because of the visual modality of sign language, it is not always easy to distinguish the linguistic from the nonlinguistic elements. This holds true especially for the present situation in Albania, where a transition from gesture to sign is under way.

The question of the distinction between signers' use of signs versus gesture is also interesting. Sutton-Spence and Woll (1999, 167) suggest that, "In the broadest sense, just as words are 'audible gestures,' signs are visible gestures with conventional form and meaning and which obey specific formational rules. Just as speakers may make sounds outside spoken language, some pantomimic signing may move signs out of signing space, so it is hard to know where to draw the line between signs and gestures." In the discussion about whether signers use gestures when they sign, Duncan (2003) describes three possible ways in which gestures might occur in a signed utterance: Gestures and signs may be coproduced, gestures may be interspersed with signs, and gestures may be produced by articulators other than those used to articulate signs.

Signs are units that belong to an agreed-upon lexicon in a codified linguistic system that includes a specific grammar, whereas emblematic gestures generally are not. In his study on contact between Mexican Sign Language and American Sign Language, Quinto-Pozos (2002) notes that the data revealed several emblems that were used by hearing people in both Mexico and the United States. Some of them were included in sign language dictionaries, where they were listed as signs. He discusses the need to examine the linguistic characteristics of commonly used gestures within a sign stream in order to define their lexical status.

In a similar way, the emblem-sign comparison discussed here raises several questions about the lexical status and pragmatic aspects of the emblems and the corresponding signs that future research might address.

Some of these issues are the following: How are Albanian deaf people using the emblematic gestures in communication with hearing people? Does their usage vary according to whether they are a part of basic gestural communication with hearing people or function as units of a linguistic system? Do the gestures become signs as soon as one deaf person addresses another deaf person, even if the second person has until then been relying on gesturing and just recently started to learn AlbSL? When does a hearing person who is learning to sign stop using the emblematic gesture and start using it as a sign? And how about foreigners, second language users who use them with both hearing and deaf people — are they signing or gesturing?

RELATIONSHIP BETWEEN EMBLEMS AND IDIOMS IN SPOKEN LANGUAGE

The lack of a written tradition for the use of both gesture and sign language makes etymology and the change in form and meaning of both gestures and signs difficult to study. What can be said about the origin of the conventional gestures that end up becoming transformed into signs? Two of the emblematic gestures from the emblem-sign study reveal something about the contact between gesture and speech. The form of the emblematic gestures and AlbSL signs MËRZITUR ("worried") and FËMIJË ("child") seems to have originated in Albanian idioms (see Figures 12 and 13).

The former gesture, MËRZITUR, is no longer known by everybody in the younger generation, and it is reported to be used more among elderly people. It can also be articulated slightly in front of the face, without contact with the nose. In AlbSL the sign can be expressed either with a head nod, stopping when the nose comes into contact with the 5 handshape (with no movement of the hand), or with a short, repeated, straight movement of the hand to the nose. The latter gesture, FËMIJË, may be articulated either with two hands on top of each other (as in the figure) or with one hand. The same holds for the sign.

Idiomatic expressions may be borrowed from one language and incorporated into another. Sutton-Spence and Woll (1999, 186) discuss idioms borrowed from English and integrated into BSL. Can idioms be transformed into gestures as well? These two conventional gestures indicate that this may be possible (unless, of course, the gesture preceded the idiom). Both MËRZITUR and FËMIJË are articulated with a 5 handshape. The Albanian word meaning "palm" is *pëllëmbë*, which also means a

FIGURE 12. MËRZITUR *"worried."* *The hand does not move.*

FIGURE 13. FËMIJË *"child."* *The hands do not move.*

measure equaling the size of a palm (i.e., a span of about six inches). The word can also be used in a figurative sense to mean "small amount or number" or "handful." The hand measure of pëllëmbë (the measure from the thumb to the pinky when all of the fingers are extended) was used especially by the older generation for measuring fabric and clothes. Thus the handshape of the gesture (5 handshape) directly reflects the function and meaning of the Albanian word *pëllëmbë.*

The Albanian idioms *turi varur* (literally, "face hanging"), *vari hundet* (literally, "hanging nose"), *me buzët varur* (literally, "with lips hanging"), and *i vari hundët (buzët) një pëllëmbë* (literally, "the hanging of nose (lips) by one span") all mean "be worried." (The last one means "being very worried.") The gesture MËRZITUR (the hanging of the nose by one span) can therefore be considered as a visual reflection of this Albanian idiom.

Another Albanian idiom containing the word *pëllëmbë* is *nje (dy) pëllëmbë njeri* ("one [two] span boy"), meaning "little guy," is often used to mean "he is only two hands high, but he is already behaving like a man." As in the case of MËRZITUR, the gesture FËMIJË (the one [two] span height of a boy) can be seen as visualizing an idiomatic expression. These examples reflect contact between spoken language, gesture, and signed language.

SUMMARY

The language of Albanian deaf people is characterized in large part by language contact. (A summary of the sources and examples of the outcome of contact is presented in Table 2.) Because language contact for signed languages means that people who use one sign language come in contact with people who use another language (or another system with linguistic features), a social aspect of power hierarchy is always involved. One cannot overemphasize equality between languages: No natural language is "better" than any other language per se. However, when working with deaf people and sign language in a developing country, there is a serious risk that the power hierarchy between the donor country and the target country will be reflected in the language. The World Federation of the Deaf has published a policy paper titled "WFD Work in Developing Countries." Section 3 in the policy paper emphasizes the importance of respecting the indigenous sign languages (emphasis mine):

B. The co-operation should as much as possible be based on the principle of mutual respect for cultural, language and social economic realities, e.g. in sign language work. *The objective should not be to export the sign language of the developed countries, but for developing countries to research and/or develop their own sign languages based on cultural realities.*

C. Deaf people from developing countries should be encouraged to receive training in specific areas (e.g. sign language and management) in developed countries. However, *the training should be tailored to enable them to work with the languages in their own countries.*

In the early days of developmental work among Deaf communities, the sign language of the donor country was sometimes exported to the recipient country. This issue of language influence has also been on the agenda during the work with deaf people in Albania. Even though most of the borrowing from International Sign has occurred out of a need for

TABLE 2. Summary of source and outcome of contact in the language use among deaf people in Albania

Source of Contact	Examples of Outcome of Contact
Before 1990	
Gestures in use in the Albanian hearing society	Emblematic gestures became signs
Fingerspelling words from the Albanian language	Lexicalized fingerspellings and initialized signs
After 1990	
International Sign (from deaf Albanians visiting Finland in 2000 and foreign advisors visiting Albania)	Signs borrowed into AlbSL for concepts that previously lacked signs. New signs were also coined parallel to indigenous signs that existed earlier.
Libër me Shenja [Book with Signs]	Nonindigenous ways of coining initialized signs
Other sign languages (from signing foreigners visiting the country and Albanian deaf people who went abroad after the collapse of Communism)	A sign for a city based on the two-handed alphabet used in Auslan; the use of foreign signs by deaf individuals who return to visit Albania after moving abroad

signs (for concepts that previously had no signs), the foreign signs are occasionally favored at the expense of existing indigenous ones (e.g., DEAF and WORK, as discussed earlier). I recommend that signers who work with deaf people in other countries be especially conscious of the language that they use. I am referring to imbalances of power between languages and to issues of language prestige, such as in the case of the unbalanced power hierarchy between AlbSL and foreign sign languages or International Sign, both of which have more prestige.

Since the trend among deaf people in Albania today seems to be to abandon the fingerspelling tradition in favor of AlbSL, many former isolated deaf people are now learning new signs.[21] From my point of view, the training that is given in linguistic awareness and language policy, for instance, is a crucial part of sign language work, and the growing level of linguistic awareness within the community is one of the successes of the sign language work that has been done in Albania. With linguistic awareness training, the risk that a nonlocal sign language will dominate at the expense of the local one can be decreased. When working with deaf people's language, one should emphasize equality between languages and lobby for a preservation of the local sign language based on its own cultural realities.

CONCLUSIONS

This first account of AlbSL provides a glimpse into the situation prevailing in the Albanian Deaf community, whose language use is characterized by language contact. During the Communist regime, deaf people were exposed to the gestures that hearing people were using. Many of the signs now in use originated in the emblematic gestures of the hearing society. Communication between deaf people was nevertheless dominated by fingerspelling based on Albanian, and, as a consequence, lexicalized fingerspellings and initialized signs emerged. For political and societal reasons, a Deaf community and a fully fledged sign language did not develop. When Communist rule came to an end, deaf Albanians began coming in contact with one another, and a community has since come into existence.

The results of contact with International Sign are seen both in the extension of the vocabulary of Albanian Sign Language and in the common tendency to favor new signs at the expense of the traditional fingerspelling. This transition, which can be considered an indication of the Albanian deaf people's wish to become part of a transnational Deaf community, reflects the awakening of a new Deaf identity. I hope that this linguistic minority will utilize AlbSL as a tool to advocate for their human and linguistic rights. The newly acquired knowledge that AlbSL is an indigenous natural language (even though it still is in a developmental phase) should directly benefit the deaf people of Albania by helping them to improve the status of the language through legislation and enhance equality between deaf and hearing people.

ACKNOWLEDGMENTS

I would like to thank David Quinto-Pozos and Jan-Ola Östman for their comments and discussions during the writing of this chapter, as well as Florjan Rojba and Leena Savolainen for their support and effort in producing the sketches and pictures. I also wish to thank the Albanian people, both deaf and hearing, with whom I have had the honor to work:

I am grateful for the hospitality that you all have shown me during my visits to your country.

NOTES

1. According to the 2004 *Tirana in Your Pocket* guide to Albania and its people, there are also approximately two million ethnic Albanians in Kosovo, hundreds of thousands in FYR Macedonia and Montenegro, and an estimated two million in the United States, Switzerland, Germany, Greece, Italy, and Canada.

2. This common negative attitude toward deaf people has its roots in Western history. Saint-Loup (1993, 392) discusses negative views of deafness in medieval Western Europe, where human suffering and diseases were seen as signs of sin, and people believed that those who were sick or had a handicap had earned their suffering as a punishment for wrongdoing.

3. The objective of the Organizational Support Project is to improve the lives of deaf people in Albania by ensuring equal opportunities to participate in society. The project gives financial support and guidance for enhancing organizational, advocacy, and sign language work, which has also served to strengthen the Deaf association in Albania. Activities have focused on intense training for ANAD staff and board members, as well as other representatives of the Deaf community. The training has been provided mainly by foreign organizational and linguistic advisors.

4. In this paper, I use the term "sign language work" to describe the work done in Albania that mainly consists of dictionary work (language documentation, sign language research, and application of the results of the research into publication use). It also includes training in Deaf awareness.

5. Colin Allen, a native deaf Auslan user who arrived in Albania in 2000 to work as an organizational advisor, estimated that communication among Deaf people at that time consisted of 90 percent fingerspelling and 10 percent indigenous signs. He also observed that many of these few signs were also used as gestures in the hearing Albanian society (pers. comm., Feb. 6, 2005; Mar. 13, 2006).

6. The working group members represented deaf persons who frequently took part in ANAD activities. Therefore I assume that they were using more signs than an average deaf person living isolated in the countryside.

7. Figures 1, 2, 3, 4, 6, 7, 12, and 13 are taken from *Gjuha e Shenjave Shqipe* 1, with permission from ANAD (Hoyer and Çabej 2005). Figures 5, 8, 9, 10, and 11 were created by Florjan Rojba.

8. In an initialized sign, the handshape corresponds through fingerspelling to the first letter of the written form of the equivalent word in a spoken language.

9. For example, lexicalized fingerspellings in which a modification of orientation and movement may indicate verb agreement are NJOF ("to know a

person") (only the Albanian letters *nj* and *f* are clearly articulated); TALL ("to make fun of") (the letters *t* and *ll* are clearly articulated); and GABIM ("to be wrong") (the letter *g* is clearly articulated).

10. When informally comparing the situation in 2000 to that in 2006, Colin Allen states that he has seen a noticeable increase in the number of signs in use among the same Deaf individuals (Colin Allen, pers. comm., Feb. 6, 2005; Mar. 13, 2006).

11. Contacts with other sign languages such as Australian Sign Language (Auslan) and Finnish Sign Language (FinSL) have not been examined systematically, and examples of these are therefore not dealt with here.

12. Colin Allen, Eduard Ajazi, and Florjan Rojba (pers. comm., Mar. 30, 2006; Apr. 13, 2006).

13. The international signs BOARD, HELP, YEAR, and PROBLEM are very similar to or the same as the corresponding ASL signs.

14. Interestingly, the word *shurdhër* is not considered offensive in Kosovo, where the majority language is also Albanian. The word is used, for example, in the name (approved by the local Deaf people) Projekti mbi Trajnimin Organizacional dhe Zhvillimin e Gjuhës së Shenjave në 11 Asociacionet Regjionale dhe Klubet e Shurdhërve, an organizational training project for the Kosovar Deaf community, which has an International NGO registration number.

15. For example, FUTBOLL ("football"), NJOF ("to know somebody"), GABIM ("to be wrong"), PO ("yes"), RE ("new"), FILLOJ ("to start"), and TALL ("to make fun of"), where the place of articulation is the neutral space in front of the signer.

16. Kendon (2004) provides an extensive presentation of studies on classifying gestures starting in the Roman era.

17. In fact, the Mediterranean countries are a popular vacation destination among Finnish Deaf people for this reason. There it is relatively easy for a Deaf foreigner to communicate with hearing people on a basic level using only gestures and facial expressions.

18. I am sorry to say that my attention as a linguist was first focused on *how* the children communicated with me and not on the sad fact that they were hungry.

19. According to the hearing informants, some gestures started to spread in Albania at the end of Communist domination. The thumbs-up for conveying a positive meaning, the crossing of one's index and middle fingers for "hope," and the time-out gesture used in sports for "break" were all new gestures for the country. In other words, not only did the end of the isolation mean that deaf people came in contact with signs from the outside, but the gestures that hearing people used also became subject to external influence. Due to its isolated past, Albania would be a gold mine for gesture studies.

20. See Frishberg (1975) for historical processes in ASL that result in change toward arbitrariness. Also see Battison (1978) for constraints in sign

formation and phonological and morphological restructuring that apply in borrowing.

21.   Fingerspelling is still used, however, as a complement to the signs.

REFERENCES

Allen, C., and S. Walters. 2005. Balkan Survey Project Report: Serbia and Montenegro. Finnish Association of the Deaf.

Andoni, B., I. Shabani, and A. Baçi. 2003. *Minorities: The present and the future.* Report of the Albanian Human Rights Group on the Situation of Minorities in Albania. Tirana, Albania: Grupi Shqiptar i të Drejtave të Njeriut.

Battison, R. 1978. *Lexical borrowing in American Sign Language.* Silver Spring, Md.: Linstok.

Berenz, N. 2003. The rise of the Brazilian Deaf community. In *Many ways to be Deaf: International variation in Deaf communities,* ed. L. Monaghan, C. Schmaling, K. Nakamura, and G. H. Turner, 173–93. Washington, D.C.: Gallaudet University Press.

Casey, S. 2003. Relationships between gestures and sign languages: Indicating participants in actions. In *Cross-linguistic perspectives in sign language research,* ed. A. Baker, B. van den Bogaerde, and O. Crasborn, 95–117. Hamburg: Signum.

Duncan, S. 2003. Gesture in language: Issues for sign language research. In *Perspectives on classifier constructions in sign language,* ed. K. Emmorey, 259–68. Mahwah, N.J.: Erlbaum.

Efron, D. 1972. *Gesture, race, and culture.* The Hague: Mouton. (The original English text, *Gesture and environment,* was published in 1941 by King's Crown Press, New York.)

Frishberg, N. 1975. Arbitrariness and iconicity: Historical change in American Sign Language. *Language* 51(3): 696–719.

Goldin-Meadow, S. 2003. *Hearing gesture: How our hands help us think.* Cambridge, Mass.: Belknap Press of Harvard University Press.

Hania, I., L. Klimi, A. Alikaj, and A. Abdihoxha. 1996. *Libër me Shenja* [Book with signs]. Tirana, Albania: Deaf School of Tirana.

Hoyer, K., and D. Çabej, eds. 2005. *Gjuha e Shenjave Shqipe* 1 [Albanian Sign Language 1]. Tirana, Albania: Albanian National Association of the Deaf.

Johnston, T., and A. Schembri. 1999. On defining lexeme in a signed language. *Sign Language and Linguistics* 2(2): 115–85.

Kendon, A. 2004. *Gesture: Visible action as utterance.* New York: Cambridge University Press.

McNeill, D. 1992. *Hand and mind: What gestures reveal about thought.* Chicago: University of Chicago Press.

Morris, D., P. Collett, P. Marsh, and M. O'Shaughnessy. 1979. *Gestures: Their origins and distribution*. London: Jonathan Cape.

Prifti, K. (ed.). 2002. *Historia e popullit shqiptar 1–2* [The history of the Albanian people]. Akademia e Shkencave e Shqipërisë, Instituti i Historisë [Albanian Academy of Science, Institute of History]. Tirana, Albania: Toena.

Pursglove, M., and A. Komarova. 2003. The changing world of the Russian Deaf community. In *Many ways to be Deaf: International variation in deaf Communities,* ed. L. Monaghan, C. Schmaling, K. Nakamura, and G. H. Turner, 249–59. Washington, D.C.: Gallaudet University Press.

Quinto-Pozos, D. 2002. Contact between Mexican Sign Language and American Sign Language in two Texas border areas. PhD diss., University of Texas–Austin.

Reagan, T. 2001. Language planning and policy. In *The sociolinguistics of sign languages,* ed. C. Lucas, 145–80. New York: Cambridge University Press.

Rosenstock, R. 2004. An investigation of International Sign: Analyzing structure and comprehension. PhD diss., Gallaudet University, Washington, D.C.

Saint-Loup, A. de. 1993. Images of the deaf in medieval western Europe. In *Looking back: A reader on the history of deaf communities and their sign languages,* ed. R. Fisher and H. Lane, 379–402. Vol. 20 of *International studies on sign language and communication of the deaf*. Hamburg: Signum.

Senghas, A., and M. Coppola. 2001. Children creating language: How Nicaraguan Sign Language acquired a spatial grammar. *Psychological Science* 12(4) (July 2001): 323–28.

SIL Ethnologue. http://www. ethnologue.com.

Supalla, T., and R. Webb. 1995. The grammar of International Sign: A new look at pidgin languages. In *Language, gesture, and space,* ed. K. Emmorey and J. S. Reilly, 333–52. Mahwah, N.J.: Erlbaum.

Sutton-Spence, R., and B. Woll. 1999. *The linguistics of British Sign Language: An introduction*. New York: Cambridge University Press.

Thomason, S. G. 1995. Language mixture: Ordinary processes, extraordinary results. In *Spanish in four continents: Studies in language contact and bilingualism,* ed. C. Silva-Corvalán, 15–33. Washington, D.C.: Georgetown University Press.

Tirana in your pocket 2. December/January 2004. Essential city guides. http://www.inyourpocket.com.

Washabaugh, W. 1986. *Five fingers for survival*. Ann Arbor: Karoma.

Weinreich, U. 1970. *Languages in contact: Findings and problems*. The Hague: Mouton (originally published as no. 1 in the series Publications of the Linguistic Circle of New York, New York, 1953).

WFD work in developing countries. Policy statement of the World Federation of the Deaf. http://www.wfdeaf.org/pdf/policy_work_dev.pdf.

Winford, D. 2003. *An introduction to contact linguistics.* Malden, Mass.:
Blackwell.

Zeshan, U. 2003. "Classificatory" constructions in Indo-Pakistani Sign
Language: Grammaticalization and lexicalization processes. In *Perspectives
on classifier constructions in sign language,* ed. K. Emmorey, 113–41.
Mahwah, N.J.: Erlbaum.

APPENDIX

The signs for PRESIDENT, GOVERNMENT, BUDGET, PROGRAM, and PAR-
LAMENT in International Sign.

PRESIDENT. *The hand bends
downwards from the wrist with
a repeated forearm rotation
movement*

GOVERNMENT

BUDGET. *The sign has a straight
repeated movement away from
the signer*

PROGRAM. *As the dominant hand
moves downwards it taps repeatedly on the palm of the nondominant hand*

PARLIAMENT

The Sign Language of Mainland China

at the Ch'iying School in Taiwan

Jean Ann, Wayne H. Smith, and Chiangsheng Yu

In Taiwan today, the language of the Deaf community is Taiwan Sign Language (TSL), one of the most studied sign languages of Asia.[1] Western researchers perceive the groundbreaking works on TSL to be Smith and Ting (1979), Ting and Smith (1984), Chao, Chu, and Liu (1988), and Smith (1989). Smith and Ting (1979) and Ting and Smith (1984) address the teaching of TSL to second-language learners, and their work contains glossaries, practice sentences, introductions to each chapter written in Chinese, and English glosses of each sign. The work of Chao, Chu, and Liu (1988) is similar in nature, while Smith (1989) examines TSL verb morphology. This significant body of work has led to more theoretical and psycholinguistic work (Chang, Su, and Tai 2005; Myers, Lee, and Tsay 2005). No published work of which we are aware, however, explores our concern here. Our topic, which was first described in Smith (1989), is both historical and sociolinguistic in nature

In a description of the three major linguistic influences on TSL, Smith writes of the impact of "the language that was used in Taiwan before 1895, concerning which no information is available" (ibid., 1). On this point, researchers maintain that when deaf people are isolated from one another, sign languages do not develop. On the other hand, in societies in which deaf people come together (e.g., in schools for deaf children), natural sign languages have an opportunity to develop (Kegl, Senghas, and Coppola 1999). Which of these circumstances (or permutations of them) might have been the case in Taiwan before 1895 is not clear, but if deaf people were able to congregate, it is perfectly possible that a sign language might have developed. If it did, no record of it exists as far as we know.

The second influence, according to Smith (1989), came from Japanese Sign Language (JSL), which was brought to Taiwan during the Japanese occupation (1895–1945) via Japanese teachers of deaf children. Support for Smith's claim comes from subsequent research that has systematically (and in much greater detail) examined the JSL and TSL lexicons (Sasaki, this volume). In addition, unpublished anecdotes from Taiwanese signers who have traveled to Japan (Lin, pers. comm.) suggest that JSL and TSL are for the most part mutually intelligible.

Although what we know about each of the early influences on TSL could and should be examined in much greater detail, in this chapter, we address the question of the third influence according to Smith (1989): the sign language of mainland China (MCSL). Smith explains that MCSL was brought to Taiwan in two ways after the Communists gained control of China in 1949. First, "students from Hong Kong who came to study at the schools for the deaf in Taiwan" were one source of MCSL (ibid., 2). Second, and perhaps more important, deaf refugees and former teachers of deaf people who left mainland China for Taiwan were another source of MCSL. As Smith (ibid.) notes, the deaf refugees from mainland China established schools for deaf children in several cities in Taiwan, but most of these facilities did not last very long. The one school that survived — the Ch'iying Private Elementary School for the Deaf — was located in southern Taiwan in the city of Kaohsiung and was established by a deaf man from mainland China named Chiang Ssu Nung. In fact, neither the literature nor the members of the Deaf community that we consulted during this research have identified any other serious source of mainland Chinese signs in Kaohsiung or anywhere else in Taiwan.[2]

To clarify our research, we explain our assumptions and some of the issues they raise. First, the generations of children who attended the Ch'iying School were clearly taught the signs of mainland China (Chao, Chiu, and Liu 1988). Since presumably many were from hearing families, we suspect that they arrived at the Ch'iying School without any knowledge of a sign language. Thus they may have picked up their first language at the Ch'iying School. The exact character of the signing to which the children were exposed is not clear: Was it Signed Mandarin, MCSL, some combination of the two, or some other possibility? Our first objective was to gain an understanding of the kind of signing to which the children at the Ch'iying School might have been exposed.

It seems possible that MCSL influenced the signing of TSL because many in the Deaf community have noted (if only anecdotally) that signers originally from the Ch'iying School communicate in TSL a little bit differently than do signers from other places in Taiwan (Smith, pers. comm.; Ku, pers. comm.).[3] Our second intention was thus to learn more about the differences deaf people perceive when they see TSL signed by former students of the Ch'iying School and signers from other places in Taiwan.

When the children left Ch'iying School (after sixth grade or even earlier), they either continued their education or went to work in Kaohsiung or elsewhere in Taiwan. At this point, they encountered TSL for the first time and adopted it; however, unless they went back to the Ch'iying School (the only place in Taiwan that used MCSL), they had no further occasion to use MCSL. As the older signers of MCSL at the school died out and the core of MCSL signers decreased, MCSL fell into disuse. The Ch'iying signers and members of the Deaf community in general confirm that, at one time, a small number of people (one consultant estimated one hundred at most) in and around the school used MCSL. Smith, writing in the late seventies, suggested that a small Deaf community in Kaohsiung was still signing MCSL, but by the early 1990s, Ann (2003) was unable to find many MCSL informants. Our third research question thus has two parts: first, to describe what we believe is a unique situation, and second, to learn more about the effects on deaf individuals of the attrition and loss of MCSL in favor of TSL.

It seems clear that the issues related to MCSL in Taiwan cannot now be examined directly (if indeed they ever could). Our problem, then, is a bit like that of Groce (1985), who examined the use of sign language on Martha's Vineyard, an island off the coast of Massachusetts. By the time she conducted her research, all of the deaf people who had used the sign language had passed away. Still living were hearing people who had known the sign language but had not used it for many years. In this situation, Groce obtained information from historical records and interviews with those who remembered the sign language. In like manner, to answer our questions about MCSL and TSL in Taiwan, we relied partly on general historical information. Unlike Groce's situation, we were able to locate and conduct in-depth, open-ended interviews with deaf people who had learned and used MCSL at the Ch'iying School (hereafter referred to as the Ch'iying signers).

We have divided the chapter into three main sections. First, we explore the history of signing and deaf education in mainland China, which we consider relevant to the establishment of the Ch'iying School for the Deaf in Kaohsiung. Second, we describe the founding of the Ch'iying School. Third, we report on our interviews with the Ch'iying signers. Finally, we return to our research questions and explain our conclusions.

In order to provide a sense of what the Ch'iying School might have been like in its early days, we explore the situation at the schools for deaf children in China that may have influenced Chiang Ssu Nung, who, upon leaving that country, established the Ch'iying School. Our brief history draws extensively from an in-progress work by Wayne Smith, as well as a few other sources. Smith's work (n.d.) is a deep and rich account of deaf education in Taiwan beginning with that in China and Japan. Because no published work that we have found examines these issues in nearly as much detail, we have relied largely on Smith's work in explaining both the origins of deaf education in China and the establishment of the Ch'iying School.

Before the 1880s, Smith says that few accommodations were made for the deaf in China. Around the same time, in New York State, a young woman named Annetta Thompson Mills, who had a deaf brother whom she adored, was learning how to teach deaf students. Then, in New York City, she had a deaf student whose father was a Presbyterian missionary in China named Charles Rogers Mills. After Charles's first wife died, Annetta married him in 1884. In the same year, the Millses arrived in Chefoo, (Qifu, now known as Yantai*) China. Having already acquired a great deal of training, Annetta then spent two years learning Chinese so that she could adapt her materials for use in teaching deaf students in China. Thus deaf education in China began (Lytle, Johnson, and Yang 2005 2006; Smith n.d.).

The Millses (and others before them) realized that a country as populated as China had to have an enormous number of deaf children (Mills 1890), so they decided to set up a school. An energetic teacher and advocate for deaf people, Annetta used her influence at home and in China

*Smith's original transcriptions of Chinese place names and names of people generally appear in a romanization system known as Wade-Giles, as is customary in Taiwan. Standardly and more recently in the linguistics literature, Chinese place names are written in *hanyu pinyin* which is a Romanization system in general use in Mainland China. The two systems differ in many ways; a name written in *hanyu pinyin* such as Wang Jian Guo would be written in Wade-Giles as Wang Chien Kuo. We have left Smith's transcriptions as they are in his original, and have inserted the *hanyu pinyin* rendering of only the most relevant names of places and people. Our insertions appear parenthesized in italics. Throughout this paper, tone marks are suppressed on all romanizations of Chinese words.

to solicit donations to create a school for deaf children in China — with some success. Eventually the Millses succeeded in setting up a highly influential school, which opened in June 1888, with a small number of deaf students whom the Millses recruited. Their goal was for the graduates of the Chefoo School to eventually establish more schools for deaf children throughout China. Remarkably, in the hope of inspiring people to take up the cause, Annetta traveled around China in 1908 to explain what she was doing at the Chefoo School (Mills 1910). According to Smith (n.d.), Fang (1979) says that, around 1915, most of the schools for deaf children in China were run by graduates of Chefoo. Throughout its early history, the Chefoo School struggled with financial problems, but it offered a rather varied curriculum. Smith (n.d.) offers this description:

By the time the school was firmly established, it was divided into two levels, according to the ability of each student. The first, or preparatory, course lasted three years, and the second, or regular, course lasted six years. As a new student came to the school, he or she was placed where it seemed appropriate, and the curriculum was adapted as necessary to meet his or her needs (Wang, L.-Y. [personal communication], 1980). . . .

Class size was usually quite small, averaging eight students (Westling 1936). On a visit to the school in late 1926, a man named Tung Yueh observed that, in the beginning classes, mirrors were used to teach speech, and a tactile method was used to teach speech sounds. Chinese characters were introduced along with a picture of the object they represented or the object itself. As the children advanced into higher level classes, their ability to answer questions also increased, whether they answered through speech or by writing on the blackboard. By the time a student was enrolled in the highest level classes, he was able to study many different subjects (Yueh 1927). At one time or another the school offered courses in all of the following subjects: speech, articulation, language and language drilling, Chinese characters, reading, Mandarin, romanized Mandarin, manual alphabet, visible speech, journal, letter, and composition writing, oral arithmetic, history, Christian religion, good manners, and good morals. They were also allowed to choose such vocationally oriented subjects as photography, industrial training, drawing, lacemaking, knitting, carpentry, basketry, weaving reed verandah shades, sewing, cooking, homemaking and . . . weaving.

Lytle, Johnson, and Yang (2005–2006) claim that, since the days of the Chefoo School, the dominant approach to the education of deaf students in China has been oralism. Interestingly, however, they acknowledge that, in schools for deaf children, the reality has always included the use of Signed Mandarin and MCSL. Smith confirms this claim. In a discussion of teaching methods used at the Chefoo School, Smith (n.d.) comments:[4]

> The school placed heavy emphasis on speech and oral training, although the use of sign language was not ruled out. From [the] earliest days in the school, one form or another of a manual alphabet was used. Ellerbek, who lived across the street from the school in Chefoo . . . stated . . . that not much weight was placed on spoken language and lipreading due to special and insurmountable difficulties such as the different dialects and the tones which are so important to the Chinese language. Great emphasis was placed on fingerspelling and sign language and many of the pupils were able to learn 2000 signs per year, with a record of 900 in three months. They had learned to express Chinese words in Latin letters and could therefore communicate with Europeans who understood Chinese but didn't know signs (Ellerbek 1904). . . .
>
> Mrs. Mills, herself, writing in 1907, spoke very highly of fingerspelling, "which is learned by these pupils almost immediately." And of fingerspelling, Carpenter (1907) wrote, "By this method, and with pantomime and gesture, they readily communicate with each other, and seem to get much happiness out of life." At first, the traditional American fingerspelling system was used to spell out romanized Mandarin. Later, after the use of Visible Speech became common in schools for the deaf in the United States, a fingerspelled version of it invented by an American named Edmund Lyon was adapted for use in teaching Mandarin Chinese. Most of the pure signs which were also used at the school were simple ones, suggested readily by the things they represented, such as "hair-bun" for MOTHER or "moustache" for FATHER (Wang, L.-Y. [personal communication], 1978).

In 1929 Annetta Thompson Mills, who was in her seventies, died in Chicago, and her school then came under the direction of her niece, Anita Carter. The story of the Chefoo School relates to the story of deaf education in Taiwan because both graduates of the Chefoo School and the students from the schools established by Chefoo graduates went to Taiwan in 1949. Smith (n.d.) discusses two such cases:

Important to the later development of deaf education in the province of Taiwan was the fact that two sisters, Wang Chao-ning and Wang Lu-yi, who had grown up at the [Chefoo] school, later became teachers there and picked up many of the techniques used at the school, techniques which they later introduced into the schools for the deaf in Taiwan. Wang Chao-ning was taught directly by Tyra Westling and the two of them would often work together after school hours. Wang Lu-yi taught at the Chefoo school for three and a half years, from about 1942 to 1946 (Wang, L.-Y. [personal communication], 1980). . . .

In 1924, the Ministry of Education of the Republic of China (Taiwan) promulgated a unified phonetic system for Mandarin, the *zhuyin fuhao* or Mandarin Phonetic Symbols. At this time, most schools for the deaf adopted the official government system, and many tried to adapt the old Visible Speech fingerspelling system to the new symbols. At least two fingerspelling systems grew out of this attempt. One was developed at the Chefoo School itself and brought to Taiwan by the Wang sisters in the late 1940s. The other was invented by Yeh Yung-hua at the Nanking School for the Blind and Mute which was founded in 1927. This system was brought to Taiwan by Fang Hung-Ch'ou and his deaf son Fang Ping-Mei, also in the late 1940s (Fang 1979).

Directly relevant to the establishment of the Ch'iying School is the Nan-t'ung School for the Deaf. Smith (n.d.) states that Chiang Ssu Nung was one of the graduates of this school:

[The] . . . Nan-t'ung [Nandong] School for the Deaf . . . was located in Lang-shan, outside the city gates of Nan-t'ung, Kiangsu [Jiangsu] province. The formal name of the school was the Kiangsu Provincial Nan-t'ung Private School for the Blind and Mute, and it was larger than most of the schools for the deaf in that area of China. It offered a six-year elementary school program, and also a three-year middle school program, and had as many as 200 students at one time. Being a branch of a normal school, around 1930 the school also added a three-year teacher training component, from which the first set of trained teachers graduated around 1933. Graduates of the program were sent throughout the country to establish more schools, and some of the schools they later served in included those in Nanking [Nanjing], Shanghai, Peiping (Municipal), Hankow, Canton [Guangzhou], Chenkiang, Suchow Co., Wuchin Co., Wuyang Co., Hsüchow, Nanch'ang (Mun.), Sungkiang Co., Hangchow (Mun.), and Yanchow in Shantung. Although certainly affected by the Japanese invasion of China in the late 1930s, the school did remain open, and the principal of the school around 1939–40 was Wang Ping-heng (Chiang, SN, [personal communication], 1978; 1980).

This brief account shows that education for deaf students was occurring in mainland China at the time the deaf refugees left China for Taiwan (1949–1950), that oral education was important, and that people were signing in schools for deaf children. We cannot be certain whether Signed Mandarin or MCSL was being signed in these schools, although our information suggests that some deaf people used a natural sign language, some used Signed Mandarin, and some used both. The reasoning behind our assumption is that the invention and use of signed codes for spoken languages is one way in which societies have dealt with the concern that deaf children learn to read and write in the spoken language with which they are in contact. Therefore, it seems reasonable to suppose that Signed Mandarin might have been in use. Because hearing people have always been involved in deaf education and have sometimes outnumbered deaf people, we might even suppose that the use of Signed Mandarin was extensive, but it also seems within the realm of possibility that native signers of MCSL also attended the school.

Furthermore, we maintain that, even if the school started out using *only* Signed Mandarin, a natural sign language might still have developed. Our proposal is based on the developmental psychological literature that says that deaf children, when presented with manual codes for English (which are notoriously difficult to process), seem to adjust these systems in ways that make them more closely resemble natural sign languages in their morphology, use of space, and the like (Goldin-Meadow 2003; Supalla 1991). This research suggests that, if the children were exposed to a manual code for Chinese at the Chefoo School, some of them might have invented an MCSL. On a separate note, even though Smith (n.d.) and Ann (2003) have said that TSL at present has no method of fingerspelling, it seems clear that fingerspelling was at least somewhat available at the beginning of deaf education in China and even in Taiwan.[5]

THE ESTABLISHMENT OF THE CH'IYING SCHOOL IN TAIWAN

When the Communists took over mainland China in 1949, many people (hearing and deaf) left the country. The deaf refugees went to Singapore, Hong Kong, and Taiwan, and some of them, finding no schools in their new environments, set up new ones. Smith (n.d.) gives a detailed account of the establishment of the Ch'iying School:

The first private school for the deaf in Taiwan after Taiwan's retrocession to China was the Ti-sheng School for Mutes founded in 1950 in the city of Keelung by Mr. Chiang Ssu-nung. Chiang was a deaf graduate of the Nant'ung Co. School for the Deaf, just north of Shanghai, and had previously established a private school for the deaf in the Chinese mainland before being forced to flee the mainland in 1949 in the wake of the Communist takeover. The Ti-sheng school was never incorporated and lasted no longer than one year, after which it was discontinued (Chiang, 1978). . . .

Determined to renew his efforts to found a school, Chiang moved south to the city of Kaohsiung where in the autumn of 1951 he borrowed some rooms in the Nantzu District of the city and established the Kaohsiung City Private Ch'iying Elementary School for the Deaf and Mute (Ch'iying Elementary School for the Deaf and Mute 1978; Chiang 1978; Ministry of Education 1976). The school had many difficulties, not the least of which were the poor conditions of the school rooms and the lack of money. In 1955 Chiang wrote an article urging for support for his efforts to educate the deaf in the Kaohsiung area. He noted that President Chiang Kai-shek felt that every city and province should have a well-equipped school for the blind and mute, but that, following World War II China only had at the most some 50 schools for the blind and deaf, most of which were not very large. He noted that Taiwan had two public and only one or two private schools for the blind and mute and that still 80% of the blind and mute children of Taiwan were not being served, as opposed to 5% unserved among the general population. Moving closer to home, Chiang noted that Kaohsiung contained one of the twelve most important harbors in China and was the second largest city in Taiwan, with a population of 300,000. With the addition of Kaohsiung and Pingtung counties, the number of persons amounted to over a million, meaning that there could be as many as 2–3,000 blind and mute persons in the area.

Although Chiang said his school was doing its best to educate these blind and mute citizens, its limited budget allowed the school to serve only a small portion of them. He pleaded urgently for support to be able to continue making a contribution to the deaf of southern Taiwan (Chiang 1955). . . . .

Chiang's plea did not go unheeded. A piece of land near Lien-ch'ih Lake in the Tsoying District of Kaohsiung was selected and donated to the school as the site for a new school building. Other assistance also came from Kaohsiung city (Ch'iying Elementary School for the Deaf and Mute 1978; Chiang 1978). Construction work progressed slowly, but finally by 1964 the new school building was completed and the school was moved to the new location. At the same time, the school filed its application for certification which was granted in April of 1966 and the school became formally established as the Kaohsiung City Private Ch'iying Elementary School for the Deaf and Mute (Ch'iying Elementary School for the Deaf and Mute 1978). . . .

Although the school began small, with hardly twenty students (Yang 1974), since the beginning of the 1970s the school has maintained a fairly constant student enrollment of just over 100 students, with 106 in 1970 (Ch'iying Elementary School for the Deaf and Mute 1970), 107 (66 male and 41 female) during the 1974–1975 school year (Ministry of Education 1976), and 101 (67 male and 34 female) in 1978 (Ch'iying Elementary School for the Deaf and Mute 1978). The students range in age from six to over 13 and are 90% from the Kaohsiung City, Kaohsiung County, and Pingtung County areas (Ch'iying Elementary School for the Deaf and Mute 1978). Since the student dormitory has a maximum capacity of only twenty students, the majority of the students at the school are daytime commuting students. The students are served by nine teachers and three staff members and are grouped into classes with 15–20 students per class. As of 1978, the school had graduated a total of eight classes of sixth graders. Following graduation, most of these students continue their studies at the Tainan school for the deaf, though a few go to the newly established classes for the deaf at Ta-yi Junior High School in Tsoying, and others go on to study at the schools in Taipei and Taichung (Ch'iying Elementary School for the Deaf and Mute 197; Ministry of Education 1976; Yang 1974). School funds have also been used to purchase a group hearing aid used in pronunciation training, but a lack of sufficient funds keeps the school from purchasing other needed equipment and to build dormitories for all the students who need such accommodations (Ch'iying Elementary School for the Deaf and Mute 1978; Yang 1974). The curriculum at the school is essentially the same as that in regular schools with the addition of classes in speech and auditory training. The textbooks used are also the same as those used in regular schools, but teachers are selective in using them with their deaf students. The school places emphasis on helping its students adapt to their environment. Physical education is also stressed at the school, and in March 1977 the school took part in Taiwan's first special Olympics competition, held in Tainan (Ch'iying Elementary School for the Deaf and Mute 1978; Yang 1974; Ministry of Education 1976).

Smith's (n.d.) detailed picture of the founding of the Ch'iying School is accompanied by a bit more information that is relevant here. He discusses a program at Ta-yi Junior High School in Kaohsiung, which graduates of Ch'iying might have attended, and makes two further statements about the Ch'iying School. First, reflecting the belief that no single method of teaching (oralism, manualism) would be successful for every deaf child, the Ta-yi program utilized a "total communication" approach. Because "most of the students [had] never received any speech training before at the Ch'iying school," the Ta-yi curriculum emphasized speech training, which suggests that the Ch'iying School was very much a signing environment. Second, the program set up "weekly meetings of the Ta-yi Junior High School Sign Language Research Club, which provides a forum for teaching sign language to the teachers and for bridging the gap created by the different sign languages used at the Ch'iying school and in the Ta-yi program (Ch'iu, C. C., personal communication, 1980)." This is a clear acknowledgment that different languages were in use at Ch'iying and Ta-yi.

The picture of deaf education in China and Taiwan suggests several characteristics of the Ch'iying School. First, it appears that, once accepted, students were dealt with on a relatively individual basis, and the curriculum was adjusted according to practical considerations that made sense for each child. Second, the Ch'iying School did not have sufficient funds to concentrate on speech; ideologically, it did not seem particularly wedded to the idea of oral education for every deaf child. As Lytle, Johnson, and Yang (2005–2006) assert in their discussion of deaf education in China, financial need sometimes dictates whether signing or speech will be emphasized. This seems to have been the case in Taiwan as well. Third, learning Chinese written language was a serious concern, and it seems reasonable to assume that Signed Chinese systems were perceived as a way to accomplish this goal.

THE CH'IYING SIGNERS' MEMORIES OF THE SIGN LANGUAGE OF MAINLAND CHINA

Based on Smith's recounting of the history, we estimate that the Ch'iying School might have graduated 200–300 deaf students before it stopped accepting new pupils. Compared with the schools that were using TSL, it is apparent that MCSL in Taiwan was not likely to survive and that the young signers who learned it first were at a serious disadvantage. The Ch'iying School has survived in Kaohsiung for some fifty years, and although it is still in existence, it closed its doors to deaf students in the early 2000s (Chiang, pers. comm.). For its first twenty to thirty years, students learned MCSL; then, sometime in the late 1970s, the transition was made to TSL (Smith, pers. comm.; Ann 2003).

Ann (ibid.) briefly reports on conversations with a few Ch'iying signers in the early 1990s about their memories of MCSL. They remembered the time they spent at Ch'iying using MCSL and demonstrated a few MCSL signs. When it seemed that they could be prompted to remember more, a dictionary of MCSL signs was presented, and the Ch'iying signers said that the signs looked familiar. Our 2005 research was influenced by this account and by the fact that some of the Ch'iying signers told us they were a bit nervous about being interviewed since they had used MCSL so long ago and were afraid of giving "wrong" answers. Believing that it would be difficult for them to remember the actual signs, we decided to try a more ethnographic approach rather than a strictly linguistic one (e.g., using structured language elicitation tasks). We hoped that this would ease their anxiety and help them remember more about their use of MCSL. Nothing about our approach precluded eliciting signs from the Ch'iying signers, but this was not the only thing we were interested in. We used no MCSL prompts such as a dictionary.

For the study, we tried to locate the Ch'iying signers that Ann had known in the early 1990s and others that would be willing to participate. Responses to our attempts were somewhat hesitant at first, similar to Ann's (2003) own experience. However, after some deliberation, our contacts supplied names, and we were able to locate and interview five suitable people, only one of whom Ann had known in the early 1990s. The five Ch'iying signers were males in their late thirties to mid-fifties. Two of the interviewees had graduated from senior high school; one had graduated from junior high school; and two had graduated from sixth grade. The five agreed to participate in an interview. Most of the sessions took place one evening as we gathered informally at the home of a Deaf leader in Kaohsiung. As far as we could determine, there have been no monolingual signers of MCSL in Taiwan for quite some time; they all sign TSL also. Yu, a TSL signer who is not familiar with MCSL, served as an interpreter for four of the Ch'iying signers. The fifth, who was the signer Ann had known in the early 1990s, was interviewed by Ann at a later time and in another location in Kaohsiung. After the interviews, we had many opportunities to return to the field for clarification. In addition, we were also able to chat with two or three other Ch'iying signers at various times, but, for many different reasons, none of them were interested in participating in a formal videotaped interview.

We informed each of the consultants of the predicted length of the interview and our hope of publishing any useful information. We assured them that their names would be kept confidential unless they wished them to be made public, that they could stop answering questions at any time, and that they would be paid for their services. The participants filled out a brief questionnaire on their demographic and linguistic background. Then each person participated in a rather open-ended, videotaped interview, in which they were asked to relate their stories and observations on certain points. Our goal was to ask eight related main questions. We were prepared with several subquestions to use as prompts in case the main question did not elicit as much from the participant as we hoped. We told everyone that we might ask slightly different, unplanned questions, depending on their answers.

To elicit the Ch'iying signers' memories of their language experiences at school, the series of questions we posed dealt with the following topics: their days at Ch'iying; where their Ch'iying teachers had come from; what language the teachers had signed (if they knew); their own signing experience, as well as that of their friends and classmates; acquisition of their first and second sign languages; and the circumstances under which they had become conscious of the existence of two sign languages. The questions were written in English and Chinese and were available to the participants and the interviewers before the sessions. At the time of the interview, the questions were signed in ASL to Yu, who interpreted them into TSL. Replies were given in TSL, and Yu interpreted them into ASL. At any time, if any of the consultants seemed uncomfortable or overtly said that they were ill at ease, we discussed other matters.

Our interactions took place in two connected rooms. The videotaped interviews were held in one room, with the interviewers and the consultant. Consultants who were not being interviewed were not prevented from watching what the others said on videotape, but for the most part, they elected not to do so. Only one interviewer was videotaped; the other was off camera.

With respect to linguistic background and language use, our research obtained the following results. Our consultants' linguistic backgrounds were uniform: All had significant hearing losses, had been deaf since they were very young (less than three years of age), and had hearing parents and families that did not sign; unsurprisingly therefore, they did not know any signs before attending the Ch'iying School. We have heard of only one Ch'iying signer (who was not available for an interview) who reported slightly different circumstances; he had an older deaf sibling from whom he had learned signs before attending the Ch'iying School. All of the participants began signing using the mainland Chinese signs and then switched to TSL. From the time they left the Ch'iying School, TSL had been their primary language.

We began the interviews by asking the consultants to tell a story about their experiences at the school in general (not connected with language); it could be funny, sad, embarrassing, or any other type of story. The participants easily remembered their days at the Ch'iying School; none appeared to have the slightest difficulty with this. Their tales included both positive and negative memories, which we do not report on here. A few told stories that evoked strong emotions, and some anecdotes were quite lengthy. Because of the apparent clarity with which the Ch'iying signers described their memories, we felt confident of their recollections of linguistic experiences.

We asked the consultants whether they recalled what it felt like to encounter a sign language for the first time and to sign for the first time. All described feeling surprised and even puzzled to see people signing when they were first brought (most by their parents) to the Ch'iying School. They all said that they did not understand anything at first, but little by little their teachers made things explicit and began to show the children how to name items in the environment (e.g., "we call that

TABLE, we call that DRINK"). As children, they found that they could communicate about the things in their environment and more. Once this became clear to them, each one described a certain degree of enthusiasm for this new way of interacting with the world.

We turned next to the subject of the teachers in the Ch'iying School and asked whether they were from Taiwan or China. The Ch'iying signers either recalled directly or remembered hearing that, in the earliest days, at least some of the teachers were from China and not Taiwan. Our consultants stated matter-of-factly that (through the years and by the time they attended the Ch'iying School) Taiwanese teachers were hired but were taught the mainland Chinese signs. The Taiwanese MCSL-signing teachers, in turn, taught the students using the mainland Chinese signs. When those teachers eventually retired, the new teachers hired were certainly from Taiwan, said our consultants, and all of the new teachers used TSL. We assume that this occurred around the time the school made the transition to TSL. One consultant reported becoming aware, much after the fact, that people could be from these two different places and that this could affect how they signed; he said that he understood (only after he had learned TSL) that the reason his elementary school principal signed differently was that he was from mainland China.

We asked the Ch'iying signers whether they could recall the signs they were taught as children and tell us the equivalent in TSL. Our consultants' memories of the mainland Chinese signs varied. The general result was that four of the five could recall some signs (ten to twenty) with some hesitation. The fifth consultant had sad memories of his days at the Ch'iying School and did not want to remember the mainland Chinese signs because it brought back these recollections. Most of the participants reported having no particular thoughts about having lost MCSL when they learned TSL; for them, it was a matter of the usefulness of the language. If most of those they met signed TSL, it was obviously better to have fluency in that language, but if most of the people they met had been MCSL signers, they would have signed MCSL.

One consultant had good memories of MCSL and said he felt a bit sad remembering how TSL had essentially supplanted MCSL in his life and in the small MCSL-signing community that once existed. He said, "I'm happy when I see a sign from mainland China. I still remember them passively, and if I see them I understand them. . . . I've remembered them almost forty years now. . . . I feel a strong connection with those signs because I learned them first." Upon picking up on our interest in learning more about MCSL in Taiwan, one consultant offered a few more thoughts. He said, "You'd better ask me now and get this on videotape. I don't use MCSL every day. I just remember it especially if I ever see a mainland China sign. But if you wait too much longer . . . it will be completely gone."

Of the signers who remembered the signs of mainland China, those that were mentioned the most often (and had TSL counterparts) were the number system and signs such as MOTHER, FATHER, OLDER/YOUNGER SISTER, and OLDER/YOUNGER BROTHER. One signer also remembered SON, DAUGHTER, TREE, TABLE, TRAIN, MAN, WOMAN, CHAIR, TABLE, RESTROOM, MORNING, AMERICA, YELLOW, and MAINLAND CHINA. Another recalled KAOHSIUNG and TELEVISION. These signs look very different in the two languages. A few of these signs appear in examples 1 through 6. The TSL signs are from Smith and Ting (1979), while the MCSL signs are from the Chinese Association for the Deaf and the Educational and Employment Department of the United Chinese Association for People with Disabilities (2003).

We asked the interviewees whether their teachers used Signed Mandarin or MCSL. In doing so we carefully explained that, by Signed Mandarin, we were referring to a form of signing that followed Chinese syntax, the character-by-character signing. After a short explanation, the Ch'iying signers seemed aware of the difference between Signed Mandarin and a natural sign language. Most of the consultants said that what was signed in the classroom was Signed Mandarin. They explained that the characters relevant to the lesson were first written on the blackboard, and the teachers then explained each one and taught them to the children *all of the accompanying signs*. (One stated that this procedure was the same as that to which hearing children were exposed in their educations, except that the hearing children did not learn the signs and the deaf children did not learn the spoken words.) The consultants said that, outside of class in general and certainly on the playground, they used the natural sign language. One consultant said that the teachers would use the natural sign language in class if the students did not understand Signed Mandarin. He made a point of saying that, "If the teachers cared about the kids, they used the natural sign language and Signed Mandarin, too. That way all the kids would understand."

We elicited information about the Ch'iying signers' linguistic experiences by asking them to use introspection — thinking about their own

TSL MOTHER   CSL MOTHER

Example 1

TSL FATHER   CSL FATHER

Example 2

TSL OLDER BROTHER   CSL OLDER BROTHER

Example 3

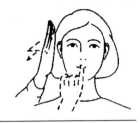

TSL YOUNGER BROTHER   CSL YOUNGER BROTHER

Example 4

TSL OLDER SISTER   CSL OLDER SISTER

Example 5

TSL YOUNGER SISTER   CSL YOUNGER SISTER

Example 6

signing first of all and then also visualizing that of the other children at the school. Were they themselves signers of Signed Mandarin or MCSL? And the other children? The Ch'iying signers all stated that they can use Signed Mandarin to some extent but that they do not always do so. Our consultants seemed less enamored of natural sign language than might be expected, although two of them commented on its efficiency in contrast to the much more laborious Signed Mandarin.

The Ch'iying signers seem to have an intensely practical view of language; they want to use the language that works for them in their society. They appear to consider their society as composed of both deaf and hearing people. If we think of manual codes for spoken languages and natural sign languages as being situated on a continuum (Woodward 1973), most of the participants described themselves as "more toward the natural sign language end." However, they also acknowledged using Signed Mandarin sometimes, both as children and as adults. All of the interviewees said that the other children variously used both Signed Mandarin and MCSL. One said that, as children, they made fun of Signed Mandarin when they were free to do so. However, for the most part, even though its disadvantages are acknowledged, Signed Mandarin is not derided, nor is TSL exalted, as noted in Ann (2003).

Having asked about the Ch'iying signers' linguistic experiences with respect to learning their first language, we then turned our attention to the end of their time at Ch'iying, when they were to graduate and move on to a different phase of life. We asked whether they recalled the circumstances surrounding their transition from MCSL to TSL. The five reported how they first came into contact with TSL. Two went on to school in Tainan, one went to a Kaohsiung school, and two began to work after sixth grade. Most of them said they were completely stunned when, upon graduating from sixth grade and leaving the Ch'iying School, they found that the signing in their new surroundings was different. They reported at first not understanding anything; after a while, however, they began to pick up the new language. All reported embracing it in the end because the community of signers to which they had belonged at the Ch'iying School was dwindling and also because, as they grew up, they found numerous uses for TSL. Our consultants stated that they had maintained contact (to varying degrees) with the Ch'iying School after graduation. When they visited the school, they again signed in MCSL. Some of the consultants said they became so used to knowing both languages that eventually they were barely conscious of their bilingualism.

We asked the interviewees whether they had ever communicated with a person from mainland China and, if so, whether they were able to communicate easily. Our consultants felt reasonably confident that they could communicate with deaf signers from China. Some had one or two experiences, and one had a great deal of experience with signers with whom they communicated rather well. All of them said that the obvious difference they encountered was lexical: different signs for the same thing.

Our consultants were all well aware that their signing is regarded as a bit odd by signers of TSL from other parts of Taiwan, and all of them attributed this partly to their having learned the mainland Chinese signs first. But they suggested, too, that significant variation exists in TSL in general, which may account for this. We asked whether they had any sense of grammatical or formational differences between TSL and MCSL. None of the participants had specifically studied TSL or MCSL. Rather, their sign languages had served as the medium of instruction, and they had never analyzed the differences. When asked what they thought other signers find strange about their signing, they mentioned primarily lexical items that they might use in conversation. The question about the differences between MCSL and TSL was regarded with some surprise; the answer was that everything is different.

RESEARCH QUESTIONS REVISITED

Returning now to our original questions, first, we wanted to gain some understanding of the kind of signing to which the children at the Ch'iying School were exposed. Our results suggest that they were exposed in large part to Signed Mandarin, particularly in the classroom, but that the children found ways and times to sign in a more natural manner outside of class. This confirms reports we have heard about a myriad of schools for deaf children in the United States and other places. In addition, Lytle, Johnson, and Yang's (2005–2006) account of the situation in China (in which MCSL and Signed Mandarin have always been used, even though the general philosophy is oral) sounds particularly reminiscent of what we have learned with respect to the Ch'iying School. Also, since the Ch'iying School had limited resources (Ann 2003), it was essentially a signing, not an oral, environment. It seems, then, that several kinds of signing might well have been in use.

We made the least headway in understanding our second research question about the differences deaf people perceive when they see TSL signed by signers from the Ch'iying School and by TSL signers from other places in Taiwan. The consultants themselves stated that they had no explanations for these variations. They could give no examples and merely asserted that there are indeed lexical differences. Our difficulties in obtaining much insight into this question are fairly easily explained. First, perhaps we have simply missed the opportunity to learn about the differences in Ch'iying signing. Because MCSL has not been taught in many years, there are now few new signers of MCSL (though some immigrants from China are MCSL signers). Many Ch'iying MCSL signers have passed away. All of the signers we know of who used MCSL learned TSL nearly thirty years ago and are certainly TSL dominant now. These circumstances might preclude investigation of the question of Ch'iying differences. Second, our ethnographic approach proved not to be effective in answering this question. A psycholinguistic or sociolinguistic approach might be more revealing. Finally, it seems possible that, given the variation in Taiwan, Ch'iying signing, despite what we have heard, is not (or perhaps is not now) appreciably different from other signing.

As for our third research question, we still suspect that the Ch'iying signers exhibit a unique linguistic situation. We believe that a more systematic approach — working with both Ch'iying signers and signers from other parts of Taiwan — might help us understand more about this. Our work thus far suggests that answers to the particular questions about MCSL might be lost to history, but they are nevertheless worth pursuing. We hope someday to better understand the story of the use of MCSL at the Ch'iying School in Taiwan. In the meantime, we have documented this fragment of the history of the Deaf community in Taiwan.

NOTES

1. We would like to thank Su Shiou-fen, Chen Yi-Jun, Ku Yu Shan, Lin Fang-yu, and Lin Chin Tang for their assistance in finding consultants and preparing materials for the interviews. Also, we gratefully acknowledge David Quinto-Pozos for giving us the inspiration to write this chapter, as well as Lourdes Pietrosemoli and two anonymous reviewers for very helpful comments. Finally, we offer our thanks to our consultants, the Ch'iying signers, for their

willingness to discuss their linguistic backgrounds and their days at the Ch'iying School.

2. Our sources, who know the Deaf community well, acknowledge that, although refugees from mainland China established several schools and some of them subsequently taught the Chinese signs, any influence of MCSL from this situation has long been lost.

3. There is a proliferation of different signs for the same referent in Taiwan (Ann 2003), a fact that many deaf Taiwanese themselves report. In fact, Lytle, Johnson, and Yang (2005–2006) state that, in mainland China, MCSL is not standardized.

4. Smith (n.d.) also discusses the schools for deaf children in China, such as the first school in Beijing, which was established around 1920 and 1921 and had a strict oral curriculum. He maintains that this school adopted a different educational philosophy from that of most of the schools for deaf students in China, suggesting that the more common philosophy was either exclusively or at least partly manual.

5. Actually, Ann (2003) discusses several cases of the use of the fingers to represent letters. However, as early as the early 1990s, the Ch'iying signers said they did not know anything about fingerspelling. Lytle, Johnson, and Yang (2005–2006) suggest that fingerspelling is currently in use in China. During the course of our research, we met a signer from China who confirmed the widespread use of fingerspelling.

REFERENCES

Ann, J. 2003. The Ch'iying School of Taiwan: A foreigner's perspective. In *Many ways to be Deaf*, ed. L. Monaghan, C. Schmaling, K. Nakamura, and G. Turner, 230–48. Washington, D.C.: Gallaudet University Press.

Carpenter, D. N. 1907. A visit to the Chefoo, China, School for the Deaf. *Association Review*: 359–62.

Chang, J.-h., S.-f. Su, and J. H.-y. Tai. (2005). Classifier predicates reanalyzed, with special reference to Taiwan Sign Language. *Language and Linguistics* 6(2): 247–78.

Chao, C.-m., H.-h. Chu, and C.-c. Liu. 1988. *Taiwan Natural Sign Language*. Taipei: Deaf Sign Language Research Association of the Republic of China.

Chiang, S. N. 1955. *Kao-hsiung shih ssu-li Ch'i-ying lung-ya hsiao-hsüeh kai-k'uang* [Introduction to the Kaohsiung City Private Ch'iying Elementary School for the Deaf and Mute].

———. 1978. Interview by W. Smith. Ch'iying School, Kaohsiung, Taiwan.

———. 1980. Interview by W. Smith. Taipei.

Chinese Association for the Deaf and the Educational and Employment Department of the United Chinese Association for People with Disabilities. 2003. *Zhong guo shou yu* [Chinese Sign Language], Part 1. Beijing: Hua Xia.

Ch'iying Elementary School for the Deaf and Mute. 1970. *Kao-hsiung shih ssu-li Ch'i-ying lung-ya hsiao-hsüeh kai-k'uang, wu-shi-chiu hsüeh-nien-tu* [Introduction to the Kaohsiung City Private Ch'iying Elementary School for the Deaf and Mute, 1970 Academic Year].

———. 1978. *Kao-hsiung shih ssu-li Ch'i-ying lung-ya hsiao-hsüeh kai-k'uang, liu-shi-ch'i hsüeh-nien-tu* [Introduction to the Kaohsiung City Private Ch'iying Elementary School for the Deaf and Mute, 1978 Academic Year].

Ellerbek. 1904. Letter in Danish from a medical missionary, dated Chefoo, China, December 28. *Småblader for Døvstumme*.

Fang, P. M., 1979. Zhongguo zaoqi de long jiaoyu lishi (A history of early deaf education in China). *Longyou Huixun* (Newsletter of the Deaf Alumni Association), 1979, Vol. 2, p. 6.

Goldin-Meadow, S. 2003. *The resilience of language: What gesture creation in deaf children can tell us about how all children learn language.* New York: Psychology Press.

Groce, N. 1985. *Everyone here spoke sign language: Hereditary deafness on Martha's Vineyard.* Cambridge, Mass.: Harvard University Press.

Kegl, J., A. Senghas, and M. Coppola. 1999. Creation through contact: Sign language emergence and sign language change in Nicaragua. In *Language creation and language change: Creolization, diachrony, and development,* ed. M. DeGraff, 179–237. Cambridge, Mass.: MIT Press.

Lytle, R. R., K. E. Johnson, and J.-h. Yang. 2005–2006. Deaf education in China: History, current issues, and emerging Deaf voices. *American Annals of the Deaf* 150(5): 457–69.

Mills, A. T. 1910. China through a car window. *Volta Review* 12(6) (September): 327–39; 12(7) (October): 421–33; 12(8) (November): 499–517.

Mills, C. R. 1890. Deaf-mute instruction. *Chinese Recorder and Missionary Journal* 21: 243–46.

Myers, J., H.-h. Lee, and J. Tsay. 2005. Phonological production in Taiwan Sign Language. *Language and Linguistics* 6(2): 310–60.

Sasaki, D. This volume.

Smith, W. H. 1989. Morphological characteristics of verbs in Taiwan Sign Language. Ph.D. diss., Department of Speech and Hearing Sciences, Indiana University.

———. n.d. A history of deaf education in Taiwan. Working paper.

———, and L. Ting. 1979. *Shou neng sheng chyau* [Your hands can become a bridge]. Vol. 1. Taipei: Deaf Sign Language Research Association of the Republic of China.

Supalla, S. 1991. Manually coded English: The modality question in signed language development. In *Theoretical issues in sign language research*. Vol. 2, *Acquisition*, ed. P. Siple and S. Fischer, 85–110. Chicago: University of Chicago Press.

Ta-yi. 1976. *Kao-hsiung shih-li Ta-yi kuo-min chung-hsüeh ch'its'ung pan gai-k'uang* [Introduction to the class for the deaf at Kaohsiung Municipal Ta-yi Junior High School]. Kao-hsiung shih-li Ta-yi kuo-min chung-hsüeh, Kaohsiung.

———. ca. 1979. *Kao-hsiung shih-li Ta-yi kuo-min chung-hsüeh (ch'its'ung) t'o-shu chiao-yü shih-yen pan kai-k'uang* [Introduction to the experimental special education class (deaf) at Kaohsiung Municipal Ta-yi Junior High School]. Kao-hsiung shih-li Ta-yi kuo-min chung-hsüeh, Kaohsiung.

Ting, L., and W. H. Smith. 1984. *Shou neng sheng chyau* [Your hands can become a bridge]. Vol. 2. Taipei: Deaf Sign Language Research Association of the Republic of China.

Westling, T. M. 1936. The school for the deaf at Chefoo. *Volta Review* 38 (January): 23–26, 56–57.

Woodward, J. 1973. Implicational lects on the deaf diglossic continuum. Ph.D. diss., Linguistics Department, Georgetown University.

Yang, T. C. 1974. Kao-hsiung shih ssu-li Ch'i-ying lung-ya hsüeh-hsiao chiao-yü [Education at the Kaohsiung City Private Ch'iying Elementary School for the Deaf and Mute]. *Hsiang-kang Lung-Ya Hsieh-hui Nian-k'an* [Hong Kong Deaf and Dumb Association Annual Journal].

Yueh, T. 1927. Chefoo School for the Deaf. *Volta Review* 29(2) (February): 103 (reprinted from *Yih Wen News*, Temple Hill, Chefoo, Shantung, China).

Contributors

Jean Ann is an Associate Professor at the State University of New York at Oswego. Her primary area of research and publication is sign language linguistics. Her most recent publication is a book entitled *Frequency of Occurrence and Ease of Articulation in Sign Language Handshapes: The Taiwanese Example* (2006) published by Gallaudet University Press. In addition, she has published articles with Long Peng on the structure of world Englishes and linguistics in K-12 education.

Jeffrey Davis has worked as an interpreter, teacher, and researcher in the fields of signed language linguistics and deaf studies for the past twenty-five years. He holds a Master's degree and a Ph.D. in Linguistics; served on the faculty of Gallaudet University in Washington, D.C. (1987–1990); and on the faculties of the University of Arizona (1990–1994) and Miami-Dade College (1994–2000). He has been a professor at the University of Tennessee since 2000. In addition to fieldwork and research, he teaches ASL, Linguistics, Interpretation, and Translation.

His research involves the linguistic analysis of ASL, interpretation processes, and translation studies. For the past two decades, he also has been researching the historical and current use of American Indian Sign Language. He presents internationally on a variety of topics related to sign language, linguistics and interpretation. He can be reached through http://web.utk.edu/~jdavis49/.

Karin Hoyer holds a Master's degree in General Linguistics from the University of Helsinki, Finland. She is a doctoral student at the University of Helsinki, and has also got a degree in sign language interpreting. She has previously worked on a research project on the lexicon of Finland-Swedish Sign Language. Currently she is involved in sign language dictionary work in Albania and Kosovo as part of Balkan developing cooperation projects carried out by the Finnish Association of the Deaf.

David McKee is Research Director of Deaf Studies Research Unit and Senior Lecturer in Applied Linguistics at Victoria University of Wellington, New Zealand. David has taught and conducted research in the United States. In 1992 he and Rachel Locker McKee established and taught New Zealand's first full-time sign language interpreter training course at Auckland University of Technology.

David's main research interests have been in Deaf Studies, including the corpus-based description of New Zealand Sign Language, sociolinguistic variation and NZSL lexicography, and comparative studies of sign languages (American, Australian, British, and New Zealand sign languages). He was consulting editor for the *Concise Dictionary of New Zealand Sign Language* (Bridget Williams Books, 2002).

Rachel Locker McKee is Programme Director of Deaf Studies in the School of Linguistics and Applied Language Studies at Victoria University of Wellington. Her professional experience as a sign language interpreter in New Zealand and the United States from 1985 led to her involvement in Applied Linguistics and the establishment of training programs for interpreters and for Deaf people as teachers of NZ Sign Language (NZSL). Her research publications have focused on analysis of the structure and use of NZSL, sign language interpreting, and the culture of the New Zealand Deaf community.

Karen Pointon is a Māori member of the New Zealand Deaf community. Karen is a qualified teacher of NZSL who has taught at Victoria University and in other community settings. A former president of the Deaf Association of New Zealand, Karen has an active role in Deaf advocacy at national and local levels.

David Quinto-Pozos received his Ph.D. in Linguistics from the University of Texas at Austin and is currently an Assistant Professor in the Department of Speech and Hearing Science at the University of Illinois at Urbana-Champaign. In addition to his research and teaching, Professor Quinto-Pozos is an RID-certified sign language interpreter and has participated as a content expert for the development of certification exams (both ASL-English and ASL-Spanish-English). His research interests include language contact and related sociolinguistic phenomena, cases of atypical sign acquisition in deaf children from signing households, and the interaction between linguistic and gestural devices in signed languages.

Daisuke Sasaki completed his doctoral studies in linguistics at the University of Texas at Austin, and is currently an Assistant Professor of Linguistics and English at Hokusei Gakuen University, Sapporo, Japan. He is also a board member of the Japanese Association of Sign Linguistics. His research interests include grammatical aspects of sign languages, such as phonology, morphology, and syntax, and he is working on his dissertation on the lexical comparison of Japanese Sign Language with Taiwan Sign Language and Korean Sign Language.

Kirsten Smiler (Te Aitanga a Mahaki, Rongowhakaata, Te Whakatohea) has recently completed her MA thesis (Applied Linguistics) which focuses on issues of language and identity for Māori members of the New Zealand Deaf community, and is currently working on her PhD thesis (Applied Linguistics) in the area of early intervention for Māori deaf children. Kirsten has worked with the Deaf Studies Research Unit and the Health Services Research Centre at Victoria University of Wellington, and has research interests in Māori Deaf people, deaf children, linguistic variation in New Zealand Sign Language, Deaf families, rangatahi Māori, youth wellbeing, disability studies and Māori health.

Wayne H. Smith received his Ph.D. from Indiana University in 1989 where his research focused on verb morphology in Taiwanese Sign Language. He has spent a total of six-and-a-half years living in Taiwan promoting awareness of TSL, serving as an advocate for the Deaf community in the areas of education and employment, conducting research into the history of deaf education in Taiwan, and authoring, along with members of the Deaf community in Taiwan, a two-volume textbook of Taiwanese Sign Language entitled *Shou Neng Sheng Qiao* (Your Hands Can Become a Bridge). He is currently director of the Learning Unlimited Language School in Surry, Maine (www.mrlanguage.com) where he has offered individual and small-group instruction in over twenty different spoken and signed languages. He may be reached at wayne@ mrlanguage.com.

Judith Yoel is currently a doctoral student in the Department of Linguistics at the University of Manitoba in Canada. She did her BA and MA at the University of Haifa in Israel. She is presently researching Canada's Maritime Sign Language.

Chiangsheng Yu is a Deaf man who grew up in Taipei, Taiwan, in a hearing family who did not know anything about TSL. His first language is Chinese; he learned TSL at age thirteen. He figured out that to get a good education and have a successful career, he would need to find a way to get to Gallaudet. Eventually, he came to the ELI at Gallaudet and began to learn English and ASL. He still remembers the feelings he had the first time he heard that "deaf people can do anything but hear" and the inspiring American Deaf people he met. Chiangsheng earned two degrees at Gallaudet University: a BA in Studio Art/Secondary Education, and an MA in Deaf Education. His education was important to him because it qualified him to work with deaf senior high school students in Taiwan. Since 2001, he has been a teacher at Kaohsiung City Municipal

Index

Italian Sign Language (LIS, Lingua Italiana dei Signi), 15–16
Italy, 218

Jankowski, K., 74
Janzen, T., 16
Japan Association to Promote Speech for the Deaf, 127
Japanese Federation of the Deaf, 131
Japanese Sign Language (JSL), 7, 8, 9, 98, 118*n*9, 235–36. *See also* Taiwanese Sign Language (TSL)
Japan Institute for Sign Language Studies, 130–31
Jefferson, Thomas, 103–4
Johnson, K. E., 240, 246, 255
Johnston, T., 217
Jordan, I. K., 155–56
JSL. *See* Japanese Sign Language

Karaj, Brunilda, 198
Kaufman, T., 42
Kauppinen, Liisa, 209
Kawamoto, Unosuke, 127
Kelston Deaf Education Centre (New Zealand), 37, 61, 74
Kendon, A., 217, 231*n*16
Kennedy, G., 8, 131, 134, 145*n*23
Keresan of New Mexico Pueblo, 88
knowledge, effect of new areas on signs, 208
Komorova, Anna, 159, 167, 197
Konishi, Shimpachi, 126
Korean Sign Language (KSL), 123–24, 128, 142–43*n*1
Kosovo, sign language in, 215
Kroeber, A. L., 91, 110, 117*n*6
Kumura, Kingo, 125
Kumura Education Center for the Blind and the Mute, 125
Kuschel, R., 129
Kyle, J.G., 96, 97
Kyoto Institute for the Blind and the Mute, 126

Landry, R., 157
language attrition, 3, 7, 13, 155–65. *See also* Russian Sign Language (RSL)
language contact
    characteristics of signed language that influence contact in visual-gestural modality, 14–20
    interlingual structural similarity of sign languages, 19–20
    prevalence of iconicity, 14–16
    utilization of gestural resources, 16–19, 20
    considerations for study of, 1–28
    sign language literature, 3–4
    contact between signed and spoken/written language, 4–7
    contact between two or more signed languages, 9–14
    lexical similarities between sign languages, 7–9
    spoken language literature, 2–3
language decline and death, 3, 4, 13–14
language family, 94, 117*n*3, 128–29
language shift, 3
Language Skills Attrition Project (LSAP), 160–61
Levinson, S., 17
Lewis and Clark expedition (U.S.), 103
lexical borrowing. *See* borrowing
lexical comparisons, 3, 8, 129–30, 131. *See also* North American Indian Signed Language varieties; Taiwanese Sign Language (TSL)
lexical gaps, 156, 178–83
lexical innovations, 173–74
lexicalization process, 220
lexical knowledge, 155
lexical similarity
    described, 7–9, 93–98
    Native American Indian Sign Language varieties and, 107–10, 115–16
    TSL and JSL and, 124

McKee, David, 7, 8, 31, 32, 33, 131, 134, 145*n*23
McKee, Rachel, 7, 13, 31, 32, 33
McNeil, D., 118*n*10, 217
MCSL. *See* Mainland China Sign Language
MD. *See* Māori Deaf people (MD) and Māori signs (MS)
media, 166–67
medieval Western Europe, 230*n*2
Meier, R.P., 8, 124, 141
metaphorical construction, 15
Mexican immigrants' language experience, 156
Mexican Sign Language (LSM, la Lengua de Señas Mexicana)
ASL and, 184
code switching vs. borrowing in, 10
emblematic gestures in, 17–18
emblems and, 224
foreign instructors and, 21
interference and, 11–12
lexical similarities between sign languages and, 7, 8, 9, 130
lexical similarity in, 98, 118*n*9
shared symbolism in, 97
Mills, Annetta Thompson, 238–41
Mills, Charles Rogers, 238–39
Ministry of Absorption (Israel), 163, 168
miscues, 172, 174, 178, 179–81, 184
missionaries, 13
Mithun, M., 92
mixed languages, 216
Modern Classics Cultural Enterprises (MCCE), 125, 126
Morford, J., 17–18
Moscow Bilingual School for the Deaf, 167
motivated new coinage, 47–48
mouthing
ASL and, 6
attrition and, 175–76
described, 185–86*n*11

interference and, 12
language contact and, 5
Māori Deaf and NZSL, 73
RSL and ISL and, 175–76
semantic importation and, 42
movement in signs, 131, 134
MS and MSL. *See* Māori Deaf people (MD) and Māori signs (MS)
mutual intelligibility, 94–95, 124, 143*n*2, 236

Nagoya Municipal School for the Blind and the Mute, 127
Nakamura, K., 124
Nakota language family, 88
name of sign language, 70–71, 73, 205–6
Napier, J., 13
National Anthropological Archives, 100–101, 104
National Archives, 99
National Association of Deaf (Israel), 163
National Deaf Māori Deaf Hui conference (2005), 32–33, 69
Natural language attrition, 154–55. *See also* Language attrition
natural sign languages, 253
Navajo (Diné) language family, 88
negation, 12
neologisms
ASE and, 56
Māori Deaf (MD) and, 49, 52, 54, 55, 58–60, 61–62, 73
Newell, L. E., 117–18*n*7
New Mexican Pueblo Isolates, 88
Newport, E. L., 19
new varieties of languages, emergence of, 3
New Zealand English (NZE), 38–39, 42, 46
New Zealand Sign Language (NZSL), 8, 130, 145*n*23. *See also* Māori Deaf people (MD) and Māori signs (MS)

semantic loans, 42–43, 50–51, 54, 55
semantic mismatches, 134
"semi-creolization," 2
semiotics, 117n6
Senghas, A., 205
sequential switching, 5
Shabani, I., 195, 197
Shaffer, B., 16
shared symbolism, 97, 124, 134
Shiga Profectural Oral School for the Deaf, 127
Shou neng sheng qiao (Your Hands Can Become a Bridge; Smith & Ting), 131
Signed English, 44, 55–57
Signed Hebrew, 177
Signed Mandarin, 242–43, 251, 253, 255
Signed Russian, 166, 167, 169
The Sign Language: A Manual of Signs (Long), 104–5, 106
sign language contact. See language contact
sign language defined, 90
"Sign Language of the Indian Nations to the West of the Mississippi River" (Jefferson), 103–4
sign vocabulary lists, 118n8, 129–30, 131
similarly articulated signs, 100, 144n17. See also phonologically similarly articulated signs
simplification, 140
simultaneous combinations of linguistic devices, 5
Siouan language family, 88
Slutzky, Emmanuel, 163, 164
Smiler, Kirsten, 7, 31, 32, 33, 67–68
Smith, Wayne H., 21–22, 125, 126, 127–28, 131, 235–36, 238–46
Smithsonian Institution, 90–91, 99, 100–101, 112
social aspects of language contacts, 2
social bilingualism, 3
social contact, 43

social evaluation, 64
Southeast Asia sign languages, 13
Spanish expeditions to Florida, 117n5
Spanish sign languages, 7, 8, 64, 96, 98, 130
spatial descriptions, 19
spoken language
   contact between signed and spoken/written language, 4–7
   language contact in, 2–3
   semantic importations and, 42
Stokoe, W.C., Jr., 129
Strang, B., 43, 60
substitutions, 52
subtractive bilingualism, 157
Supalla, T., 12, 19, 88, 206
Sutton-Spence, R., 21, 95, 217–18, 224, 225
Swadesh, M., 129
Sweden, 218
Swedish Deaf minority in Finland, 51
Swiss German Sign Language, 6, 51
symbolism, 124
symmetry, 140

Tainan School for the Blind and the Mute, 125, 126
Taipei, 125, 126, 128
Taiwanese Sign Language (TSL)
   dialects of, 128
   historical background of deaf education in Taiwan, 125–27
   Japanese Sign Language (JSL) comparative study, 9, 123–50
   current study, 130
   discussion, 133–39
   handshape differences, 134–39
   historical perspective on changes in signs, 139–41, 235–36
   methodology, 130–32
   previous studies of language comparisons, 129–30
   results, 132–33
   Mainland Chinese Sign Language (MCSL), 21–22, 235–59

arrival in Taiwan, 127–28
Ch'iying signers' memories of
MCSL, 246–55
establishment of Ch'iying School
in Taiwan and, 243–46
genetically related languages and,
128, 142
origins of Deaf education in
mainland China, 238–43
research questions, analysis of,
255–56
sign language in Taiwan, 127–29
Taiwan Provincial Taichung School
for the Deaf, 125
target language, attempt to master, 4
Tarone, E., 174
Taylor, A.R., 90, 92
temporary production errors, 184
Te Reo Māori (TRM). *See* Māori
Deaf people (MD) and Māori
signs (MS)
Thailand, indigenous sign languages
in, 14
Thomason, S. G., 42
Ting, L.-f., 128, 131, 235
Tino Rangatiratanga movement (New
Zealand), 36–37, 64
Tokyo Oral School for the Deaf, 126–
27
Tokyo School for the Blind and the
Mute, 126, 128
Tomkins, W., 110, 111, 113–14,
118*n*11
topicalization, 4
topic markers, 16
torso movements, 17
trade languages, 90
transference, 3
trilingual setting, contact in. *See*
Māori Deaf people (MD) and
Māori signs (MS)
TRM (Te Reo Māori). *See* Māori
Deaf people (MD) and Māori
signs (MS)
TSL. *See* Taiwanese Sign Language

TTY conversations, 5
Turian, D., 181

United Kingdom, 8
United States, 8, 20. *See also* North
American Indian Signed
Language varieties
Uzbek Sign Language, 159

Valli, C., 4, 5–6, 9–10, 11, 19
Venezuelan Sign Language (VSL), 17
verbs
agreement, 12
auxiliary, 19–20, 128, 144*n*13
"nonagreement analysis" and, 23*n*4
plain verbs, 19
victimization, 203–4
visual-gestural modality
characteristics of signed language
that influence contact in, 14–
20
code switching and, 5
effect of, 1–2
interlingual structural similarity of
sign languages, 19–20
prevalence of iconicity, 14–16
utilization of gestural resources,
16–19
visual homonyms, 47, 52, 58
visual iconicity, 3, 15–16. *See also*
iconicity
visual perception in signed language,
178–80
vocabulary lists. *See* sign vocabulary
lists
Voeglin, Carl, 91, 117*n*6
VOG (All-Russian Federation of the
Deaf), 162, 164
Volterra, V., 15–16
VSL (Venezuelan Sign Language), 17

Waas, M., 161, 175, 177, 180
Walters, K., 8, 124, 141
Washabaugh, W., 203–4, 224
Weatherwax, Martin, 113–14

Webb, R., 12, 206
Weinreich, U., 206
Welsh variety of British Sign
   Language (BSL), 51
Weltens, Bert, 153
West, LaMont, 91, 92
Williams, H.W., 76n2
Winford, D., 208
Woll, B., 21, 95, 96, 97, 129–30,
   131, 134, 145n23, 217–18,
   224, 225
Woodward, J., 4, 13, 106–7, 129,
   131

word order, 12, 20, 128
World Federation of the Deaf, 197,
   227
Wright, Dutton, 126
Wurtzburg, S., 90, 117n5

Yanagida, Kunio, 142
Yang, J. H., 240, 246, 255
Yoel, Judith, 13, 153
Yu, Chiangsheng, 21, 235

Zaitseva, Galina, 159, 164
Zeshan, U., 217